sovereign
bones

sovereign bones

NEW NATIVE AMERICAN WRITING
VOLUME II

Edited by Eric Gansworth

NATION BOOKS
NEW YORK

SOVEREIGN BONES:
New Native American Writing, Vol. II

Compilation Copyright © 2007 Amerinda

Published by
Nation Books
116 East 16th Street, 8th floor
New York, NY 10003

This publication is made possible in part with public funds from the New York State Council on the Arts, a state agency.
Nation Books is a copublishing venture of the Nation Institute and the Perseus Books Group.

State of the Arts

NYSCA

Nation Book titles are available at special discounts for bulk purchases in the United States by corporations, institutions, and other organizations. For more information, please contact the Special Markets Department at Perseus Books Group, 2300 Chestnut Street, Suite 200, Philadelphia, PA 19103, or call (800) 255-1514, or e-mail special.markets@perseusbooks.com.

Library of Congress Cataloging-in-Publication Data is available.

ISBN-13: 978-1-56858-357-0
ISBN-10: 1-56858-357-5

9 8 7 6 5 4 3 2 1

Book design by Astrid E. deRidder
Printed in the United States of America

For those whose stories

We remember,

And for those who will

Remember ours,

And for all the

Bumblebees who keep

Our voices thriving

While we're here

contents

one

Repatriating Ourselves

two

Speaking through Our Nations' Teeth

three

Snagging the Eye from Curtis

four

Rolling Those Sovereign Bones

acknowledgments

The poem "The Unauthorized Autobiography of Me" is reprinted from *One Stick Song,* © 2000 by Sherman Alexie, by permission of Hanging Loose Press.

The essay "The Meaning of the Music I Sing" was published in *Iroquois Voices, Iroquois Visions,* Treadwell, New York: Bright Hill Press, 1996. © Michele Dean Stock. Used by permission of the publisher.

The essay "Writers on Writing; Two Languages in Mind, but Just One in the Heart" was published in the *New York Times,* May 22, 2000. © Louise Erdrich. Used by permission of the author.

The essay "Comings and Goings in Indian Country: Spiraling from a Blog" was culled from Joy Harjo's blog at www.joyharjo.com and from Joy Harjo's "Coming and Going in Indian Country" column for the *Muscogee Nation News,* the newspaper of the Muscogee Creek Nation of Oklahoma, 2005, 2006. © Joy Harjo. Used by permission of the author.

The essay "Haksod" was published in *Iroquois Voices, Iroquois Visions,* Treadwell, New York: Bright Hill Press, 1996. © John C. Mohawk. Used by permission of the publisher.

The Ted C. Williams selection, "From *Big Medicine from Six Nations,*" was published in *Big Medicine from Six Nations,* Syracuse, New York: Syracuse University Press, 2007. © Syracuse University Press. Used by permission of the publisher.

I am thankful to Canisius College for its continued support of my work, specifically President Reverend Vincent M. Cooke, S.J.; Vice President for Academic Affairs Herbert J. Nelson; Dean of Arts and Sciences Paula M. McNutt; English Department Chair Sandra P. Cookson; and the Joseph S. Lowery Estate for Funding Faculty Fellowship in Creative Writing.

Nyah-wheh, thank you, to those who have put forth the effort in this collaboration among Amerinda: American Indian Artists Inc., particularly Diane Fraher; the New York State Council on the Arts, specifically Kathleen Masterson, Director of the Literature Program; and Nation Books. *Nyah-wheh* to the writers, artists, and editors who contributed to and supported this volume during the process, and who helped with perspective, to Rush for thematic inspiration, and *nyah-wheh* to the Bumblebee, for encouraging me, as always, to roll the bones.

L anguage is the soul of a Nation. It provides the foundation for identity and, with land in place, this provides a sense of family and security. It is the storehouse of indigenous knowledge.

Our Nations and societies are steeped in oral tradition: ceremonies and speeches that go with it; songs; medicines and medicine societies; laws; histories; stories; *Gayanehsa'go:nah* and *Gaiwiio*—these are our instructions and the foundations of our great confederacy. Because these instructions are oral, we are always a generation or two away from losing our languages altogether.

The key for language survival is usage, the continuation of traditions and ceremonies. Traditional governments require language to function in the Longhouses of the Haudenosaunee, the Kivas of the Hopi, the Longhouses of the Hiada-gwaii Tulalip Coastal Nations, the Sundance Grounds of our western brothers. The United States government knows this; that's why they attacked the language, as well as our culture and our spiritual ways of life.

The Bureau of Indian Affairs and the Department of the Interior elective systems of government don't need Native languages. They use English. It is the same for our ceremonies: change our people to Christians and they no longer need their language—they will now use English.

Our oral traditions provide their own dynamics for continuation and survival. Our elders are the libraries of our Nations. As they grow old and come near to the time when they will cross over to the "Other Side Can't" as the Lakota say, there is an urgency stirring in the next generation down to acquire knowledge from the elders.

John Mohawk's story, "Haksod," illustrates this quite well, as does Scott Lyons's story, "In Vine Veritas." This dynamic creates great energy and the drive to learn by the younger generation, and creates the same energy and drive to teach by the elders. Rick Hill's story, "Transitions in Haudenosaunee Realities: The Changing World of the Haudenosaunee as Seen in Historic Photographs," is a reality we all face. Each generation is responsible for itself and it is its charge and choice to continue.

When the Great Peacemaker completed his instructions of the *Gayanehsa'go:nah* (The Great Law of Peace), after he had installed the leaders of the five Nations—Mohawk, Oneida, Onondaga, Cayuga, and Seneca—after he had planted the Great Tree of Peace with the four white roots of truth, after he had set the eagle on top of the tree as the guardian and watchman for our new league of peace, after he had laid down the new constitution of this great confederacy, on the shores of Onondaga Lake, a thousand or more years ago . . . a woman approached him and asked, "Now that you have done all of this, how long will it last?" and he answered, "That's up to you." So far, our will to be who we are has lasted into the twenty-first century.

Language is the cultural bond for National identity; that's why our languages became the primary target of the United States government, Catholic and Christian denominations. It was a symbiotic relationship: the United States government wanted our language, and the Christians wanted our souls. In order to convert us as Christians, they first had to destroy our languages and cultures. They had to reinvent the "heathen red man" who was as free as nature into a "civilized" human being, compliant to their will.

Colonel Richard H. Pratt was the officer in charge of Fort Marion in Saint Augustine, Florida. The fort had been changed into a prison and concentration camp for the Apache, Cheyenne, and Arapaho leaders and men and other American Indians still fighting to defend their land against the expansion policies of the United States government.

Boredom was a serious issue in this prison, with the Indian men so far from their homelands. Colonel Pratt tried various programs such as shoemaking to occupy their time. He was astonished by how fast they learned. Impressed with their intelligence, he went to Washington, D.C., to see if he could convince them to deal with Indians in a different way. He said it was too difficult to change the adults, who were implacable in their resistance. He said it would be easier to change their children. He convinced them that this was a more practical way to "kill the Indian and save the man."

He convinced the powers that be in Washington, D.C., that this was a more humane way of dealing with Indians, and he was given leave to establish the first Indian boarding school. This was a psychological experiment in social engineering that has to rank with some of the Second World War Nazi experiments on human beings.

Thus, Carlisle Industrial Indian School was established in Carlisle, Pennsylvania, in the latter part of the nineteenth century, and the process of destroying American Indian languages and cultures began in earnest. Other boarding schools followed quickly: Hampton Institute in Virginia, Chilocco in Oklahoma, Haskell in Kansas, Riverside in California, Brainerd Indian School in Hot

Springs, South Dakota, Quaker schools in Philadelphia and New York, Santa Fe Indian School in New Mexico, and the Thomas Indian School in New York.

Indian Country was shocked by these events, and the trauma is still reverberating today. Some schools have been closed, but some continue into the twenty-first century. This federal policy scarred children for life and punched deep holes in the spiritual heart of American Indian Nations. Fortunately for the United States, the experiment was not completely successful.

The greatest irony of all was that it was the world-famous Code Talkers of the Second World War, American Indian soldiers, who used their Native languages over open airwaves to send and receive vital military information and instructions to their commands. This heroic service saved thousands of American lives and was strategic in helping to bring victory to the Unites States and allied Nations in the Second World War.

We are now in the beginning of the twenty-first century and we collectively face the rest of the world's greatest threat to life as we know it—global warming. Ironically, again, the world is listening to the voice of indigenous people. They are reaching for our philosophy of responsibility to the seventh generation— our traditions of long-term thinking, respect, and support for the natural world and our understanding of the great life-giving regenerative systems of the universe. Can they change, and can we hold?

Only time will tell, and time has now become a factor. I hope that this provides some background to the anthologies, perspectives, and experiences of our Native artists and writers of our times, who now direct our attention to matters of importance.

Native Nations are still here, but our peoples have suffered mightily in the process. We must understand the message used against us by our brothers from across the sea. They are fierce and unrelenting in their quest to wrest from us title to our lands. As long as we remain who we are and keep our languages, cultures, and lands, we will continue to stand and fight for the next seven generations.

Peace,

Oren Lyons (Wolf Clan, Onondaga Nation–Haudenosaunee)

introduction

SOVEREIGN TO THE BONE

Eric Gansworth

When I was approached about developing a follow-up volume to *Genocide of the Mind*, my initial inclination was to pass. Sequels generally seem like a bad idea to me, and sequels to groundbreaking work an even worse idea. My writing and painting projects were definitely enough to keep me busy without my taking on another. It had never occurred to me that I might at some point end up in the position of editing an anthology, though it should have. So many other writers I have admired over the years had taken on similar tasks, and while I remembered the pain of being shut out of some anthologies, I also knew the strong feeling of community I had when I would look at a collection for which I'd had work accepted. Writing is a lonely activity, and if anthologies do one thing for the writers included—aside from the obvious benefits of exposure—it is to give them a construct that allows for an increased sense of community. Through the varied courses of culture and history, some common element marks the contributors in any anthology.

Sometimes, I discovered that an anthology invitation was an opportunity for growth, as well as exposure and a sense of connection. I remember when MariJo Moore, the editor for *Genocide of the Mind*, approached me about participating. I think we must have gone through a series of five or six exchanges in which she asked me to write a piece of creative nonfiction for that book, to which I replied that I didn't do that; then I tried getting her to consider some other form, fiction or poetry, even painting. Those were aesthetic arenas where I had a firm footing and a long track record. I had last written an essay in college, and couldn't recall ever writing anything I would consider creative nonfiction. Throughout, she was supportive, encouraging, but unrelenting.

It was partly MariJo's insistence that I try something new that led me to discovering I had another tool available—the essay. It was one I'd had all along, but somehow I had not fully appreciated the potential of the form, relegating it to critical analysis alone. I found that I was already writing what would eventually become "Identification Pleas," my piece for *Genocide of the Mind*, in the form of a report I was required to deliver as part of the internal grant requirements at Canisius College, where I had recently been hired. Had MariJo not been patient and encouraging, the piece would have gone only into my permanent file at work, satisfying the requirements of my travel and research funds, and that would have been that. This series of events allowed me to focus on the opportunity she offered.

Around the time I was reconsidering the invitation to edit this anthology, I began watching the collected DVDs of a television series featuring interviews with contemporary artists, focusing, naturally, on their work, their process, and their motivation. Though the producers were judicious in representing the multicultural experience among the artists they selected, I didn't see any indigenous artists represented. In fairness, perhaps I missed that episode. One thing I began to notice, though, was that nearly all of the artists profiled had enormous, beautiful studios in almost magical settings and that their materials—brand-new cars, specifically designed neon lights, incendiary materials, custom-shaped synthetic materials—were all not materials the average artist had readily at hand. I know a large number of artists, and none of us have twelve spare brand-new cars to destroy for an installation. It gradually dawned on me, after an experience in a residency program, that there are a fair number of contemporary artists who can afford to be serious about their work because they are supported by financial situations and cultural institutions that were long in place before they decided to pursue the work of their lives. Would they still be destroying twelve cars at once for an installation if they had to make monthly payments on those cars like everyone I know?

I still cannot fathom this liberty. I began drawing when I was three years old, on the insides of grocery bags. When I was nine or ten, my oldest brother bought me a set of watercolors for Christmas, and one of my cousins gave me a pen and ink bottle, teaching me primitive stipple techniques he had learned in a college drawing class. I got a job working as a laborer, cleaning toilets and washing vomit from school buses, when I reached the legal age to work—twelve.

When my paycheck arrived two weeks later, I bought my first-ever new pair of jeans, three canvases, three paintbrushes, a small bottle of turpentine, and as many tubes of oil paint as the cash in my pocket would allow. At the time, I lived with my mother and my uncle, in a house that had one electrical outlet box and no running water. We drank water from a hand pump outside and wired our house with strategically placed extension cords, all trailing back to that one two-plug outlet box. It seems like some of my siblings should have been living with us then, but I don't think any of them were. Perhaps one of my brothers was in and out, the rest of the time living in Buffalo. In my bedroom I set up an easel someone had donated my way, breathing in the fumes when I slept, painting whenever I had a few hours between school and work.

My story is not uncommon. The details perhaps are, but the drive to make art, to record our lives without the benefit of trust funds or culturally well-supported institutions or families where contemporary art was commonplace, makes for much common ground in the indigenous arts community. There are arts families, to be sure—but often, the children from those families of traditional artists, if they continue in the family tradition, carry on the work their families have made for generations, and their dedication is to the act of exact perpetuation, not variation. Upon realizing the commonality, I accepted the invitation to edit this book as an invitation to host a party, something familiar to most folks in Indian communities.

I understood it as an opportunity to host one of those big, sprawling family parties, where you get to hear the greatest unexpected stories from people sitting in the shifting half-light around a huge bonfire, watching smoke and sparks fly into the night sky, a greeting sent off to Grandmother Moon. This party's invitation list was to be made up of the most interesting and creative people I knew or whose work I knew and, selfishly, I got to eavesdrop on their conversations. I consciously sought out members of "writing families," as that integral relationship speaks volumes itself about the ways we learn to survive and rely upon one another in the process.

As happens with every party, some people were unable to attend. We miss their presence, and the magic they would surely have brought with them. I was delighted to invite some new voices, as well, broadening our circle with their insights, carrying on our work. As is also true of any party that stretches to generations, I wanted to acknowledge absent friends who will not be returning, some of the voices that have left in this time. Ted C. Williams, Michele "Midge" Dean Stock, and John Mohawk are all members of our community whose absence is significantly felt, and their voices here remind us of what we have lost. Vine Deloria, the generous spirit who wrote a foreword to the first volume of this series, is glimpsed throughout the book, not with his own words explicitly, but in the impact he had on the lives of others here, who keep up our much-needed work. Even as flesh fails, we understand that the parts of us we leave behind are the support structures. Those elements of our beings, stolen for so many generations, like voices, ideas, cosmologies, come back to us—those sovereign bones.

Sovereign Bones: New Native American Writing, Volume II, evolves out of the critical success and significant contribution of the first volume—*Genocide of the Mind. Genocide* explicitly documented the effects of systematic attempts to assimilate indigenous peoples into the broader American culture. *Sovereign Bones* focuses on the ways in which those same groups have maintained separate, individual identities under the weight of history and aggression, and the key role of writers and visual artists, both established and emerging, in that struggle.

Contemporary indigenous art is, at its core, inherently political, but this book also concentrates heavily on the hallmarks of literary nonfiction and the ways in which this form allows for the personal and cultural to be explored from an aesthetic vantage point, emphasizing the key role of the artist in maintaining, protecting, and nurturing a continued cultural identity. In personal essays, memoir, and reflections on individual history, these artists explore the ways they arrived at their life's work, making significant contributions to sustaining indigenous identity. These artists address the issues as they apply to different facets of a very broad community, identify the difficulties of this mission, and, finally, reflect on the ways in which they have chosen to make contributions.

In essence, this anthology is offered as a monument to the survival of indigenous cultures and the integral contributions artists make to that survival. It is divided into four sections, introduced in the next few pages. I invited people who were primarily working in photographic media to offer pieces that might open each section, informing it visually, confronting the false and stereotypical images by which we are often defined, and at the suggestion of one of them, invited them to also contribute a shorter text concerning their work that would accompany their images. In the cases where writers are largely known as visual artists, I encouraged them to submit a representative image with their text, and if they chose to do so, it appears embedded in the text. The following sectional descriptions offer orientation to each area heading within the book.

Repatriating Ourselves

Though issues surrounding repatriation almost always concern static material objects, we know the power of understanding our own times and places, as well. Most of those items indigenous nations want returned to them represent specific eras in tribal time lines, and the memory of those things is central to remembering the history of this continent. Those catalogued bones, those climate-controlled personal effects, they speak in the ways they can, of the loss and of their time. We, contemporary indigenous people, often look toward the past nearly to the point of discrediting or devaluing our own experiences as critical places on the continuum of indigenous life on this continent. Understanding that our own lives and actions are significant as well, and taking back our own stories, as these artists do, is as much a linchpin in our cultures as anything else.

Speaking through Our Nations' Teeth

While an impressive number of indigenous languages still have many intergenerational fluent speakers, in parts of this continent the survival of an alarming number of languages rests in the hands of fewer people than nearly anywhere else in the world. Despite the reality that carrying on a legitimate conversation in many indigenous languages is possible for fewer than ten people, writers and artists are often significant players in reflecting on their ancestral languages, and the ways in which those languages endure, despite the overwhelming use of English in most indigenous households. They understand that idiom is often a large part of culture, revealing in its idiosyncrasies the ways in which people think. The survival of a language and idiom is the survival of a culture, and the artists represented here have made the incorporation of their language a key component in their work, understanding the interdependency of language, idiom, and culture.

Snagging the Eye from Curtis

Indigenous artists almost universally deal with identity and representation in their work, to varying degrees, and as such, must contend with issues of intellectual property. The long-standing tradition of others representing indigenous cultures and peoples stems heavily from the Edward Curtis images so entrenched in the broader culture. It is a strange time to be an indigenous artist in a culture that responds with a prevailing thought that the work in question is not "Indian enough" if it does not explicitly include indigenous imagery defined by an "other." Consequently, our work is often dismissed if someone else decides it does not fit authoritarian parameters of indigenousness. These artists understand that their work is cultural defense and that continued transmission of traditional ideas and contemporary manifestations of the culture are cornerstones to cultural survival.

Rolling Those Sovereign Bones

The bone game is, indeed, a gamble, an entrenched part of many indigenous cultures. As in any form of gambling, risk is inherent, and those people from indigenous communities who have chosen the artist's life understand that theirs is a gamble for survival. Their subversive acts, keeping their cultures alive, by necessity, use the tools of the oppressors: the English language, written forms of communication, Western publishing models, digital technology, film, the blog, installation, and myriad other forms of current information transmission. The risk inherent in learning to use the oppressors' tools so fluently and naturally that even they will not be aware we are rebuilding ourselves with their tools, is that often, our own people become suspicious of our motivations. This is the struggle of these indigenous artists, wrestling with the nature of audience and the reasons for creating.

This volume opens and closes, as many gatherings of Indians do, with acknowledgment of a Thanksgiving Address, the first from Ted C. Williams, and the second, as part of a fragmentary epic by Phil Young. Phil's work is at its core an exploration of body, memory, culture, and history, and the indignities we accept in our celebration that we are still here, transforming those difficulties into the art of the life we live. Ted's book *The Reservation* was published in 1976, an early work of contemporary American Indian literature, and it showed me that our stories, as they existed, were as rich and as beautiful as anyone else's. Over the years, when I would see him at gatherings, I always asked when I was going to see that second book. It had been rumored to exist for many years, though I knew of no one who had actually seen it. I believed it to be more reservation rumor, *ee-awk*. When I would ask him directly, he would consistently respond that I would see it when the time was right for me to see it. And then, he passed on.

One heavy weight I had in accepting the invitation to edit this collection was that it had come too late for me to ask Ted to write something for it. His voice had played such a significant role in my committing to the artistic life that I had an overwhelming desire to recognize the debt formally. Then, literally days after my accepting the invitation, an e-mail came to me from Syracuse University Press asking if I would consider reviewing the manuscript of the very book I had quit believing existed. I agreed immediately, and when it arrived a couple of days later, there, on the book's first few pages, was Ted's contribution to this volume. It was the beginning of his book, naturally, but it also spoke so eloquently to why we all pursue this life, and was so appropriately an acknowledgment of the gift we have been given, that it had to open this one as well.

An Opening

FROM *BIG MEDICINE FROM SIX NATIONS*

Ted C. Williams

I hear that the older I get, the farther I will have walked to school as a boy. I was born on April 6, 1930. My mother, Amelia, was a Tuscarora, as was my father, Eleazer. The Tuscarora Nation is part of the Six Nation Iroquois Confederacy. The other five nations are "charter" members of the original Five Nation Iroquois Confederacy, which formed under the persuasion of an enlightened person called The Peacemaker. The laws of the Confederacy say that whatever the mother's nationality is, her children are that nationality. So if my father, Eleazer, had been Mohawk or Oneida or Seneca or Cayuga or Onondaga (original members), I would still be a Tuscarora.

We consider the designation "Iroquois" as being improper because it did not come from any of our six languages. At the same time, people of the English speaking "world" who have gone through quite a bit of schooling and who would like people to use the "proper" naming of things, don't want us to call ourselves "Indians." But we do anyway, because Columbus, not wanting to admit to a booboo in navigation, said we were.

In the early days of my life, we didn't have electricity, so we didn't have any radios or telephones. Today, if someone were to visit without first telephoning, we might think they were barging in on us. Back then, it was exciting to hear the dog bark and see someone coming to our house, for any reason. Maybe they had news.

This was a magical time. Time? There is no Tuscarora word for time (and likely in no other Indian language, either). If we asked anyone the time, we said, "*Det de waa ni(t) deh?*" What we were saying was, "How many times does the iron strike?" So that phrase must have come about after the hearing of grandfather clocks tolling out chimes. But there were very few man-made noises.

There was a church bell in the Baptist Church. If someone died, the bell ringer would be told. We would first hear a rapid "ding-dong-ding-dong-ding-dong . . ." and then silence. Then single tolls would come. We counted them because each toll represented a year of the dead person's life. We often easily guessed who it was that died. Again, "How many times did the iron strike?"

Two or three generations before my time, the Federal Government began wondering what to do with all these Indians (of the whole United States of America). Federal Indian schools were set up, and Indian children were forced to attend them. The idea was that there would be a subtle assimilation of these Indians into the mainstream society. Part of the message to the Indian was, "We will educate you. Hey, you might even become the president some day." The other part of the message was, "You are pagans, heathens, but we will rescue you. You won't have to go to hell if you renounce your traditional beliefs and ceremonies." No speaking of a native tongue allowed. No traditional songs or dances allowed. This system was close to legal genocide. Many kidnapped children died of heartbreak and homesickness.

My father attended Carlisle Indian School, but my mother went to public school. She became so adept at reproducing the sound of the English language that she would be asked to "read" to the class though she had no idea what she was saying.

Someone told me that at one school, a teacher was determined to get an Indian boy to read. "Look at the words in this book. I'll say three or four words, reading from left to right, then you repeat aloud right after me those same words."

All went well for a few sentences, when suddenly there was a disturbance by two other children in the room.

"You be QUIET back there!" the teacher said.

"You be QUIET back there," the boy read.

————

My father was fifty years old when I was born. His friends, of his age and older, could therefore be two generations ahead of mine.

At night, when I was supposed to be in bed asleep, I'd be on the floor with my ear over the grille of the air register, listening to the talk between my father and his friends. My father was an "Indian doctor," so many of his friends, even from other reservations, would be talking "Medicine talk." Today, we might describe that kind of talk as "extrasensory perception (ESP) oriented."

Most of the experiences in which Indians drifted out of physical consciousness (went into ESP mode) took place before television, music-playing devices, video games, and the computer began occupying everyone's daily time schedule.

Nevertheless, it is very interesting how the ancient concept that the Universe is one big family touches base with "discoveries" made by science.

With the thought that if I studied hard enough I might become President of the United States, I dug into my grade school studies. My father's brother, Theodore, like many other Indians, could not assimilate the forced textbook path to enlightenment and came back from Carlisle Indian School neurotic, a polite way of saying "crazy." A sister, Minnie, made the grade and became a registered nurse. Another sister, Lizzie, though she became a schoolteacher, had a nervous breakdown and became more like Theodore than Minnie.

Minnie told me about Confucius and Taoism, and that people studying this philosophy had reached enlightenment. But she said that there were other ways to enlightenment. One was "the textbook way." Einstein had taken it. A physicist was considered "the brains" of our society.

Although the Longhouse became my way, I tried to keep track of Einstein's way, too. When I heard that subatomic particles exhibited a behavior that didn't jibe with mathematical formulas, and when physicists came up with "The Uncertainty Principle," I said, "Goody! They're back to square one." "Square one" to me was Medicine people saying, a thousand years ago, "All things are alive and have a consciousness of their own. We are all part of the Great Cycles of All Things."

So, because I like the verification of the Six Nation Great Law by science, my references to some scientific orientation in my version of the Thanksgiving Address will likely be considered "too modern" by some traditionalists. But I have recited an approximate version of this Thanksgiving Address every morning and every night for the past four years and am in good "touch" with these Elements, and they have given me only encouraging feedback.

I also feel that humor is good Medicine, and I spend a lot of my time in my "child." One time, at the great Native American Writers Conference at Oklahoma State University in Norman, a little Eskimo woman recited her poetry to us. So beautiful was it that we excitedly leaped to our feet and gave her a standing ovation.

Three hundred Indians clapping and whistling and doing the Indian "Lalalalala . . ." accolade salute.

It was too much for her. She stood there transfixed for a moment, and then she acknowledged our kudos by going into her "child." She began racing around the stage with her arms out, "playing airplane."

I think we all cried. But we also screamed our approval. We all became "children." And pandemonium ensued.

So maybe "a child shall lead them" . . . and we will place within the sod each sacred kernel of white corn . . . when the Red Oak's leaves resemble a squirrel's hand.

Love,
Ted

―――――

Prelude to the Prelude

In each of the Six Nations (Iroquois) areas of the United States and Canada, each nation or reservation that observes the traditional activities of the Great Law of the Great Peace has a sacred meeting place called the Longhouse. Before any traditional event takes place within these buildings, a powerful statement is recited, at both the preceding and closing of each day's event. This statement is called the Thanksgiving Address. Its importance is pronounced by a sort of "drum roll," a prelude of words that has (by someone) been interpreted in English as "The Words Before All Else."

The opening and closing can be embellished by the speaker, or it can be shortened (sticking to its essence)—for example, when the twenty-one-day Mid-winter Ceremony is ending near the witching hour with a social dance, and everyone is sleepy, and babies are whining.

Pretend, when you open this book, that you are entering one of the Longhouses, that you understand all six languages. If you are a man, when you get through the door, turn to the left, sit down, and behave yourself. If you're a woman, sit on the right side.

Maybe the ghost of Emerson Waterman will holler, "*SI 'DITE!*" Then, in the quiet that prevails, someone will stand up and in a sedate manner recite the Prelude (opening words) and then the Thanksgiving Address.

The Prelude

As you know . . . as we all inherently know . . . we are all just part of the Great Cycles of All Things.

And because we are all from the same Cosmology, we are all part of one great family, not only within the Element called People, but as intimate kin to all the Elements of this Divine and Harmonious Universe.

So tremendous, so magical is the Divine and Harmonious Universe, that the greatest of scholars . . . physicists . . . philosophers . . . astronomers . . . have not been able to calculate the immensity and complexity of this Great Mystery; but our Faithkeepers tell us that "GRATITUDE IS THE BEGINNING OF KNOWLEDGE AND UNDERSTANDING."

And so . . . before any significant occasion, we always open and close each day's ceremony with the Thanksgiving Address; and so powerful is it that the Faithkeepers say it is the life force of their teaching . . . because:

When we do the Thanksgiving Address, as it progresses into Divineness, it automatically brings forth the Creator or the Essence of the Creator or that Highest of Consciousness into our midst.

And when this happens, some of our secular thoughts, engulfed in unworthiness, and in awe of such a Presence, automatically drift off, leaving room for some of what we call the Good Mind to come in.

And when this happens, if we have decisions to make, they won't be made by our own know-it-all selves, but with some of that Divine intervention.

As Creation became completed, we, the Element called People, being the last Element to be created, have been given the task of caretaker of all the other Elements of our Divine and Harmonious Family.

And we have been given four tools to do this with:

We have our Good Thoughts

We have our Good Feelings

We have our Good Words

We have our Good Deeds

Because our ancestors used these tools admirably to make this a better Universe for the unborn, they have left us with a great good feeling.

And so it is, then, with happy hearts, we thank *Soong gwi oo dee sut eh* (Creator) that this is so.

The Thanksgiving Address

In the interest of not giving away the sacred secrets of our philosophy, this description of the Thanksgiving Address is meant for the reader to get a basic grasp of why it is so important to us. The speaker may expound to any length or just hit the "high points" in a late-at-night closing. The Thanksgiving Address "starts" and "ends" each day's ceremonial event. Also, the order of first-to-last-spoken-about has no hierarchy, but rather, for easier memory and so as to not skip some Element, we start with the surface of the Earth and go upwards. Some of our ancestors are "planted" underground so that's where we start. Also, in each Longhouse, after the "Thank you" to each Element, the audience responds with a word meaning, "agreed."

one

REPATRIATING OURSELVES

There is no need
for you to give
back to us
what we already own

This is who we are
in the present
tense

no climate control
no tatters of cloth
no catalogued bones
no beads on loan
no boxes
no labels
no ceremonial tables
no tags
no medicine bags
no hermetic sealers
no deadly disease
no hypotheses

no educated guesses
no dioramas
no dramas
no arrays of diaspora disconnects
no displays of personal effects

in the present
tense
this is who we are

what we already own
there is no need
for you to give
back to us.

Annabel Wong: *Self Portrait*

Taking Aim—New Directions in Tribal Media

Annabel Wong

P hotography is the contemplation of space and time. Photographs are still and safe and ultimately offer the viewer an
objective experience. As a photographer, it is both the experience of creating an image and viewing it after its creation that continually inspires me. Composition and tension are often what
determine the substance of a moment in time. The perpetual practice of this ritual in both still photography and film continually
engages me in my work.

Photography is a physical and emotional experience. The development of a narrative through one's body of work defines who we
are as artists. The desire to capture what we cannot see but rather
feel is most often my goal. Although beauty in imagery is part of
the pleasure of looking at something or someone, the feeling that
an image emotes is far more important. Does the image ask a question, or does it tell you something?

Self-portraiture has been a recurring theme in my work.
Although contemplative at times, I choose, rather, to experiment
with the idea of the placement of myself in the world and how this
shapes the viewer's experience of the image itself. The subject, in
the case of self-portraiture, is not solely the self but the context

within which the photograph is made. It is in this way that I develop a photographic vocabulary to describe myself.

In the context of Native American art and photography, I have chosen to explore a variety of subjects from portraiture, landscapes, and abstract imagery. Through my photography I hope to contribute to the contemporary view of Native people, places, and things. The Native experience is far more complex and difficult to understand or explain than any single image or film can convey. For the first time in history, the marriage of technology and art is allowing more and more Native people to show their visions and tell their stories. Whether it is through reflections of myself or others, I find great value in commenting on and portraying the contemporary life of Native people. By contributing a new set of images and ideas in the diaspora of Native people today, I believe that the redefinition of Native culture and people through art, photography, and film will allow for more positivity and understanding within the larger society.

Ironically, however, some of the greatest misunderstandings about Native people have been created through photography and film. The Native intellect and aesthetic can be translated contemporarily through these powerful mediums. The reclamation of tribal culture and religion in contemporary society is not only remembering the past and maintaining traditions but also creating a new meaning of what it is to be Native in the world today.

THE INDIAN LIST

Alex Jacobs (Karoniaktahke)

Los Indios, Indian, Indien, Indianer, Americans, American race, injuns, redman, redbone, redstick, baton rouge, peaux rouge, roht haut, redskin, salvage, savage, sauvage, salvaticho, skraelings, wild men, pagan, heathen, infidel, primitive, barbarian, cannibals, Caliban, new world man, brother to the wolf, sons of another Adam.

Red devil, tawny devil, darkies, greasy heathen,
copper colored, copper skin, red nigger, dusky devils,
smoky, backward, godawful, lowly, undeveloped,
Indian giver, Indian lover, sly as an Indian, praying Indian,
Indian captive, white savage, friendlies, hostiles, renegades,
the Indian menace, Indian peril, savage barrier,
vanishing Indian, Lo! The poor Indian, Mr. Lo,
digger Indian, stand around the fort Indian,
blanket Indian, blanket ass, feather head, la plume,
lazy Indian, wooden Indian, cigarstore Indian,
Indian princess, Indian summer, firewater, debased,
debauched, scalp, scalplock, scalpknife, warclub,
Mohawk haircut, bloodthirsty, massacre.

Fate worse than death, save a bullet for your wife,
natives are restless, throbbing drums, bury the hatchet,

smoke the peacepipe, red children visit the great white father,
low man on the totem pole, buckskinners,
too many chiefs and not enough Indians,
the Indian question, the Indian problem,
the only good Indian is a dead Indian,
nits make lice.

Siwash, chollo, chief, brave, buck, squaw, papoose,
gut eater, dog eater, puppy basher, scalp lifter,
hair lifter, wagon burner, teepee creeper, wahoo,
yahoo, wild as an Indian just off the reservation,
dirty Indian, drunken Indian, ugly as an Indian,
meaner than an Indian, Indian burn, Indian wrestling,
Indian paint, Indian sidekick, Tonto, kemo sabe, Indian scout,
Geronimo, Hiawatha, Minnehaha, Pocahantas, Kawliga, Lamanites,
Lost Tribe of Israel, el fatalismo del Indio,
give it back to the Indians, you can not change an Indian,

warpath, warpaint, war pony, war whoop, warrior,
war chant, war cry, timber nigger, prairie nigger,
save a fish—spear an Indian, Indian load, tomahawk chop.

Witch doctor, medicine man, kokopellians,
shaman, shamaness, shaman poet, buckskin guru,
spiritual advisor, spirit guide, new age Indian,
new age tribe, wannabees, wopahoes, wigwamers,
gone injun, turned red, pink Indians, beige Indians,
my grandmother was an Indian princess,
I was an Indian in another life.

American ghosts, American blood, blood on the land,

spirits on the land, bloody frontier, westward ho!
Manifest destiny, eminent domain,
Scourge of the west, pesky redskins,
keep them on the reservation, off the reservation,
kill the Indian to save the man.

And this is what we call ourselves:

Metis, mitchif, mestizo, coyote, creole, lobo, genizaros,
gente de razon, mestizajes, guajiro, californio, campesino,
la raza cosmica, Guarani, Concho, Cubano, Manitos, Casitos, Opatas,
Mingo, Mingoes, breed, mixed breed, mixed blood, half blood,
half people, owl eyes, full blood, bloods, whoops, skins, joes,
chips, nishnobs, honyas, 24 hour Indian, pure girl, pure boy,
rez bunnies, mongolian tourists, red muslims,
red power, aim, aimsters, assholes in moccasins,
red earth color people, red clay people, red pipe people,
cliff dwellers, rabbit chasers, cactus munchers, stone dreamers,
fierce ones, deer dancers, salmon smokers, shape shifters,
shaking tent, shaking the bush, bush dance, skin dance.

Tomahawk rock, Radioactive Indians, Skin Radio.
Apples—red on outside, white on inside, malinchistas,
uncle tomahawks, Indian cowboy, tourist Indians,
government Indians, I'm just a poor Indian,

I'm just a dumb Indian, commodity Indian, commod-bods,
road allowance people, leave the blanket, buckskin curtain,
corporate Indians, sellouts, New Deal Indians, Real Indians,
Gallery Indians, Minority contract Indians, ethnic Indians,
generic Indians, Weekend warriors, going home to help my people,

Navajo flu, mohacks, mohogs, put on your Indian,
Moccasin telegraph, smoke signals, yatahey boys, heya heya music,
Heckawees, beaver scalpers, Cherokee Love Medicine, buckskin gigolos.

Skindian, NDN, fancy dancers, powwow club, casino Indians,
casino creepers, billy jacks, ghost dancers, sage burners, sundancers,
frybread eaters, scones, bush scones, city scones, sconage, buffalo
humpers, buffalo jumpers, good grease, greasy faces,
better red than dead, fur bangers,
round, brown, and low to the ground, spiderwomen,
Rez mamas, antelope legs and buffalo hips,
Aaa! Gaw! Weh! Buh! Ayze! Init! See how you are?
REZ, CIB, IHS, PHS, FBI, BIA, IAIA, AA.
Road men, pledge men, button eaters, peyote eaters.

Another Indian bites the dust, flaming arrows, broken arrows,
Columbus-cide, genocide, biological warfare,
Smallpox blankets, American holocaust, extinct,
You call it discovery, we call it recovery,
Rehabilitated Indian, validated Indian,
Boarding school indian, christianized indian,
civilized indian, down on his luck indian, TV Indian,
proud indian, powwow highway, powwow queens.

Euro-Indians, Paleo-Indians, hunter gatherers, indigena, indigenous,
autochones, OPs, original peoples, original Americans, American
originals, Native American, Native North American,
Native North American Indian, indigidude,
American Indian, Amerindian, Amerinos,
First Americans, First Nations, Fourth World,
All my relations.

I wrote "The Indian List" for 1992, as a performance piece for the Columbus Quincentenary. It actually started as research in part of Rick Hill's "American Indian Stereotypes" project, art exhibit, book/publication, teaching course. I wanted to call the book *American Mythology, 500 Years of Native American Stereotypes*. Rick Hill at the Institute of American Indian Arts Museum in Santa Fe was funded by Jeffrey Bronfman (of the Canadian Seagram family) via his Southwest Research Center. Politics at the IAIA from 1992–93 left the project shelved, locked up, in question, and unpublished until recently. In 2006, Charles Dailey, the longtime IAIA museum director/museum studies instructor, staged an exhibit on the IAIA campus called "American Holocaust" based on Rick Hill's stereotype project and the research of Dorothy Grandbois and myself. Dorothy is now photography instructor at IAIA. Rick Hill teaches in New York and Canada and does work for the Haudenosaunee (Iroquois Confederacy). Rick still teaches the course in New York colleges and may be trying to get it published in some form; there was also talk about a traveling show. Hopefully the Chuck Dailey exhibit at IAIA (done by his museum students) may be the first such aspect of any traveling show. I researched the names, titles, epithets, designations, assignations, nicknames, that all types of people, including ourselves, gave to the Native inhabitants of the Americas. While the project languished in a political dead end, I developed my list into a performance piece and would read it at various "Columbus 500" events, poetry slams, and as part of my regular poetry and spoken word readings.

The topic of names is addressed in several books, and as I was researching different historical areas and authors, I kept notes and compiled my list. I do recall Jack Forbes had a few pages in one of his books (my research was in 1991–92). There were also names and epithets that I did not include because they were too broad or too specific, in that they included all races and not just Native Americans. I included some Spanish terms because I am exposed to it, but of course there would be much more available about Mexican and Central and South American Native peoples. I have also left out some derogatory terms that are not helpful and only inciting. The few such terms I did include are enough to get the point across. I would bet the topic of names and epithets comes to every Native writer in at least one of their own books, essays, or research projects. You can glean a few names from just about any book on Native peoples. David Stannard's book *American Holocaust* was a great source for a number of topics. Also doing research at that time (in 1992) were Hank Momaday, Peter Nabokov, Alvin Josephy, and Kirkpatrick Sale.

Every time I would perform the piece, people would come up and say, you forgot this, what about that, it reminds me of a certain time, place, situation, or event. All kinds of people, Native, white, black, Hispanic, young, old, would approach me after a reading. Educators said they could use it in class and asked for copies. My dear friend and former partner Dara McLaughlin, a disability advocate and poet, created her own list for the disability and wheelchair culture in her book of poems *A Map of This World*. There is supposed to be an actual video clip of me performing the piece at the Taos Poetry Circus, around 1992–93, on the Taos Poetry Circus/World Poetry Bout Web site.

When I read the piece at the Taos Poetry Slam, an old primo, some local uncle who drank, wandered in with his drink in a plastic cup and sat in the audience at the auditorium in front of the stage. We think he may have fallen asleep only to wake up and hear some strange man calling down Indians on stage, so he flung his drink at me; it hit the stage in front of me and the mike, ice cubes scattering and clinking toward me—I was told later that I did not skip a beat in the delivery of the names. It is a cathartic piece in which we all start at the same place and we end up healing together at the end. We really need *skins in the house* to make it work, because Anglos (the term for whites, or all Americans really) get nervous and don't know when to laugh or how to react. The poetry of Peter Handke revealed to me (in 1978) that a list could be made into a major piece of poetry. "The Indian List" lives best as a spoken word performance piece.

Ridge Notes, Summer 2006

Allison Adelle Hedge Coke

In the motion of ceremonial dance, one moves into clearer thinking. The veil of supposed reality lifts, allowing accessibility to greater scope. Absolute stillness can bring about the same effortless revealing. Though, in stillness, pause sometimes presents itself by invoking revelations of contemplative memory. Memory serves well enough on a cool day, seasons of years past the time my children were conceived here. On this unexpected return, turning back to where I've been, so long before, memory kindles in each rise of ridge surrounding me. Some memory not of this life, but of my blood life before . . .

———

A moment ago, I was writing about this morning, where ridges fold into one another with great puffs and heady ripples, holding blue smoke and mist within plummeting eddies. The sun, hidden by folds in the slate gray above, still shines white light through one softened atmospheric opening above layers of more gray and beige-sepia horizon. Today, the woods below are evident even by the time crows settle back in. A single leaf skips across the grass, feeling its way home. Vines cradle stone, snugly. My sister's namesake, the one-who-cries-for-acorns—the dove—takes a higher perch, almost to the hickory top, above coarse crows weighting morning with their heaviness. The lightness of ever-present gray mist, pure smoke, causes each branch to seem abrupt, ominous as the light soon surrounds this peak. Swathed in its embrace, its silky essence of wakening, welcoming me home, here to sit: relishing.

Days before, I was in archives, running over lists of Final Roll applications, in an attempt to commemorate, in some strange way, the actuality of the one-hundred-year toll of treatied identity rights and lack thereof for Indian people. Contemplating the rigidity and wrongfulness of (White) District of Columbia bureaucrats' decisions over matters of peoples not yet citizens of the 130-year self-identified State, oppressively surrounding and dictating perfectly capable nations of aboriginal American civilizations, who preceded U.S. identity by tens of thousands of years before them. How in that day, in 1906, all it took to imprison or put to death an Indian person was a White person's accusations, and all it took to take Native rights and belonging from existence was a White person's say. Surrounded by the very beauty of the Appalachian Mountains, wherein my grandfather's (along with his Eastern mother's) Final Roll application was made, rather than the Western rolls his father (of Eastern and Western blood) could also qualify him (where ten years before the federal government had reduced Indian territory to two entities—Oklahoma Territory and Indian Territory—and just a year prior to the Final Rolls, the territory citizens attempted to gain admittance to the union as the State of Sequoyah but were rebuffed by Congress) . . . I was contemplating the sheer madness of it. The Final Rolls in general. In the end, Grandpa Vaughan refused to log in as Western, partially because we are maternally inclined, but more due to his disgust with Western politics altogether. Pun intended.

Born in 1878, Escar Vaughan HedgeCoke was twenty-seven

when the Final Rolls were orchestrated, already a father of four years and working, like many other southeastern peoples, in the fields, farms, and railroads springing up every which way. My father told stories of decisions made for them and how difficult it was for his father to grasp Americana, ownership—greed. His mother a Huron root-woman/midwife and his father's mother a dreamer/seer and root-woman Cherokee, what was for them a given, now for decades a given for the others to decide. A hundred years this very year, the Final Rolls have been logged, and slight attention has been paid to that fateful time of final decree by officials with little or no knowledge of what The People were as people. Instead, the Final Rolls were just another of hundreds of feigned gestures, meant more to detach people from place, from spiritual and intellectual space which by Creation Story (or, in some cases prophesizing the coming of Whites, migratory journey), by all rights, was surely home.

———

Ours was no tertiary-distanced, thirdhand childhood. We grew up primarily conditioned in the knowledge of our ancestors. Versed in the knowledge of our ancestors' removal from their traditional homes, immersed in the lives of those who stayed, and familiar with all who hid out, taking refuge in other regions, with numerous Cherokee (Kituwa) people. We were raised with eco-ethos consciousness in an econ-ethos era. Knowing trade barter and nurture-to-nurture social structure far surpassed anything feudalistic, capitalistic, money and resource/surplus-driven societies had to offer. Raised knowing our ancestors worked wherever they could find sustenance to support their children, regardless, in what my father considered our dark ages, from the 1720s to 1978. And here in 2006, the culmination is still astounding. Since 1720, a treaty had existed with Whites/Brits. Since the settling of Jamestown for timber to blow European glass, lands were continually over-used and disgraced by them, then ravaged throughout multiple land grabs. None was more devastating than the war waged to take over extensive Eastern Indian homelands—the American Revolution.

Dad would say there was no bloodier time for Native people than the patriot fires set to eighty-some Cherokee towns, the Clinton Campaign jam floods and fires set upon the Hau-denosaunee, the outright holocaust upon Eastern tribes under the name of freedom for people who were British by blood (and by colony) but now reidentified themselves, in name and totally fab-ricated culture, as American. The reidentification of colonists from British to American was utterly devastating for Indigenous Ameri-cans—for tribes already under treaty with the British and forced to fight to protect the homeland from unlawful taking—expansion. From the identity-fraudulent Boston Tea Partiers on through to 1778, Eastern peoples were swept into the vortex of heavily weaponized war so that expatriates could name themselves patriots and destroy (or use) whoever had prior claim to what they desired. And now during the count of Final Rolls, for seventy years, the diaspora had existed as well, simply put upon for rich soil and gold in the hills of Appalachia, the then Georgians, the prison colonists, and Jackson's lot, wanted White-might on.

Our grandfather believed the entire Final Roll system was con-strued to create what he, and others like him, believed to be a "pet Indian" status, especially in the Territory, where one would appear to be what Whites believed them to be regardless of actuality of humanness once logged and pedigreed. We learned that the only reason Grandpa Vaughan went through the legal motions in the traditional Eastern heartland (despite the bureaucracy in Eastern enrollment, outright poverty, and continuing oppressive conditions), was to keep our blood noted where we truly belonged—despite what he perceived to be the ease of enrollment in Removal lands by anyone who showed up to take what was promised to Cherokee people forever in exchange for their leaving the Eastern home. He was vehemently against the enrollment of Whites as Western Cherokee, something he believed was occurring specifically in Oklahoma as a territory-grabbing tactic, and despised the idea of Washington conducting Indian politics in general.

His wife, born in 1882, was of the time when Canada conducted policy meant to strip a woman (and her children) of status rights, if she chose to marry other than a status Native. Conversely, if a First Nations' man married out, even to a White, his woman would be considered status appropriate. Having met in Indian Territory, due to their travels with relations and to work, and wishing fully to be home with their own respective peoples, Grandpa filled out the paperwork with his mother, despite his feelings about the entire legal scheme.

Other than work by Jolene Rickard, I really haven't seen many gallery shows, heard any music notations, nor read anything in the general media regarding this hundred-year anniversary, now nearly ending, and I wonder why it is so unnoticed when millions of Native peoples were affected, and their descendants forever regarded by these Final Roll decisions related to those so-called final days. My son surmised that those who fell on the short end of the tally (no CDIB—Certificate of Degree of Indian Blood) are afraid to note such publicly, and those who were ordained by D.C. Whites in the end feel less need to note the reality of White decisions over Native Nations and peoples less identified by Whites during the extensive land-grabbing era the Final Rolls represent, since it doesn't affect them now personally. Or does it? I expect he's right in many degrees of discomfort, and wonder then why that time seems something we should all take notice of, though the anniversary is quickly passing us by.

Being Canadian and Native on both sides of my family as well as being indigenous in these lands, and having a parent born on each side, respectively, in 1921 and 1922, we were definitely versed in the differences in tribal law across the Northern border and physically spent a great deal of our childhoods on both sides. My father always inspired us to think of the well-known purposeful fragmenting caused by U.S. blood degree: Two full-bloods from separate nations marry. Their kids are now half by law. Another generation comes and marries full-bloods from other nations, and their kids are only listed as a quarter by degree. Thus in three generations, for tribes existing on U.S. quarter-blood enrollment, though full Native, Indigenous people are stripped of many rights guaranteed by treaty in exchange for land and (supposed) peaceful cohabitation—forever. Knowing my dad's shirttail cousin, Gillespie Wilson, we grew up knowing that the one-drop rule for Blacks was an obvious ploy to place in servitude anyone, in White/Black society, not fully White. Yet, if the same were originally applied to Native peoples in this manner (a rare consideration even in post–Civil War White/Black society), the sheer number of Indians would have secured gross land tenure rights emphatically. Instead, most people without favorable blood degree decision (despite ridiculous bureaucratic inaccuracies and fallacies) lost affiliation and community ties/familial knowledges, and feigned White to survive as the otherwise and, most sadly, literally became White, by most means despite the blood truth, within a very short period of time.

Culture can be a very powerful weapon if android-amassed assimilation allows for survival of generations, and "resistance is futile," after all. The Americas have been the largest playing field for gross assimilation, primarily due to Euro-colonists turning on their own and needing to create a place they could rule over—the entire Western Hemisphere. Thankfully, we have the heaviness of crows in mornings of smoky mist and tall trees to contemplate, and, personally, I thank the earth I sit upon, here and now, for the simple fact that even on our Southern side, my father retained who we are despite the disadvantage, or curse as some of the older people called it when I was young.

Maybe as a response to this schizoid commemoration and the taxing upon the soul it insists upon, it is good to challenge the entire concept of belonging within a truer sense of Indigenous civilizations in North America. It concerns me that I personally know of people who have been involved with illegal activities against the identity of Native Nations from many different ethnic backgrounds—including tribal. That, in this particular hundred-year commemorative day, especially, information disputing the image bureaucrats in D.C. have constructed of the United States itself, with the Patriot Act and other frighteningly familiar fascist tactics, that those who stand against the machine, like our ancestors a hundred years ago, stand, once again, to be eradicated from the face of the planet by official decree. That noted, though Indian people have continually repeated the Creation and Emergence stories, and though Native Nations' orators back one another's stories up consistently, it has only been a very short time since White America finally "discovered" that glaciers rolled matter far underneath in their mighty waves of ice throe and flow. That most of the entire Northern portion of North America's First Nation history is far below the surface of the soil we stand upon in this day due to the glacial pummeling movement and pushing of surface to mountainous heights and/or to places underneath whereupon we now stand. In one particular incident this summer, while mining, workers found an ancient fishing village cache still in perfect order, along with other village remnants, far below the surface we exist upon, in a place considered arid today. Upon marveling over the find, they immediately destroyed it, like all the others in their careers, because the site would be closed and their good paychecks cut off during a dig to distinguish just what is actually only beneath the veil of our view today. Despite the fact that the find was so old that the fish were unrecognizable as contemporary species, the workers seemed only to lament loss of pay, and so, duty to the dollar.

The stories are true. The world below us is real and the people upon it the descendants, by blood, of those whose lives are far below today. When the horses and camels left this hemisphere for the Oriental hemisphere, ten to fourteen thousand years ago, the glaciers were forming and already turning the world upside down. The vast caves interlinking lands far below the current topsoil sometimes held escape routes insomuch as the land was quickly turning into something people could not deal with as well. In the time following return to homelands, now forever geologically changed, the stories of "this world" relay the emergence and return to reclaim living latitudes in a world now often devoid of anything remotely familiar, and yet here the people were and here they remain.

I've been loosely at work on a novel, *Digs*, for fifteen years now. I've published numerous chapters from it, mostly as short stories, but also as novel excerpts, and in this hundred-year-anniversary year, I'm drafting the screenplay as well. In this, still without divulging the secret and/or sacred, I am (like many others) tackling the task of bringing to light actualities that simply need be known in order to assert livelihood here in the Occidental hemisphere, the

Americas, which by all rights are ours by nature and belonging despite the 230 years of the occupying U.S. regime. I've decided to move ahead with the full volume and to release what small bit I have to offer the conversation, to punctuate the literary conversation in which we do exist and to allow generosity of knowledge to do its bit to correct and correlate that which is just under the surface here. I'm inspired by Indigenous nations delegating in international circles, by Indigenous people presiding over nations in the Americas—by Evo Morales's courageous leadership and insistence for full freedom and respect for Native Nations and traditions. I'm excited that the proclaimed "Decade of the Indigenous Americas, 2005–2015," has taken hold; that people are returning to prominence in places they have been stripped away from; that, Eurocentric government sanctioned or not, are asserting themselves into positions that will inspire future generations to be less complacent/wounded/assimilated and more true to traditional form, in assuming self-governance policy and place in the world.

Indigenous poets have begun the process of reclaiming traderoute (aboriginal American) ties and working to unite and reunite Indigenous poets (writers, artists, musicians, and others) through our work and publications and through our very being in this day. Upon initial request by Hugo Jamioy and Ariruma Kowii, Hugo Jamioy, Ariruma Kowii, Sherwin Bitsui, Bienvenido Arroyo, José Gabriel Alimako, Gladis Yagari, James Thomas Stevens, Jorge Miguel Cocom Pech, Leonel Lienlaf, Al Hunter, Joy Harjo, and I have all jointly committed to proclaiming this Trans-continental Indigenous American embrace. We are speaking together and for one another at the United Nations and at festivals and conferences in Medellín, Caracas, Maturín, New York, Santa Fe, and around the globe. Roberta Hill Whiteman, Karenne Wood, Gordon Henry, Carolyn Dunn, Marcie Rendon, LeAnne Howe, Simon Ortiz,

Santee Frazier, Orlando White, Mark Turcotte, Rich Van Camp, Jeannette Armstrong, and Eric Gansworth are among U.S. and Canadian Native poets invited to join us in the near future. And thus, the gathering of Indigenous creative comrades will continue from here and collectively invite unity, as we stand for one another when need be in the continual onslaught upon the Western Hemisphere, in a biological as well as social sense. Language contains essential keys, including trade-item clues, e.g.: corn in Cherokee is *selu* and in Kitchua is *semu*. Who better than poets to begin the reconstructive work ahead?

In an era when Indigenous poets in Colombia are literally existing under the colonizing gun and weaponry of capitalist greed (the so-called War on Drugs), wherein the poets, as messengers, as orators, of the people still stand to be silenced first and foremost by oppressive regimes (circa Laura Bush) when the word is ultimately imperative . . . in this era, our collective work is essential.

In this we also seek to publicly free ourselves to commit to poetics of our own linguistic and Indigenous language-based influences despite the offense of English and Spanish aggressively upon us. To proclaim that canting, rhythmic, lyric, orally inspired poetry of the Indigenous Americas stands as important on the page as lyric metered verse including sestinas, sonnets, and villanelles from the Eurocentric canon. That Indigenous image (poetic device) is vitally important to the sustainability of the world. That perspective is what it is for a reason. To proceed with purpose for the people, for poetics, versus succumbing to self-promotion-induced ranks of egocentricity and divisive measure. To proceed with love of language, of linguistic arts, among and for, the greatly diverse Indigenous populations of the Americas. To extol poetics of brotherly nations surrounding us all and note ourselves free to experiment and expound poetically as we so choose, despite the attempted labeling of Native poetics/literary guise often imposed upon us.

Sister nations we once were and in this day, I so mourn the early loss of The Great Peacemaker and the peace movement spreading throughout the Northeastern nations from the Wendat to the Haudenosaunee and intended to unite nations to the South and on so until we all lived unified in The Great Peace. Yet his purposeful intent lives on and the visions of his mother and grandmother continue as well, as do the stories, and it is our work to insist that we continue contemplating and acting toward a united Indigenous future wherein our children's children have say over themselves entirely. It is, in essence, our duty to work for peace while protecting ourselves when necessary. (Duty in traditional sense of acting for love of the people/planet versus duty as directed by industry and/or the state.) Ours to note whom we are from as well as who we are, as well as to enjoy the aboriginal privilege of living on the earth in all her glory and to fight to protect her right to exist in peace as well.

Though working continually in community mentorship and teaching, I did take a short break from book publishing following the release of *Dog Road Woman* and the chapbook *The Year of the Rat* (due to private matters, as well as public and community commitments). Meanwhile, during the past three years, in an attempt to punctuate the conversation, I've offered three new volumes of work. One to articulate the distinguished reality of being the second daughter of a mother suffering schizophrenia in a schizoid contemporary Western culture (*Rock, Ghost, Willow, Deer*). One to pay tribute to the continual work ethos of a nurture-to-nurture eco-ethos people living in an econ-ethos labor world and as testimony to labor writing as literary art (*Off-Season City Pipe*). The latest (*Blood Run*) to honor the civilizations here preceding the current Occidental dominator. Particularly the traditional mound cities, unnoticed now for a criminal length of time. This volume challenges the mainstream perspective of where these cities actually exist and what took place despite their presence, as enhanced through verse play.

In all, the volumes work to establish actualities where there are little truths, to fill the gorges of informational deletion in the conquest of the Americas. With North America being the primary area of my traditional concern—by blood—but with actuality of the Americas, in their entirety, my greatest concern in this time. Yet, none of these works fit what is commonly accepted as representational of contemporary Native literature by many of my academic non-Native colleagues, and for that I am grateful. Other people expecting stereotypical/contrived representation cannot properly register the breadth of writing by Native peoples. Somewhat identifiable by shared tendencies (versus tenets), the thousands of poets/writers of Indigenous American blood and belonging offer much more than may fit the acceptable mold fashioned by those far removed from actualities of being Native here today. Insomuch, those tendencies do not preclude variances and do not include all there is to contemplate in a creative Native mind, thus will not hold sure anything easily fit into constructs of expectations and oftentimes are truly in opposition to what is most anticipated by Borg-ettes. Would one imagine lumping all of the literary genius of the Eastern Hemisphere into one mass convention? Hardly. And so it is with Indigenous American poets and writers. And yet the need to serve our truths, to restore dignity while witnessing the beauty of the world and the fragility of human condition.

And so we work to serve our ancestors in this way. In the meantime, when it gets down to it, the luscious bounty of these rolling mountains holds forever this spark in me, my true privilege, having come of age in this motherland and having been seasoned on the Northeastern home of my grandmother, and the blood homes of my mother's people as well. That here, in this day, my life is a wonderful tangle of North America, despite the enemy's borders. And the Eastern peoples from whom I do descend, still live with me here and now, continue through my children and grandchildren (along with their Northern Plains Nations blood ties) and will know who we all are through my father, now eighty-four, and mother, now eighty-five, and through me. So in 2006, that the son of a Final Roll applicant is here to speak for himself, as a Real Person, a human being, without constraint is enough for me to relish in this great Smoky Mountain morning, even though I'm just passing through. And though my deepest interests truly lie within each rock and root below me and each crow and crest above, to better secure their place in the contemporary world (so that I may continue contemplating their beauty as a human being), my own duty is among The People and their struggles are my own, and so goes the work in which we live and who actually has the final say. While crows' wings spread and shield, their heaviness blankets all below—memory. Ah, purpose!

WHY *DO* I CONTINUE TO WRITE?
AN EXHAUSTIVE QUESTIONING

MariJo Moore

September 25, 2006

Some mornings I wake up and wonder, why even bother to continue to write? Many contrite books—such as those by the spurned husband of a twentysomething teacher who had sex with her thirteen-year-old student—are being published to ensnare readers. Is this what the general public wants? Or, are they more interested in the gush of books coming out of Washington concerning our decrepit or non-decrepit government, depending on where the authors' loyalties are positioned? Who wants to read books written from an Indigenous point of view? Are there people really interested in what I have to say?

Then, inevitably, I will receive a letter or e-mail from someone who has read my writings, thanking me for the hard work and honesty. For instance, in 1998, a Western Cherokee man attending the University of Arizona called me after reading my poem "Disturbed Journeys," in which ancestral bones stored in a museum are waiting to be poked, pierced, and carbon-dated. In a conversation with the walls of the museum, the spirit voices of these bones state that those who continue to disturb them will never totally understand the unsettling of nature or the pain caused others by doing so. This poem voices my longtime disgust with and disapproval of the grave robbing and sacred-ground desecration suffered by American Indians. The young man shared an experience he had had while working with a repatriation project in Alaska. It seems he was invited, along with local aboriginal people, to "view" skeleton remains of a fresh dig. He was helping an elder walk through the museum when, upon reading the name tag attached to one of the skulls, she gasped in horror and almost passed out in his arms. The name was that of her great-aunt.

"People have no idea the hurt that goes with this sort of discovery," the young man told me. Then he thanked me for writing the poem and said he hoped others would read my writing and become more respectful of American Indians.

And so, I continue to write. I shouldn't let feelings of despair overtake me. I should be stronger and realize I don't write for the masses: I write for those (Indian and non-) who believe that even though American Indians are a minority in today's world, we still have a right to be heard. I write so that my granddaughters will know the truth. I write because I have to.

October 2, 2006

This morning, yet another senseless murder of children is in the news. A man went into an Amish school in rural Pennsylvania and killed little girls. My heart aches for these families as I write this. What has gone wrong in the world? Are people becoming more evil, or, are we so "connected" by media these days that we have access to more information than our grandparents, or even our parents? And even though most of the news we receive has been "watered down or up," as it were, it is indeed logical that truth can be much stranger than fiction, as the old adage goes. But is the general reading public interested in nonfiction as much as fiction? I am certain that by next spring, some onlooker will write a book concerning this tragedy. Will there be an Amish—who are definitely a minority—book written as well? Since they are such a tightly knit community, and tend to stay away from modernity, this is highly improbable. Of course, the outlook is different when it comes to American Indians: modern-day matters do impact and shape our lives.

During one of my numerous interviews with the late Vine Deloria Jr., I asked how he thought Native nonfiction writings were impacting modern social issues. He answered that much depended on how people perceive social issues and what issues are important. "Culturally, there is a big revival in terms of dances, celebrations, and so forth, but you don't see a corresponding interest in restoring kinship ties and acting in the traditional manner," he added. His book *Red Earth, White Lies* had just been published, and he wanted this book to bolster belief in traditional teachings by showing the factual side of them. "I see far too many younger Indians pretending that the 'oral tradition' is composed wholly of spiritual sayings, whereas much of it is historical memory."

Obviously Deloria felt Native nonfiction to be extremely important in the matter of continued existence. He wrote to motivate future generations. Which is why I worked so hard on the two anthologies: *Genocide of the Mind: New Native Writings* and *Eating Fire, Tasting Blood: Breaking the Great Silence of the American Indian Holocaust.* During those days I mentioned at the beginning of this essay, a number of the comments I received concerned the moving writings in these anthologies.

Recently, when I was interviewed about *Eating Fire, Tasting Blood,* I was asked why this book is so necessary and timely. I referred the interviewer to an excerpt from the introduction:

"Because our historical truth is a fire that assiduously burns, a fire that demands recognition, a fire whose flames still scorch. In order to subsist in today's mêlée of war, injustice, economic deprivation, and senseless slaughter, we need to be aware of what human beings have done to each other, and are still capable of doing. We need to know ourselves as well as we know our enemies."

Yes, there are days when I question my life's path. Nevertheless, after twenty years of dedicating my life to writing, lecturing, and teaching, I can emphatically stress the following: it is imperative that American Indians write their own literature; that they write from their hearts the truth concerning their experiences and concerns. We owe this to our ancestors, as well as to our descendants. Consequently, all writing is political in one sense or another, and one can never fully imagine the effect his or her words might have on another.

October 9, 2006

This morning I awake with my stomach churning and my heart hurting. I know this is because I am holding back tears. I feel I have no right to cry, but I need to. I know I do.

Charles Frazier, who is from North Carolina and the author of the now famous book *Cold Mountain*, has written his second novel, *Thirteen Moons*. Yesterday, I watched the *CBS Sunday Morning* segment in which he was interviewed. When the interviewer stated that Frazier had been given eight million dollars as an advance, he smiled and agreed that this is a ridiculous amount. "It is just a book," he added.

This afternoon, I continue to think about the words "just a book." Perhaps to Frazier it is just a book, but to me it is a fictional account of Cherokee history, including the Trail of Tears. A book that will possibly be read by thousands, if not millions. A book some of these readers will no doubt believe to be historical fact. Another book written by a non-Indian about Indians.

I question myself: am I envious of his success? Perhaps. What contemporary writer wouldn't be? Am I hurt by the fact that the chief of the Eastern Band of Cherokee has given his approval of this book, and stated on national television that even though Cherokees are not presented in a favorable light in Frazier's writing, that it is OK because that was then and this is now? Does it trouble me that the Eastern Band is going to translate this novel into the Cherokee language? I read on the Internet where Frazier has made a donation to the Museum of the Cherokee Indian to develop their Cherokee Literature Initiative, and there are plans for a movie of *Thirteen Moons*. I have not read *Cold Mountain*, but I have begun reading *Thirteen Moons*. Honestly, I find the writing tiresome and overloaded with detail, and am losing interest.

Don't misunderstand my ramblings to think I am totally an outcast. Many people from the Eastern Band have read my books and told me how much they appreciate what I have done and am doing. I have spent a good part of the past twenty years encouraging and helping Indian people to write their own literature. I know I have Cherokee blood, but I am not a "documented" Indian. So why do I choose to write from an Indigenous point of view? Why do I feel it is so important for Indians to write their accounts of history? Why did I not choose another path? Because my path chose me and I didn't have the guts to refuse it. I was not born on the Qualla Boundary. I was not raised there, and I have never lived there. I am not a part of that community. How dare I question the tribe's motives in accepting the writing of others? I suppose I have no right to question why the chief is lauding Frazier's book and not any of mine. This whole ordeal of deep hurting concerning Frazier's new book makes me tired, makes me question why I have worked so hard. I wish with all my heart that Vine Deloria Jr. were still alive to discuss this with me. I miss his encouragement and guidance terribly. Finally, the tears are coming.

What this episodic event has done is make me go deeper into myself and question why all this publicity for Frazier's new book is hurting me so badly. Through prayer and tears I find myself asking an appalling question. I get an answer, and although it is not a pretty one, it is my answer. Therefore, everything does happen for a reason.

Do I want acceptance from others and more acknowledgments for my writings because my Indian blood comes from my dad and he never accepted me? Because he continually told me I couldn't make any money writing? Is that why I am hurting so badly and questioning why Frazier's book is receiving the attention I wanted my books to receive? No doubt there is some connection. When I discuss this with an old friend, he reminds me it is not a good idea to compare my success as a writer with the success of others. Thinking about this, I am made aware I do not understand the world of business, the world of money. I don't understand why this is what makes the world go round. It doesn't matter who is a better writer, who strives to tell the truth, it is who you know and how much money you can bring in that matters to people who do understand the business world. People need money to survive. People need money to keep cultures alive.

I continue to question myself deeper and realize I have spent most of my life trying to either prove my dad wrong, or achieve some sort of success so he would notice me. He left when I was four, and I didn't see him again until I was almost seven. He eventually left again, and this time for good. What I remember most about him during my teenage years are the phone call promises that never materialized, and spending my birthdays wondering what I had done to keep him from sending me a present, or even a card. Through my adult years, I attempted to make connections with him to develop what I thought was a "reasonable" father–daughter relationship. However, I never felt like he accepted me, or understood why I felt writing to be so important. He'd rather I had a job in computers, something that brought in steady money. Instead of comforting myself with the fictitious thought that he just didn't want to see me struggle, or realizing the fact that he thought me incompetent, I planted what I thought to be an achievable idea in my subconscious: if I could become highly successful, I would attain his approval. In reality, he was more intent on my making money than making the truth of history known.

Regardless, I am grateful for all that has been done through me, for all the people who have appreciated my writings, and for being able to fulfill my dream of being a writer. I dry my eyes and hear Vine's spirit telling me, "Go forward." A memory comes to mind.

A few months ago, as I was walking through the back door of my cabin, I heard the screams of a hawk. Looking up into the hot sun, I saw two red-tailed hawks circling effortlessly on the wind. One was screaming; over and over, she screamed to get my attention. I went inside, got some tobacco to offer, and realized what she was telling me. She was reminding me of a poem I had written several years ago:

Underneath the Hawk's Scream

I stood underneath the hawk's scream
long enough to know I didn't understand
long enough to know I needed to go deeper

long enough to know that the crows crowding her,
distressing her, tearing at her with their indifference
were there for a reason as were the blue jays quietly listening.

How badly did she want her nest in that tree?
What would she endure to make sure her cries were respected?
Her creations were born?

I stood underneath the hawk's scream long enough to realize
she was not screaming from frustration
she was screaming to be heard

long enough to know she was teaching me how to persevere.
"Carry on!" she shrieked at me.
"You have a right. It came with birth."

I realize parts of this essay are as disjointed as the lyrics of a Bob Dylan song, but that is the way of my writing life: disjointed, but beautifully so. I know if I pay attention to all the lyrics, one verse will stand out that makes sense of it all. This will be the verse that will expound the interconnectedness of all the nonsense. And this verse will give me a deeper understanding of my life's song in exchange for having paid attention. After all, my writings seem to always take integral meanings, and creativity has brought healing and deeper understanding to my life. If I am not creating, I am stagnating, and a stagnating soul is a starving soul.

Publishing will continue in its business-minded way: some outsider will cash in on the horrible Amish incident, trying to speak for that community without their permission, and more books will be published by spurned husbands, "not guilty" politicians, and so on. Regardless, I will continue to write and encourage others to do the same. I don't want to starve for anything, even a father's acceptance, ever again. I wish I could say it doesn't matter now that my dad didn't accept me, but that would be a lie, and I am determined to get to the truth. I am sure what is written through me will reach those to whom it should go. I am also confident some will read what American Indians have written, and continue to write, and realize our viewpoints are just as important as those of non-Indians. And now, I know myself better than ever before. I am the one who has to accept me. I am the one who has to accept life on life's terms. Through writing this essay, I have grown spiritually, which for me, seems to be the reason for creativity. The tears are gone and I am smiling. And believe it or not, the hawk is back, circling my house. I must go and stand underneath her screams once again. I have a right to carry on; it came with birth.

IN VINE VERITAS

Scott Richard Lyons

L ate one night in the fall of 2003, as I was reading yet another depressing article about the dismal state of our world, I received a strange, cryptic e-mail from an unfamiliar source: DOGHARPER. There was no other signature, no specific address to me, and, aside from the ID, no capitalization at all in the message. If I received it today, I would probably assume it was hawking cheap prescription drugs from Mexico and delete it without a second thought. Still, the message caught my attention. It read, quite mysteriously, "Go to your browser and type in _____." A woman's name.

Curiosity always gets the best of me, so I dutifully did exactly as I was told. She turned out to be an attractive Native scholar roughly my age. Nothing else was self-evident. Slightly creeped out, but also admittedly enthralled, I wrote back: "Who are you?"

DOGHARPER ignored my question and replied, "She's tired of dating idiots—just think you two might make a nice couple— that's all."

"I'm sorry," I responded, "but I'd like to know who I'm dealing with here." I was stern but secretly relieved that my interlocutor apparently didn't consider me an idiot.

Again DOGHARPER refused my request for identification and

instead offered unsolicited advice: "Just go to the same conference as her—strike up a conversation—tell her you know me."

"And just who is this 'me' that I supposedly know?"

Silence. No answer. For two weeks. But by then I had already figured it out. It was Vine Deloria Jr., and this was his way of setting me up on a date.

———

When Deloria passed on November 13, 2005, there was an outpouring of praise from people around the world who had studied him, respected him, contended with him, or often all three. Major newspapers published glowing obituaries of the sort typically reserved for Very Important Persons, and research universities from Syracuse to Tucson presented formal tributes in his honor. All agreed that his death constituted a major intellectual loss.

London's *Guardian* newspaper hailed Deloria as "the twentieth century's most important scholar and political voice in Native American affairs." The *New York Times* called him a "champion of Indian rights" and quoted Charles F. Wilkinson saying, "In the last 100 years, he's been the most important person in Indian affairs, period." Writing in *American Anthropologist*, for an audience Deloria often combated during his career, Raymond J. DeMallie flatly proclaimed, "His legacy is enormous."

Indeed. But for Native folks, Vine's legacy was already considered enormous. Less than a year before his death, *Indian Country Today* presented Deloria with their American Indian Visionary Award and published an accompanying series of reflections on his life written by such Native notables as Wilma Mankiller, Hank Adams, John Mohawk, and others. Norbert Hill called Deloria his "hero" and "idol" for his integrity and brilliance. Suzan Shown Harjo remembered the first time she met Deloria in the 1960s, "not so much because of what was said, but more the fact of it." She was a young mother with a kid on her hip, but he listened to her. My personal favorite, though, was the touching memoir penned by his son, the historian Philip Deloria, who spoke of his father's curious fascination with the occult, love of dogs (one of whom, I learned, was named Harper), and probably aggravating habit of replaying the same recorded songs over and over late into the night. The son's memories of his father were a deeply human reminder that even a Very Important Person like Deloria is still, after all, a person. Yes, very important—but also for reasons that rarely appear in published tributes.

It is good that Deloria's life and death received the notice it got; he deserved every word of it and more. And it seems important to note that much of the attention his passing received came from the non-Indian publishing world, especially when we recall the ways that Indian deaths were comprehended not so very long ago. (*The only good Indian* . . .) Insofar as his life's work compelled the world to take Indian lives seriously, Deloria seems to have benefited from his own legacy: when he died, and perhaps for the first time in history, non-Indians all over the world personally felt the loss and paid the same respect they would to their own. When you think about it, that's really something.

Better still is the fact that Vine's life and work were praised by Natives before he left us. It's a truism that funerals are social events where people say nice things about the departed that they really should have said when it mattered most—while the person was alive—but Vine did receive at least some of his due. I'm thankful for that.

But I also think it fairly uncommon. It's no secret that, as Native people, we don't praise each other as often as we could or should. When it comes to criticizing or blaming each other—oh, at that we are absolute masters. But praising? Not so good. There's something self-loathing in that, and I think Vine knew it. So, for me, one of his most important legacies—in addition to all of the Very Important publishing and political work he did—was the way he actively helped younger Native scholars, writers, and activists take their rightful place in this world; how he encouraged us—often in his own peculiar, tricksterish, and even curmudgeonly manner—to love ourselves.

———

This is how Vine helped me. I was a recently minted PhD and a second-year assistant professor still trying to find my way around a large national university when he visited my campus in 2003. During his visit, Deloria gave a standing-room-only lecture, lunched with other Very Important Persons, and met with several regional tribal leaders, all of whom greeted him with the same exuberant reverence one might reserve for an old war buddy who once saved the entire platoon. On the first night of his visit I was invited to join Vine and a handful of Native American Studies scholars for dinner at an elegant restaurant that I could never justify on my own budget. Now, most people would appreciate an invitation to such an enlightened, epicurean feast. But to be honest, I was feeling increasingly nervous about meeting the man.

Here, after all, was the last century's most important person in Indian affairs, period; the author of two dozen books and countless articles, the recipient of every major award people have ever given to Indians, and a name I first encountered as a little boy during the Red Power years, when my father and uncles passed around a dog-eared copy of *Custer Died for Your Sins*. (If I tried reading it then, I don't recall. But I do remember being fascinated with the cover and noticing that my father and uncles were uncharacteristically reading and discussing a book.) Here, in the flesh, would soon be the most influential author I had ever read, a scholar whose work had saved me in graduate school by giving me a language, a reading of history, and a way of thinking that I had not found in my seminars: first through *Custer*, then *We Talk, You Listen*, then *The Nations Within*, then *American Indians, American Justice*, then *God Is Red*, and then *Red Earth, White Lies*. It was only after reading those books that I could start thinking for myself. Deloria, I realized while getting ready for dinner, had serendipitously brought me to Deloria: his books had led to the completion of my dissertation, which led to my present job, which led to my imminent dinner with Vine.

Which was now leading to a decisive knot in my stomach.

As I ironed my crisp new khakis on the kitchen table, long-dormant insecurities started to revive within me. This surprised me, because at age thirty-eight I had figured them licked; but there they were, evil little things, climbing my spine like tiny bears and giving me a sudden case of self-doubt. *I wasn't smart enough.* No, I had somehow faked my way through graduate school, finished only because my department hadn't paid enough attention, but would soon be exposed in all of my intellectual vacuity. *I wasn't political enough.* Sure, I could holler sovereignty with the best of them, but maybe I really didn't know what I was talking about, and perhaps I benefited a bit too much from colonization—just look at these nice new khakis!

Most disturbing to me, however, was the surprising return of every younger Native academic's über-insecurity: *I wasn't Indian enough.* My skin was too light, my hair too short, my language fluency too English, and my petty bourgeois lifestyle too close in appearance to *Trading Spaces* (as opposed to, say, *North of 60*). During my upcoming dinner with Vine, that most Indian theorist of Indianness, I felt certain that I would quickly resemble Pierce Brosnan at the end of *Grey Owl,* when he strips off all of his buckskin and feathers in front of a bewildered audience and looks, well, really white.

Why the insecurities? On one level we can probably just chalk them up to my individual biography: a sometimes troubled childhood in a border town that made it clear that Indians were a problem, an underfunded rural school, an Indian father who didn't read (at least until Deloria), a white mother who did, or maybe just the fact that I wasn't exactly raised on the fast track to academe. Sometimes old feelings will revisit you.

But aren't biographical data also the products of history? So perhaps it's fair to speak of history, as Deloria often did, which for centuries described Natives as savages, warriors, and heathen—then later drunkards, welfare cheats, and gangbangers—but never as intellectuals; a history that turned Indians into what Audre Lorde called capitalism's "surplus people"—meaning "excess" or "waste"—and subsequently saw fit to underfund our schools and sequester us from scholars. Perhaps we can admit that, at least until Deloria, the dominant historical message to Indians has been this: *you are not smart.*

So too, perhaps, for the identity issues that can still plague younger Native people. Through centuries of assimilation policies, paternalistic social programs, and persistent stereotypes, history gave us a grand paradox regarding identity: first, *you are too Indian,* but more recently, *you are not Indian enough.* Perhaps Indian academics, oft touted these days for rebuilding our identities and cultures, sometimes feel compelled to acknowledge the hard fact that the word *rebuilding* implies a present state of wreckage.

Yes, we can talk a good game about our radical politics, our various nationalisms and sovereignties; but sometimes tiny bears scale our spines and remind us that we do not live with our people, speak our heritage language, or remember what real poverty is like. So we worry about who we are, at what cost we came to be, and subsequently, how we are perceived. We worry, that is, about our *authenticity.* Perhaps Deloria captured this dilemma in *Custer* when he wrote, "Indian life, as it relates to the real world, is a continuous attempt not to disappoint people who know us."

He was talking about Indians disappointing whites. Was I now worried about disappointing Deloria?

I put on my freshly pressed new pants, forcefully repressed my insecurities, and drove to the restaurant to meet Vine Deloria Jr. There he was—not as physically large as I had heard him to be, and looking rumpled and travel-fatigued. He looked old, actually—a thick shock of white hair—and carried a hefty cane in a manner that made it seem like a potential weapon. He greeted everyone politely, ordered tournedos of beef, and ate quickly, head tilted down, without signaling much interest in conversation. People talked to him anyway. Meanwhile, I inconspicuously munched my pork ribs as intellectually and Indianly as I could.

Finally, as our plates were cleared, Vine, surprisingly, spoke to me.

"Do you have a dog at home?"

"What?"

"A dog. If you have one, he might like those rib bones."

"You're right." I requested a doggie bag and wondered if the bones might not be too much for my eight-pound Pomeranian.

"Do you smoke?" he asked. This was not a question normally asked during academic dinners.

"Uh . . . sometimes." *How did he know?*

"Well, that's certainly a bad habit. Let's go outside and have a cigarette."

And we did.

That smoke break was the first of many we shared during Vine's stay at my campus, and one night it lasted past 1:00 A.M. During our conversations, he talked, I listened. He told wild stories about his time with NCAI (National Congress of American Indians), opined without an inkling of self-censorship about the Red Power movement, and gave advice on how to survive at a university: "Do your minimal service, don't try to change your department, and do your work. Draw a circle around yourself, and *don't let them in!*" To my great surprise, he also wanted to gossip about Native academics. Who was sleeping with whom? Would so-and-so ever finish his book? Want to know the real reason that X argued with Y? About an older established scholar, he actually said, "Next time I see that guy, I'm going to kick his ass." (I knew I was right about that cane.) To the extent that there is a meaningful difference between community-building gossip and community-destroying backbiting, Vine seemed to know exactly where the line was drawn and often walked right up to it. He was edgy, for sure, but also funny, self-deprecating, and refreshingly frank. But mostly, for me, he was generous with his time and attention. His visit was a completely validating experience, and I will never forget it.

Two weeks later he sent me those unsettling dating e-mails, and even though I didn't take his advice, they initiated a regular correspondence that lasted until his death two years later. Mostly I sent him my articles to read, and he would respond with short but substantive criticism. Sometimes I would ask him about events in the news, and he would provide frank assessments and often shocking opinions. And he continued to solicit gossip, enthusiastically researching the entire background to any public controversy I shared with him. It wasn't always a happy exchange. Sometimes I irritated him—like when I publicly defended Ward Churchill, who, I quickly learned, was not Vine's favorite person—and he would refuse to write me back for a while. But such behavior was rare, and he never shut me down. On the contrary, even if only in the form of cryptic, gossipy e-mails from DOGHARPER, his attention always encouraged me to keep going.

I don't think he thought me special, or an irresistibly scintillating e-mailer. Frankly, I would be amazed to learn that anyone in Vine's inner circle had ever heard my name before. What I believe motivated him to give me his time and attention was only this: he knew from experience that younger scholars could use some affirmation and support, so he gave it. Such a small, simple idea, but in our manic world, increasingly uncommon. And in our Indian world, where we remain quick to snap eyes at one another, it actually feels counterintuitive.

At that particular time in my life, however, it made all the difference.

When I learned of Vine's death, it didn't feel like I had lost a "friend," exactly. Nor do the words "mentor" or "teacher" accurately describe our brief relationship. Rather, I felt like I had lost what the Ojibwe call a "namesake": the elder who names you, instructs you, sometimes teases you, sometimes sets you up on dates, and sometimes gets annoyed when you are clearly slow on the uptake, but who, through instruction, example, and praise—and mostly through the sharing of precious time—helps you realize the potential of your name and find your way in this

world. There is love in such self-giving, and like all real manifestations of love, it possesses the power to combat feelings of alienation, insecurity, and self-doubt. And because the principal act of
a namesake is to give you a name, another gift you receive is your
identity.

––––––––

Vine should be remembered as pro-traditionalism and anti-
authenticity. Never conceiving of tradition as some static artifact
frozen in the distant past, he wanted Native scholars and activists
to push through Western education and find—perhaps *make* is the
better word—tradition on the other side. Having "transversed the
Western body of knowledge completely," as Deloria wrote in his
1991 essay "Higher Education and Self-Determination," Indian
intellectuals and leaders would one day establish a path on which
"the rest of the Indian community will walk right on through the
Western worldview and emerge on the other side also." Such was
his vision for us.

What did tradition mean to Deloria? Not some new Indian fun-
damentalism, nor another round of authenticity games played by
the insecure for dwindling rewards. Not a call to defend the inde-
fensible in the name of sovereignty, nor a mandate to embrace old
cultural forms that possess an unclear function in today's world.
What tradition meant for Deloria, I believe, was primarily the ethical force described in his foreword to *Genocide of the Mind*: that
changing but no less powerful body of sustainable community
values that enable Indians to feel like Indians in places like large
cities. And even large research universities, where sometimes your
namesakes are accessed through e-mail.

No one ever loved Indians more than Vine did, which apparently gave him hope. "Indian communities are achieving a stability that projects an improved life ahead for the people and their children," he optimistically wrote in *Genocide* during the winter of his life. "Adaptation, not accommodation, has become a reality."

Adapt, don't accommodate. Blaze a trail, don't authenticate. Embrace tradition on the other side. Affirm and support one another. Love Indians. Love yourself. Hope.

His legacy is enormous.

But so are the problems we face. We can't rest on his laurels.

CREATION STORY

Sara M. Ortiz

The songs, stories, poems, and advice will always
remember my father . . .

—Simon J. Ortiz

Part I

I am afraid as I am writing this. I am afraid of what may emerge. I
am afraid that the words won't come out right and that, when you
read this, you will not understand me. I will write it anyway.

I come from a place of darkness. I was told to look to the silver
lining, "over there, see that cloud on the horizon, isn't it beautiful?
Now, doesn't it make everything OK, Sara?" I have lived these days
of my life not knowing. And now that I am closer than ever *to
knowing* . . . I don't want to know anymore. I want to forget everything. I don't want to write it down, or take a picture. I don't want
to save these moments filled with a mother's neglect, homicide,
rape, and addiction, that betray logic, to my hard drive. "The world
is yours," they said. They lied.

I come from a desert region, deserted by purity and simple
shame long ago. Albuquerque, New Mexico. "Land of Enchant-
ment" or "Land of Entrapment," as it is called by some of the less
modest locals. Most of the white people had packed their things

and fled by the early nineties, the small families of them, from my tiny urban west side development. Sky View West, and the closest liquor store was a whole mile and a half away when I was born. But, of course, it's not like that anymore.

Sesame Street was my garden. I was delivered by a doctor on the south side. I was pulled from my mother by metal forceps, sterile and sharply unwelcoming on my slippery pink skin. I was pulled, just to be dropped into a playpen full of crack houses, strip clubs, Mexican restaurants, and liquor stores. I was pulled, just to be pushed into the street I was to learn my name on: *Sesame Street.* How do you get there? Don't ask me. I'm trying to forget.

The doctor brought me into this world in a south side hospital delivery room, but my mother was the one who fed me to the coyotes. I don't blame her. Not now. Not ever. She did the best she could.

Part II

I am an Indian. But even if I always was, this mattered the very least to me as a child at the end of the twentieth century. Becoming a mixed-blood Native woman at the dawn of the twenty-first century, and it all began to change. It all really changed when I began to write this narrative, when I began to "write Indian."

I hold my memories in my palm and turn them over and over, curious, in my hand—like shiny things coated in dust. I would be lost without the snapshots. I am two, maybe three. I am sitting on a plastic lawn chair, brown legs spread in a burgundy jumper made of corduroy, a white shirt beneath it. A ball, red and yellow, suspended in midair above me; I can almost hear the tiny joyous sounds my throat made then.

My mouth is open, my bright smile flashes in the early morning sun. My grandmother and great-aunt sit on either side of me, light graying hair coiffed, pantsuits pressed. Both of them laughing; my great-aunt's hands are together in front of her, her glee frozen in time. Her head is thrown slightly back in amusement.

We are all there in that picture, a backdrop of adobe behind us. My backyard overlooks the Sandia Mountains, but only our rosebush is visible in the picture; small red blooms frame the space near my grandmother's face. My aunt is in an assisted living facility in Lubbock now. She was diagnosed with Alzheimer's and Parkinson's diseases in early 1994. She used to work for the FBI in the sixties and early seventies. My mother says she wasn't a particularly generous woman, but she treated my mother well when she was younger, before she married a black man.

The last time I saw my aunt was the summer I turned fourteen. I had been sent to "Peanut Country" to stay with my grandmother in eastern New Mexico as punishment for rebelling against my mother, for lashing out at her for marrying a half-Chicano half-Navajo hustler/gangster/heroin addict without telling me. I had begun to stay out later and later. I had begun to use my voice to speak louder and louder, my own anger fueled by my disapproval of what I perceived to be her self-destructive choices for our family. This is when she sent me away to stay with my grandmother.

I listened closely to the conversations my grandmother tried to have with her sister, my aunt, whom we saw fading from us before our eyes; my grandmother, my aunt, and myself at the Tastee-Freez, plates of the night's special in front of us. I was not smiling that evening, nor do I smile now as I remember it. My grandmother talked, in her careful way, of people and happenings that I had only heard about and saw in the photo albums she kept on the glass table next to the neatly made bed in the guest room. I watched my aunt's eyes the closest as my grandmother talked, urging her to recall the places and people she spoke of. My aunt sat rocking slightly, staring at something, seemingly a million miles away, in the distance. I tried to talk to her, too, but with no real success. I wanted to make her remember me, despite the fact that I was told she never would. I was fourteen then; I returned to my neighborhood at the end of the summer, and now only think of her when my family brings up "her condition" or when we visit at holidays and special occasions.

Part III

Bad tastes rise up in my throat, and even the Pepsi can't wash them away. I remember eating oysters for the first time. I am ten. We are all sitting on the patio at the Pelican grill and bar. The evening is clear for the most part, but some clouds over the eastern horizon are moving closer, and a cool breeze blows the white linen tablecloth. It is late summer, but it is the desert, so we're dressed light. My blond lawyer mother, my Indian poet father, with graying black hair, and me; my father says, "You've never had oysters before, Sara?"

I say, "I've never wanted to."

He hands me the cold shell with the jiggly and wet opaque creature resting on the iridescent surface. I look into the shiny wetness of the thing in my hesitant hand. I close my eyes and raise it to my lips. I do not taste the small oyster, I only feel the cool smoothness of its slippery surface as it slides over my warm tongue. It is only a small wet globe in my throat, and only for a moment. I am changed. I have tasted a creature not coaxed but stolen from the vastness of the ocean. I poured my soda down my throat to rid my mouth of the remnants of its body on my tongue. I was offered them many times, but years would pass before I'd ever touch another oyster again.

Part IV

2007. Not much has changed. The coyotes cry through the mists of the river and swamps near my home. Camino Torcido: Criminal Road. She brought me here, or rather I followed her, so that I might hear their cries more clearly.

When the drug- and gang-related crimes started to increase and the Mexican families started calling every house on the block theirs, she lost her job and moved to Santa Fe to work for the public defender. My mother, she left, as she had in my most vivid and shadowed dream. She took my brother and moved to a tourist's city only sixty miles to the north of the hard soil that she dreamed, desert Mecca dreams, of growing me from so long ago. The same soil that has borne so many coke addicts and young brown prostitutes and hustlers that I've forgotten to count.

"You need to get out of there, Sar'," she would tell me over a cracking cell phone line.

While driving in the south valley, returning from an unsatisfying deal, a bullet ricocheted off of the driver's side of my mint-green Honda Civic. We were stopped at a red light at a busy intersection across from a grocery store—my baby, myself, and her dad, Antonio. I sat still, listening for more sounds. Antonio ducked instinctively. A car's tires squealing in the night; we pulled into a grocery store parking lot to examine our car. He knew we had been hit by something. I still wanted to believe that the sounds I had heard were those of a car backfiring or a tire blowing out. There was only a small indentation where the bullet had hit, only some of the paint was chipping off. All I remember is that as we drove away from the parking lot, Antonio speculated, "It was probably a small gun. Maybe a .22." All I remember was him saying things, far away, though he sat right next to me, and the sound of my breath slow and broken in my mouth. I was sixteen.

I am here, and then I am not. I am sitting in the waiting room of the Planned Parenthood. This wasn't planned. And if this is what parenthood looks like, I want none of it. I flip through pages of tabloids and glossy magazines on the table as I wait for the first round of pills and shots. I am uninterested in the skinny white women and their expensive clothes, the articles about these women and their "problems." Seems every other article deals with ways that the reader can live better. I am fifteen. I am a mother. I am brown. These articles are black words colored by bright advertisements on shiny white pages that sing empty songs to my hungry and tired eyes. But this doesn't stop me from picking up the *Marie Claire* at the bottom of the stack. I read about women, because, after all, I am one. The girls in these glossy pictures are the color of clay. They are ebony and mahogany. They are thin, and crying out to me, from the flatness of the pages.

And the pages are not flat anymore . . .

Part V

Yes, we would wait again. Weeks, weeks, months, but not those years again. O Daddy, never those years. Never again those years. Our own solution will be strength: hearts, blood, bones, skin, hope and love. The woman anger and courage risen as the People's voice again.

—Simon J. Ortiz

It was written. And it was known long before that. Spoken soon enough. All of this conjured and made magic before our coming here. And there is still so much magic to be found in it. Not all abstraction. But close to it. The better part of my humanity is all caught up in the movements of parts, and dust that has settled upon the keys of the piano in the kitchen that is never played except by the cats. Snow all covering the soil and I am thinking about the frozen swamps, and the way the moon coats that snow over the mesas and the pictures inscribed on the volcanic rocks there behind the house. Ravens and owls, here and there. But I can't see them. And I cannot hear them. But I know they are there. I am already missing the way you would disrupt my sleep, and how I would pull on the black window coverings to block out the sun just so I might steal a few more minutes of the morning with you. It's only been one day. And already I am wishing we were back in that tiny apartment near the park where I took you and Gerri to swing, to rest, to pray. You would end up sleeping there, in your car, when you had nowhere else to go. You would sleep there, even when you did. It snowed, and snowed, and snowed some more, when I was just on my way to you. But I arrived somehow, too early (or was it too late), and everything had changed while I was away. You had gone from that carefully cultivated and furnished space, or perhaps you were the same, you were still you, but I was afraid of what was living in your eyes. Perhaps I shifted my gaze. Perhaps I changed my mind, as I'd so often suggested that you do. One day I drove to the Laundromat across from the university. *She* was there. I had not seen her for some time. She was our dirty little secret. But I'd never wanted any part of her mystery, nor did I want her to want any of mine. And perhaps she never did. Who knows what she has now. I smiled when I looked up, and then away— back to your mismatched socks, my jeans and many-colored panties tumbling in that industrial dryer. I barely noticed who was looking at me back, and then away, or how. I left. I did not look back. But I did tell him that I saw her there. He wasn't surprised. He just shook his head, and vowed never to go to that particular Laundromat if he could help it. T. M. Y.'s new book arrived just after Christmas. X-Indians? What X-Indians? They believed. But not really. And only just a little bit, when everyone was thinking that they did. Just enough to bring them off the island. Just enough to bring them back to the reservations, back to the slums, back to the bars in the city, back to the back rooms of abandoned houses, back and back to where they would never be seen. And who does tell the stories of ghosts? Everyone. But not all the ghosts. Just the pretty ones. I once spoke to him about selling. About sex. About the way we would be sold to the men so the men would buy what we were selling, so that we'd have to sell more so that we might buy more so that we might sell more to them. . . . And it would go on this way for hours. Disjointed and just somehow, he stole that towel from the Chinle Holiday Inn and returned to me with little pieces of black glass under his nails, and a strange odor in his curly hair. He always smelled like various smoke, and when I neatly folded and tucked away the olive chenille throw, it would smell like him. Somehow he always knew where the soft spots were, and he always had a knife with him. Scraping and burning resin—a favorite pastime of his—would find the microsuede all under it, and it was as good a place as any to land. Burning fibers and twisted keratin. Semen and leftover tomato soup from the diner on the corner across from old Albuquerque High. Whenever we wanted to remember weightless, we floated. The hot water in the shower always went cold too soon. On New Year's Eve, 2006, I turned to him and said, "Today, just today, I'd like not to spiral." I failed. Failed again. Not sure who saw. But decided to write it here first, just to be sure. Considering Oprah in Johannesburg, her shiny new school for little black girls far, far away, and the snapping of Arab necks. Islam is Arab and Saddam Hussein is dead. James Brown, too. Gerald Ford to follow that train of death, and so many Muslim and American soldiers to fan flames in heaven with the feathers of peacocks and angels.

Open mouths of dogs and butterflies with azure and gossamer wings. I will remember Manhattan, even though I have never been there. Even though I may die before I ever take that eastbound train. I have written you all over the walls, but they are all crumbling now, and to add insult to injury there are various insects living under my skin as I am typing this—I have MySpace, YouTube, and e-mail to blame for that. Windows XP is an unstable environment. Should have listened to Ishmael and installed Linux instead. What was I thinking? I had gone to her, summoned by the unfolding of wings, but she was deader than ever when I got there. And just as cold. I thought of all the Mohawks, Oneidas, Navajos, Lakotas, Ojibwes, and Seminoles I had never known existed. There would be some new food to sustain us now. Call it End-Times Commodities. And I know Indians who drive Lexuses and VWs and mourn the loss of cheese that once came in blocks and not slices.

Part VI

this is not an end. only a beginning. do you see me? can you? i have said, and will say until my final word, in response to the question "where is the movement now?": **we are the children of the movement.** and we are dying. we are killing ourselves in record numbers. *this is where your movement is now.* what of protest, what of resistance you say? where is our movement? look now—we are turning our want for freedom, terrorist and resistant inclinations, upon ourselves, as opposed to our nations, the united states. and in doing so we are actually striking at the very heart of our nation. our message: you've left us, again and again. we are not free. but we will be. the freedom that eluded you is ours. **you cannot take this from us.** you **will not** take this from us. not now. not ever. we have no other option. you cannot take this last freedom from us. not now. not ever. you will look around you at, and with, the last fleeting light—before that blanket of night upon you—you, all elders, all survived somehow, you will finally see that your children are all dead; the last of them dying. tell me then where your movement is? light, oh light, you are dying. elders—you are too tired to sing the songs we wrote, often to you, composed by brilliant—but dying—digital light. dear ones, you deserve to rest.

Morning; it has come.

From the Reservation to *Dawn of the Dead* to James Dickey and Back Again

Eric Gansworth

A mong the most frequent questions I get when doing public readings of my work is, not surprisingly, "How did you become a writer?" It often makes me uneasy, because it seems to imply that the phrase's emphasis word could change the question's meaning significantly. For example, "*How* did you become a writer" is very different from "How did *you* become a writer" and "How did you become a *writer*" in its meaning. At least two versions of that question imply that someone in my situation—a reservation-dwelling welfare kid who grew up in a house with no plumbing and one electrical outlet—would seem an unlikely candidate to be sharing my words in public forums. It's safest to regard most of these questions as innocent, as they're frequently from students in college settings who hope to become writers themselves. That discomfort remains, though. I suspect that there are some who in fact do mean to deliver the emphasis in those dubious ways, perhaps not even aware of its tone, themselves.

Given the frequency of this generic question, one would think I might have an actual answer. However, that would not be the case. The answer is different nearly every time, but the answers are not so different from one another that any are truly inaccurate. For me, the writer's life is all about the conversation, the one readers have with each other, the shared experience, certainly.

It eventually also became about the conversation the writer tries to have with the reader, the dialogue in which I had obviously decided at some point to make an opening volley. The exact moment in my life that decision happened, though, is an event I have not, to my satisfaction, been able to accurately pinpoint. The response I usually give has some relationship to my interests at the time of the asking, and in accumulation, the answers serve as a kaleidoscope of how one becomes a writer, or at least how I arrived at that moment.

This essay originated when a student of mine, Mike, asked me if I would be interested or willing to be the speaker for the induction ceremony of Sigma Tau Delta, the English Honor Society. I told him, jokingly, that having never been invited to be a member of any sort of honor society, I felt much like I were living out that Groucho Marx axiom, in which he stated: "I don't care to belong to a club that accepts people like me as members." I then clarified that this organization seemed to be in pursuit of a relatively formal kind of academic excellence, one perhaps a little more scholarly than I have pursued, myself—in short, the views of someone not as lowbrow as I am. I further explained that I am not a particularly good lecturer, and am much more of a storyteller, in and out of the classroom, but that if he were willing to have his name associated with what I might conjure up, then I would be happy to do this presentation. Mike, who was at that time enrolled in my Film as Literature class—where we discussed film adaptations of novels we'd already read—encouraged me to approach whatever topic I wanted. He suggested, laughing, that I might even talk about *Dawn of the Dead*, a zombie movie I had been enthusiastically discussing in class the week before. With these things in mind, I wrote the first version of this essay.

In my family, I have generally been something of an alien, even from the beginning, "bookish" in a household where that was not a compliment. All members of my family are rabid sports fans, running from reservation to reservation all summer, chasing lacrosse games, and I could not in the least care for sports—playing or watching. Once, I found a photograph of myself at maybe the age of three, in lacrosse gear, holding the stick fiercely, even appearing to cradle it skillfully. I had no memory of this photo being taken, but I waved it triumphantly as proof that I had indeed belonged to my family's aesthetics and sensibilities at some unremembered point. One of my sisters looked nonchalantly at the photograph and exclaimed in a bored voice that the family had wrestled me into the outfit, and that I had remained in it only for the approximately thirty seconds it took to snap the picture. A contrarian from the beginning, I was always off dreaming in some other place, negotiating other worlds, worried more about *Lost in Space* than the loss the Buffalo Bills had endured the week before. In that light, I suppose books were a natural attraction.

Aside from a set of encyclopedias that were current sometime before I was born, when the moon's surface was still a myth and mystery in the night sky, I can recall five books in my family house when I was a child. That was probably four more than were in many households on the reservation where I grew up. There might have been others, but they are the five I remember. We, as American Indians, are members of oral cultures, for the most part, not reading cultures, and while we might have embraced the immediacy and orality of television—the voices transmitting across the air—the reading of books seemed not as natural an inclination. I have no idea how we came by those books, but I attempted to read them as soon as I could read.

Years later, at the age of fourteen, I made my first formal book purchase, the sixth book I remember existing in our house, the first one I brought in. I had loved horror movies since I was a very small child. While babysitting me one Friday night when I was five, my cousin encouraged me to stay up late with him and watch *The Blob* on the late-night scary movies on channel 7. In my desire, I even endured local newscaster/celebrity Irv Weinstein riveting western New Yorkers with stories of Buffalo Blaze Busters conquering another four-alarmer on the city's West Side. After that Friday, my life would never be the same. On Monday morning, I ran into the classroom and announced: "Man, this is the coolest thing!" and I regaled classmates with a plot synopsis, including shrieks and a pantomime of the Blob's victims, and gained instant popularity with the more prurient members of my class.

From then on, I tried to stay up late every Friday to catch the scary movie. It was easy to go unnoticed in our ancient house, with my mother and members of her generation playing quarter-ante poker in the other room. My mother, like many American Indian parents, allowed her children tremendous freedoms—and the responsibilities that came with those freedoms. I was invisible in the darkened living room as they filled the house with smoke and laughter and the sounds of quarters trading back and forth, as if a quarter didn't mean a thing to anyone at the table. The truth was that "spare" quarters were scarce, and each of them were doing exactly what I was doing—engaging their fears by risking what little they had.

Sometimes, I sat directly in front of the television, hand-tuning the dial for the duration of a film, in a desperate attempt to improve the signal I was receiving from a television station ninety miles away in Rochester. We didn't have a dedicated channel 13 on the television's VHF dial, and I often cruised through its snowy atmosphere, delicately turning the sensitive outer dial, hoping to pick up strange transmissions from other places. I found out recently that Canadian filmmaker David Cronenberg had done similar things as a child, searching out the exotic in those blank spaces, and developed the seeds for his subversive television-based horror film *Videodrome* partly from engaging in this frequency cruising. One Friday evening the Rochester transmission was a terrible film called *Plan 9 from Outer Space*. Vampira has never looked scarier than she did in those early morning hours, phasing in and out, with shifts in the wind sending her ghostly walk out to my family's finicky reservation television set.

It was the era before VCRs, and the only way to see a movie you had enjoyed for a second time was to wait for it to be broadcast on television, or read the wonderful novel upon which the film was based, or read the badly written novelization culled from the screenplay. While *The Blob* would certainly reappear, continually taunting mid-century teens on late-night television, and Vampira would likely chase Tor Johnson across a makeshift graveyard again in a year or two, a different film entered my life around the time puberty arrived. *Dawn of the Dead* is, in short, an overly graphic film whose basic premise pits a ragged band of human protagonists taking refuge in a shopping mall against a horde of lethal antagonists—flesh-consuming zombies who return from the dead and attack the living. This film was the sequel to the independent horror classic *Night of the Living Dead*. One of my cousins who lived next door had actually seen *Night of the Living Dead* at a local drive-in theater with some friends, and had lorded it over me for several years, occasionally offering fragmentary plot elements at random times and immediately growing silent if I asked for more.

Dawn of the Dead was mine, and I claimed it entirely. I went to see it on opening day, lying about my age—I was fourteen, and it was a film with the unusual distinction of having been released unrated, but with a self-imposed younger-viewer limit of eighteen. I had been so preoccupied by its imminent release that in the weeks before any commercials aired on a real television, I had literally dreamed my own advertisements for the film, and I was not at all dissatisfied when I left the theater that Friday afternoon. It was as outrageous as I had imagined, unlike anything I had ever seen before, and I tried to go back the next day to catch another showing. The ticket taker on Saturday, however, was a little more authoritarian and could see, even through my "older teen" costume, that I was indeed not eligible to enter the theater.

The film was gone a week later, and I had lost my second opportunity to see this horror film that I knew would be considered a landmark at some future date. However, given its graphic nature, explicitly the frequency with which zombies vividly devoured the living, I was quite certain, even at fourteen, that this film would not be airing on network television at any time in the near future. I could spin that dial as long as I wanted on channel 13 and I would never find it. The novelization of *Dawn of the Dead*, cowritten by the director and including eight color stills from the film, was the book I bought, the sixth book to enter my family home as a welcome addition since I had been born. I even special-ordered it from the Book Corner, an independent bookstore on Main Street in Niagara Falls, and read it in a single day when it finally arrived.

Of the five pre–*Dawn of the Dead* books in our house, one was a book titled *Coolly*, a biography of a surgeon, whose name, I imagined, was Coolly. Now, years later, I speculate that the title was an adverb, describing his disposition while exploring the innards of anaesthetized others with sharp instruments. The second was a biography that I had cashed in my babysitting savings to get my mother for her birthday. It was either Doris Day's life story or Dinah Shore's; I always confuse these two entertainers. OK, I admit: this one I never did try to read.

The third was Harper Lee's *To Kill a Mockingbird*. When I saw a book with *this* title, I avidly read it, planning my next classroom epic, only to discover there was not a single avian murder in the book. I was disappointed. I wanted the sensational. I wanted The Blob to Kill the Mockingbird. Even in my disappointment, though, I understood the implications in the book for race relations in this country, and that my future would forever involve similar cross-currents, like those strange transmissions from other places, familiar and foreign simultaneously. The balcony seats will always exist for us, as far as I could tell. The fourth book was Dee Brown's *Bury My Heart at Wounded Knee*, which was an important book to everyone on the reservation, but it was too dense and formal for me as a child. I was unable to enter that world, but knew that its examination of the ideological battle all Indians had to maintain in this country waited for me when I would be ready.

The fifth book was the only one I was forbidden to read. This edict from my family naturally made it that much more provocative. The book's title was not extraordinary or, for that matter, even interesting. My curiosity was not piqued by a story about someone giving birth, which was what I had assumed given the title. However, every time I went near the book, someone in the house directed me to put it back. When I was in middle school, I picked it up one day and no one told me to set it down.

My oldest brother said, "You know what that book's about? It's about the rape of the land." I could tell this was a statement someone else had made to him, that he was mimicking some other person's critique of the work but had not fully understood that analysis himself. I said, "Oh," and put it back on the shelf. That phrase was intriguing. It was my introduction to the world of metaphor. I came back to the book a few days later and read the inside dust jacket, which described the canoe journey of four sub-urbanites in Georgia and the trials they encountered, from horny and belligerent hillbillies to the dangerous and unpredictable landscape. I could not build the bridge between what my brother had said and this book description, so I decided to read it when I got to be a better reader, to see if I could find that connection. I hung on to it and eventually took the book with me to college. The book was, of course, James Dickey's *Deliverance*.

It was indeed as graphic and as haunting as the jacket had suggested, but the entire time I read it, I could hear my brother's phrase running through my head, and knew that he had given me a tremendous key to seeing beyond the literal, to seeing the larger thematic issues Dickey was inviting readers to engage, the uneasy tensions along socioeconomic borders in American culture, and I could never thank either of them—James Dickey or my brother—enough for these invitations through the door.

At this same time that my brother offered this key to me, I purchased an issue of the magazine *Starlog* that contained an interview with George A. Romero, the writer-director of, yes, you guessed it, *Dawn of the Dead*. I was hoping to read about the more gruesome aspects of the movie and how he had arrived at such outlandish ideas, but I received something entirely different. Romero said the film was a social commentary, a critique on the consumerist mentality so prevalent throughout the country in the mid-seventies. This was of course not an idea exclusive to Romero, but that he had chosen to play out the metaphor in a horror film, to marry two passions, the monster movie and cultural critique, caused a total perspective shift for me. Suddenly, I could see one scene vividly in my mind: the protagonists stand on the mall's roof, staring out at the thousands of zombies surrounding the building. One person asks: "Why do they come here?" Another character replies: "Memory? Instinct? This was an important place in their lives." I could not wait to see the film again with my new eyes. My world was changed forever, a second time.

I had always pictured literature as those lofty and only marginally interesting narratives we were forced to read in classes, but after these pivotal discoveries, I could see metaphor and larger thematic concerns in works I had first come to love because of the story. That new door remained open, and instead of telling my classmates about zombies biting other characters, I began showing them the elements of these books and films that made me rethink the ways I looked at the world. I delighted in having this conversation and decided eventually to find a career where I could do this full-time. Now, twenty-five years later, having read thousands of books, I am still talking about these ideas, maybe opening some minds, maybe not, but still making the attempt.

In the time since discovering these two works riding in tandem into my imagination, I have published five books, most having to do with reservation life and culture, in fiction and poetry, one of them the recipient of a PEN award, and even a book of poems, paintings, and creative nonfiction about another horror movie—*The Legend of Boggy Creek*—and the ways it explores the idea of faith. I teach courses in film and writing at Canisius College, where I am writer in residence, about a half hour from the reservation. The electricity-and-plumbing-deficient house that was home to my family for 150 years has burned down. Most of my parents' generation has gone to play poker on the other side, where the worry over quarters and a royal flush is not so great, and they return often, rise from the dead, but only as smoky voices in my heart, continuing to tell me stories. Their voices fade, like those snowy signals from distant channels, and the way to preserve them is the way I learned all those years ago. I, like many writers, am creating the novelization of a life, trying to remain as faithful to the narrative, but within the confines of a different medium. This is no way to bring those times or people back, but I can keep them in my memory, the scenes as I remember them, with a degree of accuracy that suits my needs. But you know what they say about how the more things change . . .

Dawn of the Dead was at the movies again a few weeks ago, having been remade by another director, one who has different concerns—the media's manipulation and "branding" of news, the culture's preoccupation with the formalized degradation and cut-throat sensibilities of "reality television," the ways in which societies respond to those who have been infected with viruses, HIV, SARS, avian flu, and other equally timely and relevant themes, all, again, subversively wrapped in the clever disguise of a horror movie about flesh-eating zombies and the human survivors who try to negotiate the new and hostile world in which they live. The world in its current state left an imprint on that director, and he in turn tried to contribute to our continuing story. It was sort of odd that the two biggest movies at the box office that week were *Dawn of the Dead* and *The Passion of the Christ*. I guess we each seek out the ghosts that haunt us the most. I was there, in the theater, for the first showing of *Dawn of the Dead,* waiting for the lights to go down so I could run out and be among the first to have a conversation about this interpretation. If there is a novelization, I will probably buy it, for old times' sake, and start the conversation again, ready to run into a room full of people and shout: "Man, this is the coolest thing!"

HAKSOD

John C. Mohawk

My car glided silently up the slightly inclined gravel drive, past the great sugar maples that lined the way. He was standing at the edge of his garden, about fifty yards away, leaning against a hoe, facing away from me. Before I was out of the car, he looked my way, his face a smile as I approached.

"Hello," he said, "It's good to see you," his voice flowing with enthusiasm. His name was Harrison Ground, and he had been a chief among the Tonawanda Seneca for some seventy years.

He wore a hearing aid, and his body was bent with the weight of more than ninety years. His voice was always soft, and he was a pleasant-looking man, slight, given to wearing suspenders, smoking a pipe, and carrying a cane. He was always enthusiastic, always filled with questions about how things were going in the world. One had to remind oneself that seventy years ago this man played professional baseball for a season or two, and that as a young man he traveled extensively. Somehow, now, it seemed as though he belonged to this place, as though he had never left it, and never would.

We shook hands and stood silently for a moment as we surveyed the garden. It was July, and the rich western New York soil was prolific with plant life. The garden was a marvel for a product of a man and a woman of advanced years. Maybe an acre was a patchwork of corn and beans and pumpkins, strawberries and different crops, all in small patches. Corn, potatoes, and beans took up the most room. Harrison and his wife were close to self-sufficient on this small patch, a testimony to the degree of skill and experience they shared.

"Come," he said. "Let's go into the house." We walked around a depression in the soil, some kind of man-made ditch. On one side of the ditch I noticed what appeared to be a planting, not in rows, but planted like grain. I stopped next to it.

"*Hayug* beans," he said. "I still grow some here. Not so many people grow these anymore." *Hayug* is a Seneca bean; as far as I know, no one but Seneca grow it. It is used in the summer at the time of the Green Bean Ceremony. A rich and succulent green bean, it always seemed to me a cross between asparagus and a string bean.

My friend and his wife grew most of their food on this small homestead. They had done so most of their lives. They went to the grocery store for sugar and coffee, butter and milk, and the little meat they ate mostly came from the store. But the vegetables and fruits they needed came from their little garden and were stored in the root cellar under their house.

There was usually activity here in the summertime, but never drudgery. They had very little income, yet they typically gave produce away at the end of the summer to people who were hungry. That he and his wife could suffer arthritis and the many infirmities of advanced old age and still raise and preserve so much food on a small piece of land stood as something of a lesson about the advantages of skill over energy and ambition.

Next to the beans was a trellis overgrown with vines. "Those are gourds," he explained. "I make a trellis so the gourds hang free. They grow round that way and are more useful." The gourds aren't eaten. They're prized for the shell, which can make dippers or other useful objects, and they're pretty in the garden.

In the house we sat at a table. "I have been thinking about you," and he drew out a pipe from his pocket. "I've been wondering how things are with you."

He had taught me a lot, this old man. He taught me social dance music and ceremonial music. He showed me plants and explained what he knew about the old ways, and he was always helpful, always gentle.

"I thought I'd come and ask about the old days. I've been wondering what it was like in the times before, if you knew anybody among our Seneca people who lived before we migrated to this reservation. Did you?"

He sat back in his chair a moment, and his eyes seemed to focus on the ceiling above me. After a while, he put his elbow on the table and rested his chin on his palm.

"When I was a young boy," he began, "I had a friend. He was an old man who lived in a cabin in the woods not far from here. Almost every day I went to visit him, and he would invite me inside his little cabin, where we would talk. On my first visit, when I asked him his name, he said, 'Call me Haksod.' I had many *Haksods* when I was a boy.

"Haksod was a very old man. Some people said he was nearly a hundred years old when I knew him. But wait . . ." The old man pulled himself up and hurried out of the room, up what I knew to be a staircase. In a few moments he was back, carrying a large wooden object.

"You see this?" he asked. He presented an ancient wooden corn-pounder. "Look here," he said. On one side of it were carved two words: Canisteo 1831.

Canisteo means Beautiful Corn. It is the name of a Seneca village on the Genesee which was abandoned when people were forced to move westward in the 1830s.

"Our people brought this with them and carved the date on the pounder so we'd remember. This old man, Haksod, was with the people when they moved here."

He stopped for a moment, his voice trailing off. Then, very softly, he started again. "Haksod said that when they were here, in this swamp land, at first it was very dangerous. Everybody had to hide all the time or they might be murdered. Very dangerous. But he said before that, when we lived on the Genesee, it was very pleasant, very nice. He told me once he was born just before the war with Britain.

"He and I were good friends. In those days there was no road to his cabin, just trails in the forest. This was before cars appeared in these parts. Every morning Haksod made mush and tea. And cracked-corn soup. There were other boys who visited him, too, but I think I visited the most. He told lots of stories and showed me how to sharpen a knife. I can still remember some of the stories.

"Haksod had friends, old people, when he was young. He could remember talking to people who had been in wars with the French. The Americans. The English. The people he grew up with could remember a long way.

"Then, one day, it was before noon when I went to his house. It was just a one-room cabin. There were only two windows and a door. I knocked, but no one answered. Finally, I looked through the window, and I could see a figure lying on the cot. So I went in. Haksod lay very quietly. When I touched him, he did not wake. So I ran for help."

Haksod's voice was shaky, even after more than eight decades. "He was the first friend I buried," he said, his voice lowering. "Later, I buried many, but he was the first."

two

SPEAKING THROUGH OUR NATIONS' TEETH

When you see me
for the first time
at a powwow or social
across the circle
we dance
in which language and worldview
do you form your first
impression

the one you were taught
in school, memorizing epics
and heroes of other
people, diagramming
sentences with the precision
of a surgeon, driving
modifiers and prepositional
phrases beneath the horizon
like roots or
dead relatives
or both

or the ones you were taught
hiding beneath
your mother's dining room
table, where she
and her generation
forgot you were there and
spoke of the giant turtle, the twins
the grandmother moon and said
"Jeh-oos' eh, awk-r(h)ee aw(t)-ness"
to one another, laughing
without fear of you
learning and growing
this voice they thought
would only keep you behind

I listen, for Cheweant; Skenno; She'kon;
Guuwaadze; Hensci, estonko; Boozhoo;
Dah-leh; osiyo; ready to bare these teeth
in a smile where we find ourselves
and each other.

—*Nyah-wheh* to the artists who contributed greetings in their language to this poem.

Melanie Printup Hope: *Grandmother Moon*

From *The Prayer of Thanksgiving*

Melanie Printup Hope

My work is an exploration of my Native American identity and ancestry. As an artist, I convey my personal experiences of cultural and spiritual growth through the use of drawing, beadwork, sculpture, computer-generated images, animation, sound, video, and installation.

Each new piece begins with a feeling that I want to express or a story I want to tell. As I begin to do my research, I use pencils on paper to sketch and conceptualize my ideas. Most of my pieces start with beadwork and are first sketched with colored pencils on paper, then mounted to a piece of bristol board. Using a threaded needle, I bring it up through the back of the board and string on a row of beads. I use a second threaded needle to tack down every few beads.

I learned this technique from some of the elder women who taught beadworking classes at the Tuscarora Indian School (Lewiston, New York) during the 1970s and 1980s. Beadworking has always been a big part of my community, and these classes are still taught today. Originally, the Iroquois used beads made of wampum to record a time in history. Wampum belts are woven with beads made from shell to tell a story about a particular point in time. After European contact, wampum was replaced with seed beads as trading took place during colonial times. As the land was taken and traditional ways of life were interrupted, selling beadwork to European tourists became a useful way to generate income for Iroquois families. Trading beaded souvenirs at Niagara Falls, New York, during the nineteenth and twentieth centuries became a way of life for my ancestors. It is through the process of sewing these beads that I am able to connect with the past while reflecting on the present.

Sometimes I scan the finished beadwork on a flatbed scanner and use Adobe Photoshop to manipulate the image. The finished document may be printed on paper to be viewed in a gallery. Or the image may be integrated into video to be viewed at a festival. Or it may be imported into Macromedia Director for viewing on a CD-ROM. Or it may be integrated into an interactive environment using Macromedia Dreamweaver or Flash for viewing anywhere in the world via the Web. Just as I have used the newest digital technologies over the last twenty-five years as a graphic designer to communicate my clients' needs, I use it as an artist to share my cultural ideas. It is only natural for me to fuse beads and pixels to share a story.

This image, *Grandmother Moon* (1996), is one of twenty-six images created for *The Prayer of Thanksgiving* (interactive installation). The prayer is based on the belief that the world cannot be taken for granted, and that we must thank all living things in order to align our minds with the natural world. This prayer is the backbone of the Iroquois culture.

As I weave together ancient traditional beadwork with highly advanced skills in electronic arts, I fill each piece with the wisdom of my ancestors while also incorporating present-day struggles within the community. I use my own artistic expression to share with the viewer the story of where my ancestors began and the instructions of how we must lead our lives—maintaining balance, living in peace with everyone around us, respecting and loving nature and all living things.

A Faithkeeper is selected to share the words of thanksgiving at the opening and closing of social, government, and ceremonial events. The prayer follows a general structure; however, individual speakers use their own words and expression. This prayer follows an order, beginning with the lowest spiritual forces on Earth, continuing to those in the sky, and ending with the highest forces beyond the sky. The prayer begins with The People, and is followed by The Earth, The Waters, The Fish, The Plants, The Animals, The Trees, The Birds, Our Sustenance, The Winds, The Thunderers, The Sun, The Moon, The Stars, The Four Beings, and Handsome Lake. The prayer ends with The Creator.

Writers on Writing; Two Languages in Mind, but Just One in the Heart

Louise Erdrich

For years now I have been in love with a language other than the English in which I write, and it is a rough affair. Every day I try to learn a little more Ojibwe. I have taken to carrying verb conjugation charts in my purse, along with the tiny notebook I've always kept for jotting down book ideas, overheard conversations, language detritus, phrases that pop into my head. Now that little notebook includes an increasing volume of Ojibwe words. My English is jealous, my Ojibwe elusive. Like a besieged unfaithful lover, I'm trying to appease them both.

Ojibwemowin, or Anishinabemowin, the Chippewa language, was last spoken in our family by Patrick Gourneau, my maternal grandfather, a Turtle Mountain Ojibwe who used it mainly in his prayers. Growing up off reservation, I thought Ojibwemowin mainly was a language for prayers, like Latin in the Catholic liturgy. I was unaware for many years that Ojibwemowin was spoken in Canada, Minnesota, and Wisconsin, though by a dwindling number of people. By the time I began to study the language, I was living in New Hampshire, so for the first few years I used language tapes.

I never learned more than a few polite phrases that way, but the sound of the language in the author Basil Johnston's calm and dignified Anishinabe voice sustained me through bouts of homesickness.

I spoke basic Ojibwe in the isolation of my car, traveling here and there on twisting New England roads. Back then, as now, I carried my tapes everywhere.

The language bit deep into my heart, but it was an unfulfilled longing. I had nobody to speak it with, nobody who remembered my grandfather's standing with his sacred pipe in the woods next to a box elder tree, talking to the spirits. Not until I moved back to the Midwest and settled in Minneapolis did I find a fellow Ojibweg to learn with, and a teacher.

Mille Lacs' Ojibwe elder Jim Clark—Naawi-giizis, or Center of the Day—is a magnetically pleasant, sunny, crew-cut World War II veteran with a mysterious kindliness that shows in his slightest gesture. When he laughs, everything about him laughs; and when he is serious, his eyes are round like a boy's.

Naawi-giizis introduced me to the deep intelligence of the language and forever set me on a quest to speak it for one reason: I want to get the jokes. I also want to understand the prayers and the *adisookaanug,* the sacred stories, but the irresistible part of language for me is the explosion of hilarity that attends every other minute of an Ojibwe visit. As most speakers are now bilingual, the language is spiked with puns on both English and Ojibwe, most playing on the oddness of *gichi-mookomaan,* that is, big knife or American, habits and behavior.

This desire to deepen my alternate language puts me in an odd relationship to my first love, English. It is, after all, the language stuffed into my mother's ancestors' mouths. English is the reason she didn't speak her native language and the reason I can barely limp along in mine. English is an all-devouring language that has moved across North America like the fabulous plagues of locusts that darkened the sky and devoured even the handles of rakes and hoes. Yet the omnivorous nature of a colonial language is a writer's gift. Raised in the English language, I partake of a mongrel feast.

A hundred years ago most Ojibwe people spoke Ojibwemowin, but the Bureau of Indian Affairs and religious boarding schools punished and humiliated children who spoke native languages. The program worked, and there are now almost no fluent speakers of Ojibwe in the United States under the age of thirty. Speakers like Naawi-giizis value the language partly because it has been physically beaten out of so many people. Fluent speakers have had to fight for the language with their own flesh, have endured ridicule, have resisted shame and stubbornly pledged themselves to keep on talking the talk.

My relationship is of course very different. How do you go back to a language you never had? Why should a writer who loves her first language find it necessary and essential to complicate her life with another? Simple reasons, personal and impersonal. In the past few years I've found that I can talk to God only in this language, that somehow my grandfather's use of the language penetrated. The sound comforts me.

What the Ojibwe call the Gizhe Manidoo, the great and kind spirit residing in all that lives, what the Lakota call the Great Mystery, is associated for me with the flow of Ojibwemowin. My Catholic training touched me intellectually and symbolically, but apparently never engaged my heart.

There is also this: Ojibwemowin is one of the few surviving languages that evolved to the present here in North America. The intelligence of this language is adapted as no other to the philosophy bound up in northern land, lakes, rivers, forests, arid plains; to the animals and their particular habits; to the shades of meaning in the very placement of stones. As a North American writer it is essential to me that I try to understand our human relationship to place in the deepest way possible, using my favorite tool, language.

There are place names in Ojibwe and Dakota for every physical feature of Minnesota, including recent additions like city parks and dredged lakes. Ojibwemowin is not static, not confined to describing the world of some out-of-reach and sacred past. There are words for e-mail, computers, Internet, fax. For exotic animals in zoos. *Anaamibiig gookoosh*, the underwater pig, is a hippopotamus. *Nandookomeshiinh*, the lice hunter, is the monkey.

There are words for the serenity prayer used in 12-step programs and translations of nursery rhymes. The varieties of people other than Ojibwe or Anishinabe are also named: Aiibiishaabooke-wininiwag, the tea people, are Asians. Agongosininiwag, the chipmunk people, are Scandinavians. I'm still trying to find out why.

For years I saw only the surface of Ojibwemowin. With any study at all one looks deep into a stunning complex of verbs. Ojibwemowin is a language of verbs. All action. Two-thirds of the words are verbs, and for each verb there are as many as 6,000 forms. The storm of verb forms makes it a wildly adaptive and powerfully precise language. *Changite-ige* describes the way a duck tips itself up in the water butt first. There is a word for what would happen if a man fell off a motorcycle with a pipe in his mouth and the stem of it went through the back of his head. There can be a verb for anything.

When it comes to nouns, there is some relief. There aren't many objects. With a modest if inadvertent political correctness, there are no designations of gender in Ojibwemowin. There are no feminine or masculine possessives or articles.

Nouns are mainly designated as alive or dead, animate or inanimate. The word for stone, *asin*, is animate. Stones are called grandfathers, and grandmothers and are extremely important in Ojibwe philosophy. Once I began to think of stones as animate, I started to wonder whether I was picking up a stone or it was putting itself into my hand. Stones are not the same as they were to me in English. I can't write about a stone without considering it in Ojibwe and acknowledging that the Anishinabe universe began with a conversation between stones.

Ojibwemowin is also a language of emotions; shades of feeling can be mixed like paints. There is a word for what occurs when your heart is silently shedding tears. Ojibwe is especially good at describing intellectual states and the fine points of moral responsibility.

Ozozamenimaa pertains to a misuse of one's talents getting out of control. *Ozozamichige* implies you can still set things right. There are many more kinds of love than there are in English. There are myriad shades of emotional meaning to designate various family and clan members. It is a language that also recognizes the humanity of a creaturely God, and the absurd and wondrous sexuality of even the most deeply religious beings.

Slowly the language has crept into my writing, replacing a word here, a concept there, beginning to carry weight. I've thought of course of writing stories in Ojibwe, like a reverse Nabokov. With my Ojibwe at the level of a dreamy four-year-old child's, I probably won't.

Though it was not originally a written language, people simply adapted the English alphabet and wrote phonetically. During the Second World War, Naawi-giizis wrote Ojibwe letters to his uncle from Europe. He spoke freely about his movements, as no censor could understand his writing. Ojibwe orthography has recently been standardized. Even so, it is an all-day task for me to write even one paragraph using verbs in their correct arcane forms. And even then, there are so many dialects of Ojibwe that, for many speakers, I'll still have gotten it wrong.

As awful as my own Ojibwe must sound to a fluent speaker, I have never, ever, been greeted with a moment of impatience or laughter. Perhaps people wait until I've left the room. But more likely, I think, there is an urgency about attempting to speak the language. To Ojibwe speakers, the language is a deeply loved entity. There is a spirit or an originating genius belonging to each word.

Before attempting to speak this language, a learner must acknowledge these spirits with gifts of tobacco and food. Anyone who attempts Ojibwemowin is engaged in something more than learning tongue twisters. However awkward my nouns, unstable my verbs, however stumbling my delivery, to engage in the language is to engage the spirit. Perhaps that is what my teachers know, and what my English will forgive.

Wooden Heart, *Dopwin*, Language Table

Heid E. Erdrich

Sometimes there is no table. Sometimes just desks pushed together to make room to share. Sometimes we raid another room for a dining surface. Still, we gather as for a meal. And always one appears, offering by offering: diet pop, chips and salsa, fruit, cheese and bread. On a good night there's wild rice, *manoomin*, often in more than one version. Real, hand-harvested, 1 cup dry to 2 cups water or broth, boil 20 minutes, no peeking, let sit to absorb liquid and cool, then season as many ways as there are lakes in Minnesota. Sometimes there's fresh-baked *gallette* or bannock or frybread arrives under cover of a dishtowel. Once, my sister brought amazingly tasty smoked fish she got from a Michigan Ojibwe family. People still talk about that fish. Meg Noori sent me this recipe for Language Table Feast:

Coffee (black with sugar in a bowl to be poured into coffee as needed). Cut fruit and cheese because the diabetics need something to snack on. A "Busy Mom's Pie"—select box in your grocer's freezer aisle, open at home while your coat is still on and the kids are yelling, butter the top and sprinkle with cinnamon sugar, have small children gather and focus on the pie for a minute, let them blow kisses to it, put it in the oven, bake as directed, and don't say you bought it unless they ask.

But Language Table is not about the food. It's about the romance. The attraction. The love. You can take that literally, if you wish. Couples have fallen in love over the table and gone on to marry and teach their children the language. Used to be it happened every year, my language teacher told me. I think he took some pride in those unions, and well he should have. But the true love of which I speak contains another passion, one more faithful, one whose kiss stays forever on the tongue: the love of language. That's what brings folks together each week. They come for the chance to learn just a bit more, to speak for an hour, to hear Ojibwemowin spoken and to hear it prayed. *Miigwiich manidoog, miigwich mishomisanan, miigwich nikomisanan . . .*

Someone else loves it, too. Love of Ojibwemowin the language, vibrates through her. I can feel it all the way from Michigan, where she is now. She has taken seriously the linguist's observation that a living language must not only be spoken, but used creatively. Her own teacher, Helen Roy, helps her get correct Ojibwe in her creative expression. In this part of one of her poems, Meg Noori writes to the table as to a lover:

> *N'zaagitonaa eyaa'iyang, Anishinaabemowin Dopwin,*
> We love you, Language Table
> *gdo'miijim*
> your food
> *gdo'pabwinan*
> your chairs
> *dopwini kaadan*
> your legs
> *ikidowinan*
> the words
> *enendamowinan*

the ideas
ezhi-baabiiwiyaang ezhi-maadookwiyaang ensa gizhigag
the way you wait for us and the way you share with us
every day.

Your legs? Ah, yes. Meg's flirting tone makes sense to us, although
it might seem strange to some. Flirting means a lot in our language
and it's also what can make Language Table so much fun. I'd like
to tell you more, even to confess my own flirtations, but first I have
to admit that I have not been to Language Table much this year.
There are a million busy workaday-world reasons I have not been
going, but I won't get into that. Reading Meg's poem I think, why
have I denied myself such pleasure? Oh, Language Table, wait for
me, forgive and love me once I come back. Perhaps you will, my
Dopwin, should I speak Meg's words:

> *Giishpin bi izhaamigoyin,*
> If we come to you
> *bi namadabiyaang,*
> and we sit
> *miinwa gigidoyaang,*
> and we talk
> *gdaa bi bimaadiz na?*
> will you be alive (for us)?

Why have I denied myself the pleasure, what satisfies in its stead?
Well, not going every Monday or Tuesday night does not mean I
have been cut off from other language learners. We're a cyber-
loving bunch, as well as word lovers. Sometimes my Ojibwe fix
arrives in e-mail or over the Web.

Meg keeps up the cyber table for her *Anishinaabemowin Dopwin* at Ann Arbor, Michigan, on *Nongo e-Anishinaabemjig*, People Who Speak Anishinaabe Today:

> This site represents many things, most of all, it is evidence that Anishinaabemowin is alive and well. We have created this cyber space so that the ancient sounds are not lost and can be connected to anyone willing to listen, learn, and labor with us in the effort to maintain Anishinaabemowin. We are humbled by our teachers and those who have preceded us in this work. (www.umich.edu/~ojibwe/)

The group Meg works with follows the language "nest" model, she says. I imagine myself as a baby bird with mouth open waiting for tasty bits of language to be dropped in—if I swallow enough, will my words fly? One day they will float out effortlessly, as deliciously as *N'zaagitonaa, Anishinaabemowin Dopwin*, We love you, Language Table.

————

Love, again. A young woman I know, a Dakota, tells us she is in love. She fell in love with a Dakota young man who first "MySpaced," her, then began showing up at Dakota Language Table often enough to get her attention. Think of Language Table as the modern-day equivalent of standing outside a girl's lodge with a blanket, playing love songs on a bird-shaped flute. Now an indigenous boy must make his name in the Word Wars to show he would make a good father, one who would teach his children to speak their language. How romantic is that? Imagine, once you find a man who speaks your ancestor's words, you will always have a code between you and the whole big non-Native world, words shared between you two alone. "Oh, please," a Dine friend once cried, "Send me someone to make love to me in my Native tongue!"

But the promise of love may not be enough. We may have to make some bread. You know the old joke? When the Creator was handing out butts, he asked the Ojibwe women if they wanted buns and they said, no, thanks, we'll take bannock. Some of us have regretted that choice ever since, but still we make our flat, flaky favorite, called bannock or, as we from Turtle Mountain do, *gallette* pronounced *gullet*. I like this recipe from Metiscommis-sion.com because it gives a little comment (with an asterisk) that I'll take as life advice as well as cooking instruction: 3 cups flour, 3 tsp. baking powder, 1 tsp. sugar (optional), 1 1/2 cups milk, 1/4 cup melted fat/lard, 1/2 tsp. salt. * Never overwork. Bake at 350 for 15–20 minutes until golden brown.

Even the promise of love and food is sometimes not enough. Even wanting to study Ojibwe language for myself was not suffi-cient motivation for me to commit to my study. Sure, I loved the feeling of being with others who loved the language, hearing the elders so pleased to be able to speak Ojibwe again, seeing the children running around or learning with attention, sharing the potluck meals that worked somehow. And while I enjoyed the feeling of community, I noticed that so few people took part. Where, I wondered, was everyone?

Sometimes I asked friends to come with me, but they often seemed bashful and said their Ojibwe was not good enough. I know this attitude is an effect of the boarding-school era, when indigenous languages were banned outright and children were punished for speaking even their own names. Imagine those moments: you speak your name—and Ojibwe names are beautiful, fluid states given by the spirits in a dream—your name given to you in a ceremony, you are asked who you are by some forbidding figure, a nun or matron, and then slapped for saying it. How long has that slap stung? How much does relearning renew that pain?

Ojibwe elders tell us that the language is inside us somewhere, that we carry it in our bodies. That's a hopeful thought, that we can recover our language like we recover health. My sister Angie's an Indian Health Service physician, but even she knows you can get folks to do anything if there's frybread involved. If we put out a sign saying "Language Table and Frybread, Tonight Free!" we'd get a lot more takers, I am sure. But if we carry the language in our bodies, we better take some care with them:

Dr. Angie's No-Fry Frybread

Mix dough according to your favorite recipe, but swap half the white flour for wheat and place *lightly* greased rounds on a pan in a 375-degree oven until puffed up and brown. Pat on towels before serving. Serving size: 1/2 piece. Yep.

With frybread, it is hard to be good. And the Ojibwe worldview, as I've heard it called, wants aspects of our lives to come into a circle of goodness. Somehow, from within our English-language perspective, goodness equates to "good behavior" alone. Do people now associate indigenous language with spiritual goodness? I sense that many Ojibwe people, at least in the city, think that they are not "good enough" to study the language, even in the informal way offered at Language Table. Perhaps because Ojibwe language in many communities retreated, to be spoken only in ceremony, it came to be seen as a privileged language. And Language Table does treat the language as spirit. But what would be good for the leery to know is that privilege goes both ways: we may need the language to ask the right questions, but, as Meg suggests in her poem, the language may answer us as well:

Giishpin semaa miinigoyin, aaniish ge ezhi naadamoyingiba?
If we offer you tobacco, what will you help us become?

*Waabzheshii wii aawiyaang wii chi waasa waabandamaang ge
ni ezhiwebag?*
A marten looking far into the future?

Pukane wii aawiyaang wii nagamoyaang?
A grasshopper making a song?

*Gimewan wii aawiyaang wii naamademeyaang oshki-
waaskoneing?*
Rain on a new flower?

What has the language helped us to become? To engage learning
the way I have been able to do requires that I acknowledge the
privilege inherent in studying Ojibwe. Nothing stops me, really,
but my own laziness or business. No shame, no bus fare, no illness
or abuse at home, no internalized oppression. And still it is hard
for me, with all my privilege, to go and keep going. How then does
Ojibwe language recovery take place for an entire culture when so
many things stop people from engaging in such learning? What
can we do to bring others into this becoming, this possibility, this
language as alive as *Pukane* grasshopper?

If only everyone understood that Language Table loves us all. Well,
maybe that's a bit too Jesus of me. Still, they make a point of saying
they welcome everyone at Meg's Language Table, every level of
learner, from every culture or combination of cultures. That's always
seemed true to me at Ojibwe classes I've attended as well. Meg
describes her *Dopwin* as a "place where speakers and students meet
each week to make a difference." Meg is an activist and advocate for

indigenous language learning; her poetry in Ojibwemowin reveals that she strives for the "creative fluency" that, according to linguists, is needed to keep our language alive.

> *Anishinaabemowin Dopwin, N' Bazigeminaa,*
> Language Table, Our Sweetheart,
> *Gawiin pisagaag eta g'da'aawesii.*
> You are not only a flat board.
> *Wii Nakweshkodaading, ingoji g'daaw.*
> You are a meeting place.
> *Kinomageng ingoji g'daaw.*
> You are a university.
> *Kina nda'anamewinaanin miinwa nda'bwajigewinaanin*
> All our prayers and dreams
> *Ndo maamaawi'iyaami*
> gather there
> *biinjiiying kiin e-ayaawiiyin mitigo'ode.*
> inside your wooden heart.

To say those words, *mitigo'ode,* to say *Wooden Heart,* means almost the opposite of what we hear in English. Wooden-hearted is what I was, and often am, in spiritual terms. But in Ojibwe, that wood is alive and that heart is not just a core but it beats with story. Wooden heart, *mitigo'ode,* sounds open, spirited even, in Ojibwemowin.

Beginning to know a language that brings wood to life was a long time coming for me. For many years my only chance to hear the language my grandfather spoke was when, on occasion, I listened to Ojibwe spoken at ceremonies, or if I played Ojibwe tapes. Then, ten years ago, I moved to Minnesota and began to hear the language more. Then I began to have dreams in which Ojibwe words came to me. Some were spoken aloud, others were printed

in images—once on the license plates of two Volkswagen bugs—
Ojibwe words whose meaning escaped me at the time. I wrote
them down. Although I asked others who studied Ojibwemowin
to help me understand these dream words, I learned that I would
need to study Ojibwe myself if I ever really wanted to understand
the Ojibwe words that came to me. Harder still for this wooden
heart, I needed to take the language into my head and, something
more, I had to be open to the words in a spiritual way.

Now, not only as charge and price for my learning, but in a kind
of pact of faith with my dreams, I share my interest in Ojibwe
through my writing. It was not, at first, easy for me to approach
this learning (an intellectual activity) with anything spiritual in
mind, because the word *spirit* has always seemed, well, not at all
intellectual. What does *spirit* mean? Religion? God? Ghosts? These
questions crept in when I really wanted to concentrate on animate
and inanimate Ojibwe verbs.

Meg Noori's line, her name for Language Table, Wooden Heart,
helps it all make sense to me. *Mitigo'ode* contains the notion of
spirit as in "the spirit of the thing"—the vital force that comes from
our people's long and thoughtful history with their words. To
study Ojibwe language is to come into the presence of words that
were last spoken in my family by my grandfather. To study Ojibwe
is to take part in the recovery of a language. In sharing the experience of learning our Native language through poetry, we are in a
small way, in my case pitifully small—though sincere—way, doing
as our teachers encourage: helping to keep the language alive.

Ojibwe language has come speaking into my dreams. It arises
from me in some way I cannot explain except to trust that something within me retains a relationship to the language, that some
small part of my intelligence (what others might call my spirit)
inherited from the generations of Ojibwe speakers who are my

ancestors, was meant to know this language on some level. Perhaps I will never speak Ojibwemowin with any level of fluency, but at least its words now sound in my dreams. As Meg Noori says:

> *N'zaagitonaa, Anishinaabemowin Dopwin,*
> We love you, Language Table,
> *kaa waabaamigoo miinwa, miinwa, miinwa, miinwa pane.*
> we'll see you again, and again, and again, and again forever.

THE SOURCE OF THE DRIVE FOR MY LANGUAGE WORK

Kaihuhatati (Jerry L. Hill)

In 1987 I sat down with Amos Christjohn for the first time to work on the Oneida language. He was one of the Oneida elders for whom Oneida was his first language. There were still a few then. There are fewer now.

His devotion to the language was born out of a lifetime interest leading to a degree in linguistics at the age of sixty-nine from Lakehead University in Ontario, Canada, under the direction of Professor Bill Cook, to whom he often referred.

I returned home to Wisconsin from law school in California in 1976 with two goals: to acquire my language and to represent the tribe. I accomplished one and am still working on the other. I would be the first of more than a dozen Oneida lawyers. I knew a couple dozen Indian attorneys, but there were few in Wisconsin. That changed, but in 1976, we were few.

I earned a BA degree in linguistics in 1973, and each summer I returned home for another experience with the language. So, I would spend the summer listening to as many Oneida speakers as I could in various situations, almost always in the company of my grandma, another Oneida first-language speaker. Then I had a somewhat naive view of acquisition, not as simple but with the belief, which I still have, that the generally accepted methods of studying other languages were the least effective ways to acquire any language. There was really no place for Native languages except at the university level, where they were treated as subjects rather than as living languages. Non-Native scholars used our languages as exotic dissertation topics for their PhDs. My observation then was that there had to be a better way. Over the years I learned another way, but that was not to be for more than ten more years, after returning home.

In 1976, there were still dozens of first-language Oneida speakers—including my maternal grandmother—who grew up with Oneida as their first language. Most of these were former students of the despised BIA boarding-school system. As a child I had heard Oneida routinely but didn't appreciate that it was in serious decline as our community language shifted to English, almost exclusively by 1976. Native language extinction is one of our silent enemies.

In 1987 I organized weekly lunch meetings with some of the speakers and those who had expressed an interest in wanting to speak. This was also my first disappointment; good ideas often are not enough. So, after several meetings, Amos and I were left with each other. I was convinced that it was because of me; a paranoid delusion that is a whole 'nother story. Anyway, I tried again, with the same result. Then I had another insight; my excitement wasn't contagious, either. I realized that it was just us, so Amos and I met at lunchtime almost every day for the next ten years.

Literacy and Fluency

Our language had been extensively recorded and analyzed since 1939, with hundreds of stories and anecdotes written under a WPA project designed by a very respected linguist, Morris Swadish, and a Yale grad student, Floyd Lounsberry, who also became an eminent linguist. These linguists worked closely with first-language speakers of Oneida developing an orthography, the origin of which was derived from an earlier Mohawk orthography first created by missionaries among them in the 1700s. Because Oneida and Mohawk are closely related, though separate, Iroquoian languages, speakers of either one are able to mutually comprehend one another. Literacy in each language was a fact for many years before the Oneida WPA project came into being. In fact, when the linguists began working in Oneida, their goal was to train Oneidas to become literate in their own language within two years. That the Oneidas were able to adopt the new orthography in less than two months became a good laugh on the linguists but, more importantly, facilitated the transcription of the hundreds of stories referred to. Fluency precedes literacy: competent speakers can become literate.

This particular insight was slow in coming because of ineffective American language-teaching methods that focus on analysis rather than acquisition. Students are taught to know "about" language rather than to become conversationally fluent. For someone who wants to be able to speak a language, it becomes all the more frustrating, because learning "about" reinforces the first language at the expense of the target language. To say it another way: one can be a competent speaker and still be illiterate. And, still another way: one can be taught to read with little or no comprehension of what one has read. So, the observation that speaking precedes literacy becomes particularly important for Native people in 2006 whose first language is English and who reside in communities where the shift to English is all but complete.

Although there are systems of recording events in many Native cultures, actual written languages were only beginning to appear in Middle and South America a few thousand years ago, and only discovered recently, in the past hundred years or so. The importance of this to the average Native community member who wants to participate in their language is the realization that part of our acculturation as Americans, i.e., being literate in English, is an impediment to acquiring the language of our ancestors. The question raised is, what would be an optimal way to address the challenge?

It slowly dawned on me that one way of addressing the challenge would be to use analytical knowledge as well as practical experience. My apprenticeship with Amos Christjohn was an interweaving of both of these aspects of language acquisition. I grew up in an Oneida-speaking community but did not acquire the language and made no attempts at it until I was a middle-aged man far past the optimal age of acquisition. In college I earned a degree in linguistics with the idea that modern science could help me learn the language of my ancestors. Then I was recruited to law school, which added another three-year delay. Our history was not taught in the boarding schools then, nor is it taught in public schools now. Yet, when I returned home, my focus was on immediate legal issues facing the tribe, with only desultory attention to language until one day it simply clicked in my head that our language needed attention right now, not tomorrow. That was the beginning of my conscious focus on the Oneida language.

I first had to deal with the fact that our ways, Amos's of teaching and mine of learning, didn't seem compatible. My idea was to get directly into immersion, and his was approaching language from an analytical perspective. I finally understood this as an illustration of Amos's experience as someone who grew up with Oneida as a first language, compared to mine as someone with English as a first language. He knew what I was seeking to know.

He knew how to speak, and so writing and analysis was a natural sequence for him. For me, working from materials written in an orthography based upon the English alphabet was the opposite of immersion. Though we never argued about it, we wound up doing it his way. When I complained to my brother, he said: "Well, just do it his way. You have a degree in it." That simple observation was right to the point. From then on things got much better for both of us. Best of all, I finally realized that what Amos and I were doing was the traditional way of teaching and learning.

The Traditional Way

Amos liked working with someone who understood and was trained in analysis as he was, and I was able to join my interests with his methods and purpose; in time, I slowly realized I was acquiring the language. Some years later I understood that this was also a reflection of the old ways, in which the seeker goes to the one who knows and establishes a relationship by showing a willingness to do the work, whatever the one who knows wants done. It was truly a traditional experience; I came to him and after a couple of years he knew I was serious.

Our Languages and the Law

As an attorney working on various legal issues for the tribe, there was a need for accurate historical information. I thought how convenient it would be to find a journal or diary about what people where thinking and doing at the time of the emigration from New York, the Civil War, the Allotment, boarding schools, Indian Reorganization, Citizenship, and the like. Of course, I found nothing by such designation. There was, however, correspondence between the Tribal Council and Washington, D.C., as well as various other documents, such as a proposed Oneida Nation Constitution. These gave some of the story, but huge gaps remained. I was shocked to find exactly what I had been seeking as far as what the

Oneida people thought was important in these hundreds of stories transcribed in the new Oneida orthography. Of course, it was a quiet discovery, because it required context and piecing together. I had found more of the story reposing in these old words waiting to be resuscitated and shared. Amos was my guide to this new trove of our history.

Such was my experience, weaving together the disciplines of linguistics and law, with the direct experience in the language in the original words of Oneida people who were there. It was my personal Rosetta stone, and one that would continue to inspire me in the years to come and to share with others—those who would appreciate this cache of Oneida history and knowledge, collected by Oneida people, in the Oneida language.

He Destroys the Fields

Our history came alive as I was able to connect directly to the experience of my ancestors from before the American Revolution with its insights into the "Founding Fathers" up to World War II. For example, I learned the Iroquois perspective on the Sullivan Campaign to wipe out all vestiges of the Six Nations' resistance to the new United States under the direct, but deep-cover orders of President George Washington and the subsequent naming of Washington, D.C., as ^takalyasne ("Place of the Destroyer") and the title of all presidents from Washington to G. W. Bush as Lah^takalyas ("Destroyer of the Fields"). Another example is when the delegation from the Wannamaker Commission arrived in Oneida with the U.S. flag from Washington, D.C., to inform the Oneidas that they had become citizens under the new Indian Citizenship Act of 1924 (of course, without Oneida knowledge or consent, much less our request). The D.C. delegation asked the assembled Oneidas to post the flag, but no one would admit to understanding what the delegation was saying, so the delegation was forced to do it them-selves. Unfortunately, the flag became entangled, and the delega-tion demanded that the chief order one of the men to climb up the pole. The assembled Oneidas burst out laughing, and one of the underling delegates was forced to climb the pole himself, in his suit, to the roars of the "new citizen" Oneidas. Ironically, the cor-respondence showed that the term *citizen* was used pejoratively among the Oneidas.

These were some of the experiences that came to me with the study of our language. Some of the WPA stories were sentimental, some inspiring, more than a few humorous and ribald, and, of course, many poignant and sorrowful. I connected to the lives of my ancestors in a way that my acculturated education could never accomplish and dedicated myself to sharing this connection with my tribal relatives as well as the public in general. Knowledge is truly a power, but one that must be maintained, cultivated, and passed on for the future.

So much of the rhetoric of Native language and culture becomes susceptible to political "Buffalo" or "Unity" speeches that are enough to cause one's eyes to glaze over or embarrassed groans. Yet, it would be more than unkind to cynically dismiss these sen-timents. As an Osage colleague once said of lateral oppression: "There's enough responsibility for all of us to choke on." The obvious point needing no explanation.

Acculturation and Assimilation

To connect with the circumstances of our ancestors, it is necessary to acknowledge their hardships and historical contexts. We have been acculturated and are well on our way to becoming assimi-lated. There is a difference between acculturation and assimilation.

The influence of acculturation is hard to deny. We're educated in another system, and our present decision-making institutions of governance are derived from theirs. There are also more subtle ways of acculturation, such as our dress and unconscious use of all the nuances of American English, as well as regional dialects.

Having said all that, it remains a fact that Native communities retain and express an imperative of identity that defines them even against other very closely related communities. This individuality stands in sharp contrast to the typical generic term *Indian* and its variations, e.g., *American Indian, Native American,* and its vulgarisms, *Red Skins, Blanket Asses,* and the like. Even the Anglicized versions of our names e.g., Oneida vs. On^yota'aka, Chippewa vs. Ojibwe, Ottawa vs. Odawa, show the pattern, and we, unfortunately, have adopted the drift until we accept being Indians, which would have been an insult to our ancestors. Still, without contrary information, it is a blameless sin. Such is the incremental force of assimilation.

An interesting aside is that a number of tribes have changed their community names back to traditional designations, e.g., Ho Chunk vs. Winnebago, Tohono O'odham vs. Pima, etc.

Assimilation is the uncritical acceptance of change, as in the "great American melting pot." So, after a couple of generations, the descendants of European immigrants become Americans, with little to distinguish them from other sons of European immigrants. The other, more visible immigrants, such as the descendants of African slaves, Asians, and those from south of the border, many of whom are Native people but who are defined as Mexicans, Guatemalans, or Hondurans, collectively, can be grouped together as nonwhite. The specter of American racism is complicit in these designations and impossible to deny, notwithstanding federal laws and the claims of politicians to the contrary.

Indians Are Not Minorities

Despite this, Native people in America occupy a truly unique legal status, which begins with the U.S. Constitution and its antecedent, the colonial Articles of Confederation. We are much more than simple social minorities. Our governments have been legally recognized for as long as the United States has existed, and each of the three branches of the federal government has had its hands full in attempting to define exactly what the contours of those legal rights are. This is still true.

Culturally speaking, in 2006, Indians are bicultural and, if we're lucky, bilingual, having all the attributes of American citizens as well as the blood rights of our ancestors to our original identities. This is codified federal law and Tribal constitutions, most importantly, reflect the strength asserted in our traditions.

Inherent Sovereignty

The right of self-identification is culturally and politically inherent. This is obvious when a culture's independence is backed by sufficient force to resist unilateral assertions to the contrary by outsiders. One need only look to communications between the first English colonizers and the Six Nations in which astute appointed governors were tactful to the point of fear in requesting accommodation of any kind. Compared to the cowardly and treacherous Sullivan Campaign 150 years later, the evolution from respect to dismissive arrogance stands in sharp contrast.

The Strength of Our Languages

The point of this history and these examples is that Indian people have remained focused on facts and their ability to assess circumstances for five hundred years despite revisionist institutional claims to the contrary. However, we have been inundated for the past two hundred years by the oppressive and dishonest policies of the federal government and a generally ignorant public. The sum of these conditions compounds the onslaught against the values of our ancestors and reminders of our original identities. One might liken this to what is presently called identity theft, except with an even more sinister motive. With Indians, when they define who we are, then the next step is to define us out of existence, and we will become a "minority" with only the rights of minorities. Without our languages, the difficulty of maintaining our identities is incalculable.

The single most undeniable attribute of Native identity is language. Anti-Indian groups and individuals can argue with our history, and now, even our genomic origins, to support their claim that although we may be descended from Indians, we are no longer "real" Indians with legal rights, thus justifying their argument that Indians are simply minorities.

The dire stress under which Indian communities are presently placed can be most directly observed in the state of our languages. If linguists are to be believed, our languages are moribund, with little possibility of recovery. This may not be the mean-spirited prediction of Indian-hating linguists; it can be a simple scientific empirical observation based upon existing statistical data. Consider that other indigenous languages with as many as 100,000 speakers outside North America are considered endangered—compared to our communities, in which there remain only a few dozen or fewer speakers. The lesson one draws from this is that fine-tuned statistics are simply based upon information. If this information is used to predict the future, then it is speculation. It may, thus, be an educated guess, but in the absence of competing data, one is left to react emotionally rather than purposefully after a conscious assessment of the circumstances. My apprenticeship in the Oneida language regenerated my hope for Native people.

Working with Amos Christjohn for ten years allowed me the emotional support of an enlightened elder who respected the old way and the opportunity to use new tools to help preserve our Oneida language by speaking it. His younger sister, Maria Hinton, ninety-six, is now my mentor. My grandma always said, "Make yourself useful," and with the oversight of these respected elders I am able to assist and share with other Oneida people, including my family, what I've acquired and to encourage them in every way I can to do the same.

A Ghost Dance for Words

Jeanette Weaskus

Officer Scott could smell the wood smoke as it blew in the wind from the sweathouse. He heard the cries of the baby that had prompted the neighbors to call tribal police. It was the second day the toddler had been left alone. Officer Scott used his bulk against the flimsy doorframe. The thump against the door caused the child to cease crying and climb up to peer through the window. Black hair in day-old braids, the darkness of a full-blood, bib overalls, and most likely wearing moccasins, just like many other Nez Perce children. As the door burst open, Officer Scott found that the infant had been foraging through the sparse pantry and concocting his own meals, already able to mimic the actions of his mother in the kitchen. Officer Scott knew the young girl, only seventeen, and he was not surprised that she had left the baby alone. When Ezmarelda failed to return, the boy's fate was decided. He would be sent to the mission orphanage on the Yakima Indian Reservation. In the social climate of 1942, with the war economy and signs in store windows reading NO DOGS OR INDIANS ALLOWED and WHITE TRADE ONLY, it was not probable that this Nez Perce boy would be adopted.

———

Ezmarelda was a fluent speaker of the Nez Perce language, Nimi-ipuutimpt. She had run away from her son and the reservation to work as an aircraft riveter at Boeing in Seattle. Ez assumed that her sister would take care of the boy until the war was over, but Emeraude had eloped in secret and was motoring down Highway 101 toward Camp Pendleton with her new husband. Em would have taken the boy, but fate did not allow it. The consequences of this boy being institutionalized are still palpable, though both Ezmarelda and her son have long been buried beneath the blanket of mother earth. Ezmarelda did not pass on her fluency in indigenous dialect to her son. At only one year of age and placed in a mission, he was given English as his language, and all of his heirs were also denied fluency.

I ferry the large, porous stones into the sweathouse. My aunt has taught me which rocks will stay orange and hot for the longest time. Inside the sweathouse, the elders know what I will ask, that I will want to learn "an Inden word." Though I learned the names of animals and household items, mere vocabulary is very far from fluency in our nation's dialect. In supplement to hustling the elders for words at any chance, I have also taken the full course of Nez Perce language at college level. Now in my language capacity are verbs that can be morphologically combined with pronouns and tense affixes to produce working sentences. The only problem with striving for indigenous fluency in college is that the program comes to an inevitable end.

After graduation, I enter the realm of capitalism, a forty-hour workweek, and feel the dream of attaining fluency perish under the limited time for life outside the eight-hour day. I ponder fluency and its attainability. Capitalistic societal demands are killing tribalism and traditionalism; factored in among these aspects is the quest to regain indigenous dialect. The great holy man Smowhalla reflected on the manner in which employment killed traditional religion. He posited the impossibility of fully practicing the Dreamer religion and upholding the traditional way of hunter-gatherer life when in the employ of a farmer. Back in Smowhalla's day, hunting and gathering were still viable ways of making a living, but no more. Our tribe relies on the capitalistic way of life, though many men rebel against this by working seasonally and spending the rest of the year hunting and fishing.

With my college years over and my young boys too wild to behave in the community classroom where elders teach language lessons, I need a new method to gain language. I have passed along what I know to my sons, which is "a thimbleful," as Mae Taylor teased me. The curriculum in the community classroom is the basic stuff anyway, animal names, counting, household items, and clothing; what I need is to hear the language in motion, every day. To attain fluency one must have constant contact with a fluent speaker and use very little English. The day would come when my grandma's sister, Emeraude, would have me clean her house every day, but we spoke English to one another, though I did beg for and receive many "Inden" words.

It is alarming to contemplate that the fluent speakers of Nez Perce are below one hundred in number and that this sacred language is not available to completely learn at a time vital to its continuance. The tribe incorporates lessons in the Head Start program with the basics, beginning with colors. Language lessons are incorporated all the way through elementary and high school grade levels. Though it is a fine attempt at language acquisition, what the tribe will be left with is an amazing pidgin. I know the love for our language exists, but how can we become fluent when all of society, including our own, works against it? As my favorite history professor says, "Fluent speakers of the Nez Perce language are national treasures."

As a young woman, I often dreamed of asking one of the iconographic figures of our tribe, for example Yellow Wolf or Chief Joseph, questions about the "old days," especially my first love of traditional culture—religion. In reality, if I could manage the vocabulary to ask about religion, I would be crippled in the area of comprehension and understand very little of the answer. It would be the same stumbling conversation I have with other elders, only without the luxury of "What was that again?" As an older woman, now I desire advice from the Father, Wovoka, whose command of English included writing; he had knowledge of a precise technique used for the extraction of lost cultural information, the Ghost Dance. The Pawnee had practiced the Ghost Dance as prescribed by the Father, Wovoka, and the result was a renaissance of renewed culture. Missing bits that had been decimated through non-Indian and missionary contact were recalled, including language.

Wovokian rhetoric encompassed a view that through hard work and living in a good way, an Indian could perform the Ghost Dance with success. The benefit of a successful dance would be dead friends and relatives who relayed to the individual a piece of lost culture. Considering the indigenous traditional belief systems and religions of my region, this makes perfect sense; who better than those in temporal proximity to the intact culture to recall its lost remnants? The Ghost Dance was meant for this reason, as a revival of traditionalism and a repatriation of Indianness. I would ask of the Father Wovoka: just how much language can Ghost Dancing earn? If the Ghost Dance has the capability to repatriate tribal culture, then paint the sacred shirts in the prescribed manner and hold hands up to the sky.

————

I chip the green flakes from porous lava rock to mix a tint for the sacred shirts. The green will stain the fringe and other background areas of the shirt. The true artwork is the sacred symbols painted in darker colors: the comet, the morning star, the sun, moon, dragonfly, butterfly, and icons of one's own tribe, mine being the Chinook salmon, elk, eagle, and moose. Painting takes much time, but is blessedly simpler than beadwork. I choose a simple design with three Chinook across the back, two morning stars and a crescent moon on the front. Each son in his individuality has chosen a material for the shirt. Construction of the fringe in buckskin is easier than in muslin or cotton, the other traditional materials used for making the sacred shirts.

The Father Wovoka prescribed a dance lasting for five days, and on the sixth day to bathe in the river. I put in a request for a week off from work. My boss denies the request because the department "needs me." I wonder if the dance can be performed only on the weekends? Feeling haunted by capitalism, I must save up my vacation time and annual leave to amount to five days in the summer, because that's the best time to bathe in the river. Meanwhile I consider the math of the Ghost Dance: to perform a dance every six weeks is not possible with a full-time job. Smowhalla was right, better to practice traditionalism than to be in the employ, however there is that specter of food and rent that in contemporary life cannot be denied.

Ezmarelda succumbed to the pressures of capitalism. The money may have appeared as a relief during this depressed period of the economy; however, I would argue, as one of Ezmarelda's progeny, that the denial of indigenous dialect fluency for the future generations of our people in exchange for momentary security and monetary gain was not a fair exchange to the future tribal members. The present may be a fleeting moment to a parent within the tapestry of tribal history; however, what we teach our children about tradition and language lasts well into future generations.

INDIGENOUS LANGUAGE CONSCIOUSNESS: BEING, PLACE, AND SOVEREIGNTY

Simon J. Ortiz

Guuwaadze, gai dawaah eh tru-drai-draa-skah. Hello, how are you—I hope all have arisen in good health and good spirits.

Guuwaadze is one word, and it is literally a question that asks, "How are you?" Gai dawaah eh is a phrase which refers to your health and well-being, not only physically but also psychically. Tru-drai-draa-skah literally and technically formulates a state of being and an action having to do with rising from a prone position in the morning, i.e., at the beginning of a day.

So: Guuwaadze—how are all of you? Gai dawaah eh—hopes for well-being of your physique and your psyche. Tru-drai-draa-skah—your being is in the act of rising to your feet at the beginning of a day.

What a morning greeting!

The nature of language as expressed by Indigenous human culture has to do with an intuitive and vital connection that human beings have with the natural earth process or dynamic. In other words, we, as Indigenous people, speak language that directly comes from the natural forces all around us. Language comes directly from the natural environment—simply put, human language comes from Mother Earth, the natural environment, namely, the natural world within which we thrive.

Jeannette Armstrong, a teacher and writer from the Salish culture and a fluent Salish speaker, says Indigenous language is the voice of the geographical region Indigenous people traditionally and originally inhabit. Indigenous languages, then, are particular and unique to Indigenous peoples in regions they know as their homelands, i.e., their places of origin. For example, in the U.S. southwest area of New Mexico, where my native cultural community of Acoma Pueblo is located, the native language spoken by *Acqumeh hanu*—Acoma people—is Keres.

Keres is one of the five different Indigenous languages that people speak in their nineteen Pueblo tribal cultural communities. Other Indigenous languages Pueblo people speak are Tewa, Tiwa, Towa, and Zuni. (Very briefly, I must explain that *pueblo* is a Spanish word meaning town, community, or group of people; the word has been used since Spanish colonial times and has been generally adopted by Pueblo people as a term for their communities.) Seven of the nineteen distinct Pueblo tribes speak Keres as a native language, and they are divided into eastern and western dialects. Same language but different dialects. Five Pueblo tribes located along or near the Rio Grande speak eastern Keres, and two Pueblos, Laguna and Acoma, speak the western dialect.

It's the same Keres language, like I said, but eastern and western Keres are different dialects, and there are different pronunciations of words. For example, *Guwaadze*—that asks how you are, that I referred to earlier—requires a response. "I'm well" or "We're well" is the usual response. In western Keres, it is *"Dawaa-eh,"* meaning, "I'm well and thank you." In eastern Keres, the response is *"Rawa,"* meaning the same thing as the western Keres. In eastern Keres, the enunciation is different. An *r* sound is made—a fast and quick roll of that *r*, like "rr." People are very particular and insistent about their local dialects even when they are from the same language group. The Pueblos of Acoma and Laguna are located next to each other as sister tribal communities. Since they are sister communities, they speak the same Keres language, but nonetheless they insist on their language differences, their dialects, because it is the way they maintain their identities and their distinctiveness.

There is a *quuti*—a mountain—that is common to both Acoma and Laguna. To each of them, and according to each of their own versions of the traditional origin or emergence story, the *quuti* is sacred. Symbolically, the *quuti* is vastly important, because it sits north of both Acoma and Laguna. And north is the sacred direction from which, in mythic times past, their peoples came.

A long time ago, many years back in the past. *Meeshru hama yuu nah kahtyah-stih kah-shraitih.* From Shipapu, the origin or emergence place to the north. From there, all life arose or emerged. And north is also the sacred direction toward which the spirits of the departed-deceased travel to return to the origin-beginning place of life. The people of Aacqu (Acoma) and Kahwaika (Laguna) have the highest mutual respect for the *quuti* named Kaweshtima by Acoma people and Tsebina by Laguna people.

Since it is the same sacred mountain Acoma and Laguna people refer to in their oral traditions, prayers, songs, and story narratives, and since they speak the same Keres language and are sister Pueblo tribal communities living next to each other, shouldn't they have the same name for the mountain? In other words, shouldn't they know the *quuti* by a shared name? Why, no, they don't think so. Since their language is determined by their geographical locales, they know the sacred *quuti* by their own distinct names for it. *Daistih stutaah-ahtih-shii-neeyah, ehmee eh hehya sruuweh Kaweshtima steiu-to-neemah-stah.* That's what Acoma people say in their native language. Because we are from here, meaning from the Acoma Pueblo site or location, that's the reason we know Kaweshtima by that name. Or the English translation can also be: because we are living here (i.e., where Acoma Pueblo is located), that's why we are aware of Kaweshtima by that knowledge.

Being and place. One's awareness of being or a community's awareness of being is determined very much by place. In fact, one can say Existence is determined by being and place. Awareness of their respective beings as Acoma and Laguna is the basis of their relationship to the *quuti;* therefore Acoma and Laguna know the *quuti* in their own respective dialects of the Keres language. The sacred regard they have for the *quuti* is determined by their relationship to it, and this is the reason for their different names for the mountain.

The Acoma name Kaweshtima literally translates in English into "snow-covered female mountain." The Laguna name Tsebina translates in English into "female head covered with a scarf." Although English translations are descriptive enough, they lack the relational power residing in the original Indigenous language. That's due to necessary fact and the nature of Indigenous language: language forms and evolves from the natural and geographical environment of a cultural community. As a result, Kaweshtima and Tsebina-names not absolutely different but differing enough—are maintained as such. They have to be different because their meanings are determined by the context and locale of Acoma's and Laguna's separate and different environments and the relationship of their environments to the sacred mountain.

Being and place are conceptually linked. This is an Indigenous principle and, therefore, is maintained as such within Indigenous cultural philosophy and expressed in the most common or ordinary way. When I introduce myself in my native *dzehni* Keres, I speak in the same way I conceive of myself: *Aacqumeh stuudah*. Literally, I am saying "Acoma-like, I am." Or "Acoma, I am." Literally stating "I am Acoma," the physical Pueblo community itself not from or of Acoma or similar in likeness to the Pueblo and people of Acoma but Acoma as physical and cultural entity.

The same language dynamic occurs when I further identify myself by saying *"Dyaamih hanu studah."* I am the Eagle People. Of course, I'm saying I am of or from or a member of the Eagle Clan, but the words, in English translation, literally state: I am the Eagle People. Conceptually, to state "I am the Eagle People" and "I am the people of Acoma" is necessary. *Dzah dze-guwaah ee'shkah haitih hanu nuudah-sk'uunuh.* I cannot be any other person or people. In fact, my very Existence is conceptually founded on my awareness and acceptance of my identity as a *Dyammih hanu* of the *Aacqumeh hanu*. It is very important and necessary to express myself as my very being; that, in fact, is the only way to state my case as a human cultural being. It is the only way to fully identify and state who I am as a human cultural being. Without doing that, I do not have conceptual Existence.

Obviously, Indigenous languages have direct bearing on the conceptualization of Existence via Indigenous culture. Being and place equals Existence. Or Being + Place = Existence. In the past ten or so years in my poetry and other writings, I have been repeating a mantra of sorts: land, culture, and community. Usually I don't say Indigenous land, culture, and community, but that's what I mean. In terms of what I said about Indigenous being and place, I could actually edit and revise the mantra and say: Indigenous land, culture, and community equals Indigenous being and place. Or Indigenous being and place is land, culture, and community.

————

The greatest and most horrible trauma Indigenous peoples of the Americas have experienced and endured for hundreds of years since European settlement, colonization, conquest—yes, let's go ahead and say conquest—has been the loss of place. Especially the loss of place due to loss of land. When the equation of Indigenous being + place = land, culture, and community is affected by loss of place:land, the equation is corrupted extremely. Indigenous peoples live all over the Americas, north, south, east, and west. Canada to Argentina, coast to coast on both North and South American continents and the islands of Central America. Undoubtedly, though devastatingly affected by colonialism, the Indigenous population did not vanish like Western society and culture vainly wished and even planned for. On the contrary, the Indigenous population in the Americas numbers in the tens of millions and is constantly growing—not in leaps and bounds, but growing. Yet Indigenous peoples have felt at times "vanished" and "invisible"! In fact, in a manner of speaking, Indigenous peoples in Latin America until lately have often not dared to identify as "Indios" because they are not acknowledged and accepted as such, except pejoratively!

Loss of place and land has impacted Indigenous American people beyond the maximum. The phenomenon of loss is indescribable; it could be called physical and psychic displacement, but that would be a clear understatement. As invaders-settlers-colonizers moved into Indigenous homelands in North, Central, and South America, physical removal of Indigenous people happened.

They moved either suddenly or gradually, many times by threat and/or violent, physical annihilation. From woodland to prairie, from desert to mountain, from seashore to lakeshore, from wetland to dry land—there was no place where loss of Indigenous land did not happen!

Physical displacement is physical removal, and it is obvious enough to comprehend. Psychic displacement is more difficult to comprehend, because comprehension takes place in the realm of the abstract and intellectual. The designation of "Indian reservations" ("Indian reserves" in Canada) is a case in point. When the U.S. federal government designated Indigenous lands to have federal trust status by virtue of congressional and government authority, such designation blatantly assaulted original sovereign control exercised by Indigenous people.

Before 1851, there were no "Indian reservations" in what is now the state of New Mexico. Because the United States did not have political control over Mexican national territory. Not until the United States forced Mexico to cede its sovereign control (which Mexico had gained with its independence from Spain in 1825) by forcing it to sign the Treaty of Guadalupe Hidalgo in 1851. By the end of the nineteenth century, all New Mexican Pueblos were enclosed within "Indian reservations" as designated by the U.S. federal government. U.S. Manifest Destiny was achieved in Indigenous Pueblo country by "Indian reservization." Indigenous lands became federal trust land; Indigenous homelands were no longer controlled by Indigenous people but by the U.S. Congress and administrative decree.

Aacqumeh lands traditionally "belonging" to Acoma people and used for ages by Acoma people were no longer "theirs" to control. Not only was the traditional land area severely reduced in size, but *Aacquumeh hanu*'s caretaking rules were superseded by federal laws. *Dzah dzeenah hanu chah-haatsee-nuh.* The land was no longer people's land. *Dzah dzeenah hanu ehteh tah-o-nuh.* People no longer had access to it. *Deh-mehshru dzah dzenah hanu de-dyah te-shruunu.* It was like people were no longer able to hold and touch it.

The "Indian reservation" land was the same land *Acquumeh hanu* had lived on for centuries. It was land they had known as home for as long as they could remember and upon which they had built homes. *Ai dyu dyaa-truh eh aishtyuu tyaa-ahshtee-tra.* Upon it was their home and community. But when the U.S. federal government designated their Aacqumeh homeland an "Indian reservation," it was no longer "theirs." Simple as that. With federal governmental rhetoric in American English, namely applying the term "Indian reservation" and backing it up with congressional and constitutional powers, a vital and intimate relationship with place:land began to dissipate and even vanish. And, conceptually, Indigenous people felt dissipated, vanished, and disappeared. And placeless. And homeless.

––––––––––

Several years ago, my thirty-eight-year-old son said he wanted to go home. He was working as an attorney in Washington, D.C., and there were some personal problems he was dealing with at the time. He was gradually working through the problems, but the main thing at that point in his life was a feeling that he "wanted to go home." He spoke about the constantly fast-paced working atmosphere and pressures of the job he had with a U.S. congressional committee office. "Wanting to go home" was and is an expressed symptom of what many Indigenous American people experience when "place" has been removed or taken away from them. Or when they have been removed or taken away from "place." Even when they have removed themselves by their own volition.

I've spoken about the close, intimate relationship one has to place, especially when place is Indigenous land. To Indigenous people, this is obviously a very critical matter. Especially when physical place is literally land. Land = place. When one is removed from place, there is a literal loss of place. When one's homeland is designated by the federal government as an "Indian reservation," that is a loss of place as much as it is a literal loss of land. *Dzah dzeenah hanu ehteh tah-ah-nuh. Deh-mehshru dzah dzenah hanu de-dyah te-shruunu.* People no longer had access to it. It seemed like people could no longer touch and hold it. Although the land is still there under their feet and around them physically, it is no longer regarded in the same way; it is federal government land now, protected by federal law, which has always worked against Indigenous people. Access is gained, if at all, only after going through extensive bureaucratic procedure. Close, intimate relationship with the land is no longer the case, nor even possible. I recall elders years ago vociferously, emotionally, and painfully speaking about "the *mericano hu-chani* stealing the people's land by putting up official signs saying NO TRESPASSING: GOVERNMENT PROPERTY." And today you hear elders who are now people my age saying exactly the same thing!

My son did not grow up within a reservation community like I did. While he occasionally visited his grandparents and other relatives, he was raised mostly away from the reservation in non-Indigenous contexts. There was an Indigenous cultural context in urban areas where he grew up in Albuquerque, Tucson, and Phoenix. His mother socialized within an urban Indian community, and she took him to visit Navajo reservation relatives, and he was with her for several years when she worked teaching school on the reservation. But he did not know "home" to be the Indian reservations of his Acoma and Navajo tribal parents, although he identified closely with the social-cultural Indigenous context into which he was born. He was like many others whose heritage is Indigenous and who do not reside in reservation communities but are a part of the Indigenous social-cultural context found in urban locales across the United States. As a result, my son, like many others, claims "home" to be the social-cultural context that's clearly Indigenous with regard to Indigenous family ties, cultural customs, spiritual traditions, community gatherings, and so forth. And the social-cultural Indigenous context is "home" as an identity, no doubt about that. It is not the "Indian reservation" home, certainly, but it is a concrete Indigenous home of family, community, culture, historical and modern-day traditions, and communal identification with other Indigenous people. Without a doubt, this is an Indigenous consciousness that one calls "home."

So when my son spoke of wanting to go home, I knew what he meant. He wanted to return to a safe, comfortable, secure haven where he was born and raised. Home is where the heart is. Home is where family roots are. Home is where community is most bonded. Home is where parents and grandparents reside. Home is home. I know where that is. I knew it as an Indigenous community called Deetseyaamah where I was raised, where I spent my childhood, where I grew up as an Acoma youth. For me, it was clear where home was. And then I had the thought—and also on behalf of my son, who was not raised in the same place:home I was—"What is home for him and other Indigenous young people anymore?" And then I had a concurrent thought: "What is home anymore for Indigenous people now that there has been considerable cultural change?"

For Indigenous American people, home used to be simple. You had a home, and you could return to it if you chose to do so. You belonged to a place, and there was no question about the place to which you belonged. Your homeland was the source of your identity, and that was a major part of your identifiable place in cultural society. Returning home was a simple matter of returning to the place you belonged. When you belonged to a place, you didn't have to explain to anyone anything but that you were returning home. You returned home; you returned to place. You returned to your land. But now that your Indigenous land has been designated an "Indian reservation," are you still returning home?

That is a big, big part of the question I asked myself: What is "home" now, when there has been tremendous change?

This ultimately has to do with Indigenous language and the question of sovereignty, and, further, sovereignty has to do with consciousness of being Indigenous. In the past forty years, a great deal of concern has been expressed within Indigenous communities of the Americas regarding the viability of Indigenous languages. Some have said that because of vast social and cultural changes—many or most of them unsought and undesired—resulting in assimilation and acculturation of Indigenous peoples into mainstream society and culture, Indigenous languages are being lost. And some say that along with loss of Indigenous languages has been mainstream education that has readily replaced Indigenous languages with English, Spanish, and French, resulting in the rapid loss of Indigenous languages. The situation is dire in the eyes of most Indigenous communities, because the loss of Indigenous languages is related to the loss of Indigenous cultures.

Further, the loss of Indigenous cultures means the loss of the hold—the closeness and intimacy—Indigenous communities have on their lands, on their place, in other words. Although Indigenous culture may not depend entirely or only upon Indigenous languages, there is a strong, undying belief that if Indigenous peoples lose their languages, that will signal the further loss of Indigenous cultures.

What is really at stake is cultural and political sovereignty. While there is support and advocacy by Indigenous peoples for Indigenous language viability and continuance, in the United States there is spotty support and advocacy by non-Indigenous people and institutions. There is minimal and reluctant support by federal and state governments that fund education curricula in schools. No mainstream public or private schools require the teaching of Indigenous languages. Acoma and Laguna both have schools in their reservation communities where the Keres language is taught in an extracurricular manner, but not as a requirement. Acoma and Laguna teachers and staff work at the schools. They speak with students in their native language, but not consistently, because there is no mandate by the schools nor by the tribal governments of the reservations that would make Indigenous language use more consistent. Acoma and Laguna Pueblos are faced with gradual language loss; they realize they have to take measures to ensure the continuance of their Indigenous languages. However, they are also governed by official school policies that do not support and advocate the Indigenous languages of their Indigenous students. When schools officially do not require Indigenous language teaching and learning, this influences and determines community mores. As a result, there is less and less Indigenous language use and more language loss.

––––––––

While Indigenous language may not be the only element for Indigenous cultural continuance, it is a major force and factor because of its role in forming and sustaining cultural substance and identity. To a large degree, colonial languages have replaced Indigenous languages; this fact is realized and recognized by Indigenous peoples of the Americas. To a degree, they have molded or adapted English—and other colonial languages, like Spanish, French, and Portuguese—to their own use in order to maintain the significance and strength of their Indigenous culture and identity. The ability (perhaps another word for this is facility) to do this is dictated by necessity. Since Indigenous languages are generally ostracized, ignored, and even forbidden and outlawed by non-Indigenous governments and the schools they operate, there has to be some way to continue and sustain the core of Indigenous values and lifeways. The insistence—let's call it resistance against disappearance—on Indigenous language use as a means of expression is necessary; it is the only way Indigenous people can truly have Existence. Without Indigenous power of expression, Indigenous people like my son and me and my eight grandchildren will not have a being and place they know to be their own. In fact, without the Indigenous sovereignty held and contained in the core values and lifeways expressed by Indigenous language, they (we) will not have Existence.

MARROW MEMORY
Clifford E. Trafzer

Since the time of creation, American Indian people have known that memory is stored in the blood and bones of the people. For thousands of years before the arrival of non-Natives, elders passed on traditions in the language of the people, recording bone memories through oral traditions and on material objects made of wood, skins, rocks, textiles, basketry, and ivory. These items reminded the people of their memories, brought them to light again. The source of this knowledge is found in the bones of the people, living remains that speak in many ways to inform and continue the circle, tying the past to the present. Native story-tellers, singers, artists, writers, musicians, and others draw on their bone memory to keep traditions alive and make them live within their relatives. And like a great whirlwind, contemporary people add to tribal memories that will be preserved and treasured for generations to come. The body stores tradition in its bones, where genetic information lives beyond the life of the person and is transferred into the structural material of his or her children, grandchildren, and great-grandchildren. Deposits of knowledge, understanding, and being live in the bones of Indian people, and they share these with those who listen and learn.

At an early age, my mother instilled in her four children the fact that all of the Americas was our place because our people had lived here long before European settlers. She would say, "This was our land first and then they came." My mother's knowledge was innate, born of something deep within her, and I was impressed by her continually calm, deliberate way. She had a deep understanding of our place on earth, and she shared her convictions with her children so we could understand them and pass them on to our children. I have no doubt she also learned these things from her father and grandfather, but she also carried knowledge in the frame of her body, where you could see it in her bearing. She used this knowledge to teach us about numerous life lessons. One night, my mother asked me to run across the street to get a cup of sugar from our neighbors. I refused to go because I was afraid of the dark. My mother stopped her baking, held my hand, and led me outside. Standing behind me, she turned me east toward our neighbor's home and asked me what I saw. I told her I saw our neighbor's home and the tall trees behind the house. Then she turned me to the south and asked me what I saw. I told her I saw my Aunt Jessie's house and the woods behind the house. She turned me to the west and asked me what I saw. I told her I saw our house and garden. She then turned me to the north and asked me what I saw. I told her I saw Big Hill and the road running off to the highway. "Did you see anything out there that could hurt you?" she asked. I admitted that I had not. She then told me that nothing in the dark would hurt me and added that a host of spirits surrounded and protected me. I had heard this from her before. This time I believed her.

Mothers and grandmothers, fathers and grandfathers, aunts, uncles, and an assortment of other relatives shared their wisdom with Native children for generations, and American Indians have said as much many times in many ways. Through her own writings, Okanagan storyteller Humishuma (Mourning Dove) once wrote that she "dreamed of a home of my own where I could have all the grandmothers I wanted to tell me stories." Humishuma grew up in mat lodges and tepees where her elders told stories, but she never enjoyed a home where numerous grandmothers shared their stories and where listeners could learn. Her mother told stories and so did her surrogate grandmother, Tequalt or Long Woman, who lived with the family and served as a "teacher . . . a great storyteller." For Mourning Dove, Tequalt was a regular "Walking Indian Encyclopedia," and she told stories about the time when "animals ruled the world" before the "creation of man." Her stories introduced Mourning Dove to many animal people who prepared the world for the coming of human beings. The stories taught people "moral endings to give us the idea of doing right and honesty paid in real life." Whenever the elders spoke, Mourning Dove's mother asked her daughter, "Have you no ears?" She told Mourning Dove that "ears are made to listen through. You must listen to your elders." Mourning Dove's parents taught her ancient "truths" of the people. "This story I am telling you is true," Mourning Dove explained. "It was given me by my father," and for her, "the tales . . . were sacred." Her father had taught her many tribal stories, "honored me with them, trusted me." In return, Mourning Dove shared them orally and in writing, so that others might know of the two creations and keep the stories alive.

This is the way my Choctaw friend and fellow historian, Donna Akers, learned as a child. Each summer during the hot, humid days in Oklahoma, Donna visited the home of her maternal grandmother. She was a storyteller and tribal historian. She knew her way around words and stories, trusting in the value of the spoken word. Akers remembered that when she was a small girl, her grandmother invited all the children visiting her home to join her in the backyard where the children sat in the grass, in the shade of tall green trees. Once they were seated on the earth, her grandmother asked the children to be silent and serious. She had them close their eyes and then she would say, "Now come with me to the Old Choctaw Nation." And Grandmother took them there through her words and something more, something residing deep inside the Choctaw elder. Donna's grandmother took the children through time and space using her presence and power. The children traveled to Mississippi, where they stood beside the sacred mound Nani Wayah. The Mother Mound lived in the old woman, and through her words, she brought it alive in the minds and bodies of Donna and the other children. It lives there still within my friend and all the Choctaw people who know the story. They have a consummate and intimate memory of their origin place, the site that holds the bones of their kin.

Through the oral tradition, my mother taught me about the great epidemics that killed so many Indian people. She told me about the smallpox, measles, influenza, and other plagues Europeans brought to Native America. She also knew something of the medicine that had always lived among Indian people brought on by disobedience of tribal laws, infractions against sacred objects and places, and the purposeful actions of evil people to do harm to others. Serrano elder Pauline Ormego Murillo taught me more about this "staying" medicine by telling me a story about her mother, Martha Manuel. In the early twentieth century, a Cahuilla medicine man named Ignacio Ormego visited the San Manuel Indian Reservation located near San Bernardino, California. He left some of his "medicine" that was "something powerful" in an arroyo. The *pul*, or Indian doctor, intended this medicine for another adult who would pick it up a bit later. As Chappo, as Ignacio was known, came out of the wash, he saw two children playing close by. He warned them not to go near the wash, and then he went on to the village of Santos Manuel. When the *pul* left, the children investigated the arroyo. Martha Manuel and her cousin, Vincent Morongo, went into the wash to play. Soon Martha became ill, and by the time the children returned home, Martha had a high fever and great pain in her leg.

Martha's parents called Doctor John Evans, who visited Martha on the reservation and took her to the San Bernardino Hospital for three days. After four days, Martha got no better, and Dr. Evans told the family he was baffled by the illness. The family conferred only a short time before taking her home from the hospital, saying "this was their medicine." They placed Martha in a horse-drawn wagon and took the trail east to Palm Springs to see Pedro Chino, a high-ranking medicine man or *pul ahmnawet*. Chino was a powerful healer among the Cahuilla Indians who lived near Agua Caliente, a powerful medicine hot springs. Chino doctored Martha using the sun, waters from the hot spring, and his own special powers. Chino was a breath doctor, traveling over Martha's leg with a hah, hah, hah, hah, hah sound. Once he located the problem in Martha's little leg, he used his power as a sucking doctor, pulling an object from deep within her leg. When Martha recovered, she told her family she had seen multiples of a little man running around her leg, helping the affected area. According to Martha, the little men were all the same, tiny animated figures of her grandfather.

Santos Manuel, her paternal great-grandfather, had come to help his kin, wearing his black suit, black vest, and black top hat. He was alive and spoke to her, calling her Cath'ee and saying, "You are very sick but you will get well." Martha's story is part of her family's and tribe's history, a story still told to children on the San Manuel Reservation. This is a story that lives deep within Pauline Murillo. She tells the story so that others may know the truth, the real story of her people, not the stories concocted by non-Indians who tell Native stories without listening and learning firsthand. Martha Manuel Chacon once attended a Catholic boarding school called the Saint Boniface Indian School in Banning, California. She hated the experience, particularly being forced to work in the laundry washing blue jeans. When she protested too vehemently, a nun smacked young Martha on the face. Martha responded by slapping the nun on the face. When the nun retorted, saying that Martha was going to hell for her actions, Martha shot back that if *she* was going to hell, so was the nun for hitting Martha in the first place. A priest whipped Martha as punishment. When Martha returned home after the incident, she refused to go back to the boarding school and never did. But other Indian children were not so fortunate. After 1879, many American Indians attended off-reservation boarding schools, often far from their families and tribes. Lakota Luther Standing Bear was one of the first Indians to attend Carlisle Industrial School in Pennsylvania, far from the plains and mountains of the Dakotas. Life had changed rapidly for the Plains Indians as the United States Army and greedy capitalists set out to kill all the buffalo for their hides. The buffalo was the foundation of life for the Plains people.

Like Martha Chacon and many other Indians, Standing Bear used his education to "turn the power" and make the rapidly changing world right for Indian people. When they finished their educations, they both used it to bring balance back to their people by telling the truth about Indians through the spoken and written word. Luther Standing Bear used his ability to write English to compose books about traditional Indian life. In his writings, he reported hearing from hunters "that the Plains were covered with dead bison," and when he went to investigate, he saw "the bodies of hundreds of dead buffalo lying about, just wasting, and the odor was terrible." White people, he reported, were the "wasteful, wanton killers of this noble game animal," and he found the white hunters to be "repulsive." Arapaho artist Carl Sweezy remembered hating "the white men who slaughtered bulls and cows and calves alike and left them to rot on the prairies." As a result, "the herds grew fewer and smaller, and our scouts went farther in search of them." He lamented that "we wanted to believe what we had always believed, that the buffalo came up out of a hole in the ground somewhere out on the western Plains and that if we held our dances and used the buffalo as we had been taught to do, there would always be more. But our medicine was gradually losing its power."

Crow chronicler Pretty Shield said that after the white people killed the buffalo, "Sickness came, strange sickness that nobody knew about." She linked the destruction of the buffalo to disease and death among the people, including her own daughters. One got the coughing sickness, or tuberculosis, and died. "I did not believe it," but then "my other daughter died." Pretty Shield was convinced that this "would not have happened if we Crows had been living as we were intended to live." She lamented the loss of her daughters and the buffalo. "Ahh, my heart fell down when I began to see dead buffalo scattered all over our beautiful country, killed and skinned, and left to rot by white men." The entire land "smelled of rotting meat" and the hearts of the people "were like stones." She remarked that not even the Lakota, Cheyenne, Arapaho, or Pecunni "would . . . do such a thing as this." All of the tribes of Plains remember the time of Plenty Buffalo, storing up the stories in the marrow of their bones.

In order to deal with the tragedy, one Kiowa woman had a vision that in the "dawn mist . . . rising from Medicine Creeks" she saw Mount Scott open and a buffalo bull lead "the cows and their calves" into the mountain, where "the world was green and fresh, as it had been when she was a small girl." The buffalo disappeared inside the mountain "never to be seen again." In the years to come, the buffalo returned—not in the numbers the people had once known, but they did not die. They had lived inside the mountain until the appropriate time when they returned to the people, a symbol of life and sovereignty. Kiowas, Cheyenne, Arapaho, Lakota, Blackfeet, Pawnee, and other Plains Indians remember the time of the buffalo, when the people lived free upon the Plains. They also remember the Plains littered with buffalo bones left lying in the sun to bleach and disintegrate slowly.

In centuries past, many Indian people cared for the bones of their loved ones in special ways. Among some tribes, family members or professional bone pickers scraped the flesh from the bones of the dead before wrapping and reburying them in a sacred way. Among Wyandot people, villagers once exhumed the dead and carefully cared for the bones before moving their village to another site. They dug large grave areas near the villages and lined them with beaver pelts. Then, in a ceremonial fashion, Wyandots placed the bones of their relatives into a common grave, stirring in the remains of the dead. In this way, the dead lived again together in community in the other world. The stories, traditions, and truths of the people remained in the bones of these people and the bones of their living relatives. Their genetic material contained more than DNA and genetic markers, they contained tribal memories that live still in the bones of their descendants. In this way, the vitality of the people still lives, connecting contemporary people with distant relatives, so that we may know.

THE MEANING OF THE MUSIC I SING

Michele "Midge" Dean Stock

I grew up on what I like to call the "old" Allegany Reservation in southwestern New York State, and I had the great privilege of participating in activities in the Longhouse and the community at a time when many of our respected traditional elders were still alive. When I say the "old" reservation, I of course refer to the reservation on which we lived prior to the devastation brought about by the building of Kinzua Dam, which caused an extremely traumatic relocation of our people in the mid-1960s. Although some of the old reservation remains, the places that gave us much of our life's energy and comfort are no longer inhabitable, and have been ravaged by time, the elements, or human waste.

The days preceding the relocation and the Dam seemed simpler and more beautiful, with yearly rituals of herb and medicine gathering, weekly socials at the Longhouse, and a stronger sense of community and communal living. Though I was just a child, I was not oblivious to what was going on around me, and we were taught to learn our traditions and pay close attention to the world around us. We also had a small "Indian Village" in Cold Spring, open in the summers, at which we would dance; sell beadwork baskets and traditional foods; and share our culture with non-Indian travelers on what was then the main Route 17 between Jamestown and Salamanca, New York.

The weekly socials at the Cold Spring Longhouse were open to the community, and even to non-Indian visitors, as they were a time for community sharing, socialization, and raising funds for the foods served at traditional ceremonies. These socials often included spirited games outside, before the social, and always included food and laughter. Sometimes, legends or stories would be told there as well, with some being decidedly frightening, as I recall, prompting me to avoid going to the outhouse in the dark until urgency forced me out! I remember trying always to get several people to accompany me out of fear that I might encounter something from the stories along the way were I alone.

Mostly, however, I remember joy and happiness and the sometimes wicked laughter of the old ladies after a few off-color jokes in Seneca were told. How often I recall them noting that such a joke would lose its humor entirely if translated into the inadequacies of the English language. Their laughter and joy made the socials all the more fun, and, as a child, I sometimes felt as though I was being "let in" on the adult humor just by being close by.

Looking back, I feel so blessed to have been a part of those times. My relatives, extended and close, as well as elders of great stature—about whom much is still spoken in great respect and admiration—were around me there, and at many other events which I attended at that time in my life. Unknowingly, I was learning things from a precious resource, the likes of which I would not see again in years to come. I was also surrounded by people whose first language was Seneca, and lived in the carefree mind-set that there would always be people like that around me. The ravages of the Dam and relocation, and the natural progression of time and life, have since shown me that this was not to be the case.

As tradition has long dictated, socials were the events at which we learned the songs and dances. As children, no one ever sat us down and "taught" a song or dance steps. It was necessary and required that we get up and learn it by watching and doing. This could be accompanied by ridicule or embarrassment, but that was part of the process. The fact that there were always other children learning certainly helped, and some of the laughter was not ridicule, but pure joy that tiny tots were still learning and carrying on the tradition, and laughter was uncontrollable as the inevitable unsteadiness and teetering of children learning were observed. The socials spawned Singing Societies and impromptu gatherings at people's houses, which turned into song and dancefests in the garage, living room, or backyard. These and the summers at the "Indian Village" reinforced my and others' knowledge of the music and the dances and traditions indigenous to our Allegany community. I say it in this way because each Seneca and Iroquois community has a different, colloquial style of both song and language, and it wasn't until I was much older that I really realized how diverse these are. As an adult, I also learned how much we had "borrowed" from other nations and adapted to be our own. Though the dance might be the same, or similar, the song was somewhat adjusted to be more Iroquoian. I also learned that, with the exception of the Women's or Ladies' Dance, nearly all the traditional Iroquois social and ceremonial music remained unchanged for centuries, virtually since its original inception. The songs, therefore, become a meaningful and profound connection with our ancestors, and also thereby perpetuate an ancient and valued tradition.

Seneca/Iroquois music is also integral to the overall culture, and a means of celebration and renewal. Participating in the dances and singing the music have always given me a sense of pride, exuberance, and an indescribable connection with my heritage. With each song I sing, a memory emerges that connects me to the individuals who have gone on before me and to a history not always within my living memory. It also ignites me with a passion to dispel the stereotype that all of our music is similar to the "powwow" types of songs, as our music is much more melodious and diverse. Though "powwow" is a term commonly associated with native gatherings, it is a foreign term to us, but really symbolizes the centuries of socials we have hosted and participated in with other nations. I believe it is part of what has helped us survive and cope with the many changes that have taken place in our lives, and the hardships and threats we have had to endure.

As an adult working in education and toward a preservation of our heritage, I worked with a number of elders who helped to translate everyday songs and hymns into the Seneca language, using this as a means of learning or reinforcing language acquisition. Using music to learn language is a powerful and effective method, and seems to come easier to people than rote learning or repetition. One particular elder, Alberta Austin, enlisted me to sing songs she had translated for children in order to help teach preschoolers and small children in the Seneca Nation's day care and Head Start programs. This recording proved effective for all ages, as the familiar nursery songs and the themes therein taught full sentences and could be easily remembered in the context of familiar songs. She then took hymns translated originally in the mid-1800s by missionary Asher Wright and put them in contemporary Seneca. As a project of the 4 Corners Church in Irving, on the Cattaraugus Reservation, she translated many hymns sung in church and made them available to the communities of Allegany and Tonawanda as well. She did this until her death, leaving a legacy of beautiful hymns available to sing in the Seneca language. I have found that singing these songs in our own language is as enriching an experience to me as is singing traditional music. The bonus, also, is the fact that this contemporary music helps to retain the language, whereas the traditional songs, though untranslatable, preserve tradition.

three

SNAGGING THE EYE FROM CURTIS

The first time I saw you,
I noticed immediately
that your tones were brown
but not sepia
that there were no herds
of headless buffalo
dotting the landscape
behind you
no questionable blanket
mantled across your shoulders
no sun perpetually setting
on the mesas and plateaus
heaving themselves around you
in authenticity—
that you were not

> *a daguerreotype*
> *a tintype*
> *a stereotype*
> *a bloodtype "I +"*

percentages marked
by the yardstick
of a photographer
nearly convincing us
a century ago
we were ghosts trapped within
his snapping shutter

who was unaware
we could learn
where the F stopped
and how the light
metered out the ways
we knew ourselves
to be and not to be,
no question.

Pena Bonita: *Mo Betta Indian*

SAMO = MORE THE SAME OLE SAMO

Pena Bonita

U nable to sleep, and it's already 5 A.M. Thoughts rule, and
sleep doesn't seem possible. I worry about a granddaughter
who wants to be an artist and has few other skills. I can
think of three women artists here in the city who are homeless.
They are excellent at their craft, have degrees, and are smart
cookies. One has traveled to other countries to present her work
and has been well received, yet she currently sleeps on the sofa of
a friend, eats at a community kitchen, and uses the computers at
the library. One whose work has been displayed in numerous exhibitions within the Native community has become a resident in a
shelter for the homeless, and the other has a new temporary situation every time I see her.

These Native women are bound up in the search for acceptance.
They all have had portfolios of work that has been written about
in reviews praising them. But I have never seen any of their work
in the established galleries in New York City. As young artists we
come to New York expecting to have our work responded to in the
same arena as other graduates of the art schools. But the social
force of gallery acceptance is full of unstated issues. One. It's just
flat-out harder for a woman to find the support of a gallery. Two.
Being a Native is good for a gallery invitation to their opening, but

getting into the gallery stable is a different matter. Three. Most gallery owners aren't changing the order of how they see sales happening, and they want young white guys, as that's the place they see the future investments happening (with their support).

While some gallery owners may see a need for change in the showing of work that includes ethnic art, they wind up advising the artist to seek the special selection of segregated exhibitions— only they don't put it quite so honestly. They will regale anyone listening with how they are in the process of changing and how change has accelerated and how it is such a struggle to show art. Then they wind up the conversation with how they appreciate the wonderful art and the superb crafts of the American Indians. After that they wind up with grandiose stories about their trips to Santa Fe.

For the Indian woman artists in New York, the record of racial and sexual oppression is a bitter one. This is not a country with minority women artists hanging in its grandest museums. America doesn't want American Indian artists to be part of its mainstream art. Often we are insulted by professors paid to teach us when we struggle for integrity. They want to keep us distinctive and crafting beadwork and tourist bargains. But of such good quality as to be of enough value to bring good prices in the auction house.

For the older generation, the Indian art scene was invisible, except for pottery, baskets, and the stereotype craft work good for putting on a shelf. Today Natives are creating work that is no longer silent and submissive. Our work is unique, valid, carrying significant messages, and often shows the bitterness that the journey has involved. Picasso is lauded for his ugly paintings, but let an Indian paint something shocking, and someone is sure to say, "That's not Indian art!"

Our work is exiled to casino art galleries, unreviewed in critical theories written by people who know nothing of tradition and elegance in Native life. God knows Native artists are not into competing with the established art of our oppressors by imitating their art. But it seems being an Indian artist means having a lot of art on hand and no real marketplaces in which to sell it.

THE UNAUTHORIZED AUTOBIOGRAPHY OF ME

Sherman Alexie

L ate summer night on the Spokane Indian Reservation. Ten Indians are playing basketball on a court barely illuminated by the streetlight above them. They will play until the brown, leather ball is invisible in the dark. They will play until an errant pass jams a finger, knocks a pair of glasses off the face, smashes a nose and draws blood. They will play until the ball bounces off the court and disappears into the shadows.

This may be all you need to know about Native American literature.

Thesis: I have never met a Native American. Thesis repeated: I have met thousands of Indians.

November 1994, Manhattan: PEN American panel on Indian Literature. N. Scott Momaday, James Welch, Gloria Miguel, Joy Harjo, me. Two or three hundred people in the audience. Mostly non-Indians, an Indian or three. Questions and answers.

"Why do you insist on calling yourselves Indian?" asks a white woman in a nice hat. "It's so demeaning."

"Listen," I say. "The word belongs to us now. We are Indians. That has nothing to do with Indians from India. We are not American Indians. We are Indians, pronounced In-din. It belongs to us. We own it and we're not going to give it back."

So much has been taken from us that we hold onto the smallest things left with all the strength we have.

———————

1976: Winter on the Spokane Indian Reservation. My two cousins, S and G, have enough money for gloves. They buy them at Irene's Grocery Store. Irene is a white woman who has lived on our reservation since the beginning of time. I have no money for gloves. My hands are bare.

We build snow fortresses on the football field. Since we are Indian boys playing, there must be a war. We stockpile snowballs. S and G build their fortress on the fifty-yard line. I build mine on the thirty-yard line. We begin our little war.

My cousins are good warriors. They throw snowballs with precision. I am bombarded, under siege, defeated quickly. My cousins bury me in the snow. My grave is shallow. If my cousins knew how to dance, they might have danced on my grave. But they know how to laugh, so they laugh. They are my cousins, meaning we are related in the Indian way. My father drank beers with their father for most of two decades, and that is enough to make us relatives. Indians gather relatives like firewood, protection against the cold. I am buried in the snow, cold, without protection. My hands are bare.

After a short celebration, my cousins exhume me. I am too cold to fight. Shivering, I walk home, anxious for warmth. I know my mother is home. She is probably sewing a quilt. She is always sewing quilts. If she sells a quilt, we have dinner. If she fails to sell a quilt, we go hungry. My mother has never failed to sell a quilt. But the threat of hunger is always there.

When I step into the house, my mother is sewing yet another quilt. She is singing a song under her breath. You might assume she is singing a highly traditional Spokane Indian song. In fact, she is singing Donna Fargo's "The Happiest Girl in the Whole U.S.A." Improbably, this is a highly traditional Spokane Indian song. The living room is dark in the late afternoon. The house is cold. My mother is wearing her coat and shoes.

"Why don't you turn up the heat?" I ask my mother.

"No electricity," she says.

"Power went out?" I ask.

"Didn't pay the bill," she says.

I am colder. I inhale, exhale, my breath visible inside the house. I can hear a car sliding on the icy road outside. My mother is making a quilt. This quilt will pay for the electricity. Her fingers are stiff and painful from the cold. She is sewing as fast as she can.

———

On the jukebox in the bar: Hank Williams, Patsy Cline, Johnny Cash, Charlie Rich, Freddy Fender, Donna Fargo.

On the radio in the car: Creedence Clearwater Revival, Three Dog Night, Blood, Sweat & Tears, Janis Joplin, early Stones, earlier Beatles.

On the stereo in the house: Glen Campbell, Roy Orbison, Johnny Horton, Loretta Lynn, "The Ballad of the Green Beret."

———

1975: Mr. Manley, the fourth-grade music teacher, sets a row of musical instruments in front of us. From left to right, a flute, clarinet, French horn, trombone, trumpet, tuba, drum. We're getting our first chance to play this kind of music.

"Now," he explains, "I want all of you to line up behind the instrument you'd like to learn how to play."

Dawn, Loretta, and Karen line up behind the flute. Melissa and Michelle behind the clarinet. Lori and Willette, the French horn. All ten Indian boys line up behind the drum.

———

1970: My sister Mary is beautiful. She is fourteen years older than me. She wears short skirts and nylons because she is supposed to wear short skirts and nylons. It is expected. Her black hair is combed long, straight. Often, she sits in her favorite chair, the fake leather lounger we rescued from the dump. Holding a hand mirror, she combs her hair, applies her make-up. Much lipstick and eye shadow, no foundation. She is always leaving the house. I do not know where she goes.

I do remember sitting at her feet, rubbing my cheek against her nyloned calf, while she waited for her ride. In Montana in 1981, she died in an early-morning fire. At the time, I was sleeping at a friend's house in Washington state. I was not dreaming of my sister.

———

"Sherman," says the critic, "How does the oral tradition apply to your work?"

"Well," I say, as I hold my latest book close to me, "It doesn't apply at all because I typed this. And when I'm typing, I'm really, really quiet."

1977: Summer. Steve and I want to attend the KISS concert in Spokane. KISS is very popular on my reservation. Gene Simmons, the bass player. Paul Stanley, lead singer and rhythm guitarist. Ace Frehley, lead guitar. Peter Criss, drums. All four hide their faces behind elaborate make-up. Simmons the devil, Stanley the lover, Frehley the space man, Criss the cat.

The songs: "Do You Love Me," "Calling Dr. Love," "Love Gun," "Makin' Love," "C'mon and Love Me."

Steve and I are too young to go on our own. His uncle and aunt, born-again Christians, decide to chaperon us. Inside the Spokane Coliseum, the four of us find seats far from the stage and the enormous speakers. Uncle and Aunt wanted to avoid the bulk of the crowd, but have landed us in the unofficial pot-smoking section. We are overwhelmed by the sweet smoke. Steve and I cover our mouths and noses with Styrofoam cups and try to breathe normally.

KISS opens their show with staged explosions, flashing red lights, a prolonged guitar solo by Frehley. Simmons spits fire. The crowd rushes the stage. All the pot smokers in our section hold lighters, tiny flames flickering, high above their heads. The songs are so familiar we know all the words. The audience sings along.

The songs: "Let Me Go, Rock 'n' Roll," "Detroit Rock City," "Rock and Roll All Nite."

The decibel level is tremendous. Steve and I can feel the sound waves crashing against the Styrofoam cups we hold over our faces. Aunt and Uncle are panicked, finally convinced that the devil plays a mean guitar. This is too much for them. It is also too much for Steve and me, but we pretend to be disappointed when Aunt and Uncle drag us out of the Coliseum.

During the drive home, Aunt and Uncle play Christian music on the radio. Loudly and badly, they sing along. Steve and I are in the back of the Pacer, looking up through the strangely curved rear window. There is a meteor shower, the largest in a decade. Steve and I smell like pot smoke. We smile at this. Our ears ring. We make wishes on the shooting stars, though both of us know that a shooting star is not a star. It's just a sliver of stone.

———

I made a very conscious decision to marry an Indian woman, who made a very conscious decision to marry me.

Our hope: to give birth to and raise Indian children who love themselves. That is the most revolutionary act.

———

1982: I am the only Indian student at Reardon High, an all-white school in a small farm town just outside my reservation. I am in the pizza parlor, sharing a deluxe with my white friends. We are talking and laughing. A drunk Indian walks in. He staggers to the counter and orders a beer. The waiter ignores him. We are all silent.

At our table, S is shaking her head. She leans toward us as if to share a secret.

"Man," she says, "I hate Indians."

———

I am curious about the writers who identify themselves as mixed-blood Indians. Is it difficult for them to decide which container they should put their nouns and verbs into? Invisibility, after all, can be useful, as a blonde, Aryan-featured Jew in Germany might have found during World War II. Then again, I think of the horror stories that such a pale undetected Jew could tell about life during the Holocaust.

———

An Incomplete List of People I Wish Were Indian

Kareem Abdul-Jabbar
Adam
Muhammad Ali
Susan B. Anthony
Jimmy Carter
Patsy Cline
D. B. Cooper
Robert De Niro
Emily Dickinson
Isadora Duncan
Amelia Earhart
Eve
Dian Fossey
Jesus Christ
Robert Johnson
Helen Keller
Billie Jean King
Martin Luther King, Jr.
John Lennon

Mary Magdalene

Pablo Neruda

Flannery O'Connor

Rosa Parks

Wilma Rudolph

Sappho

William Shakespeare

Bruce Springsteen

Meryl Streep

John Steinbeck

Superman

Harriet Tubman

Voltaire

Walt Whitman

1995: Summer. Seattle, Washington. I am idling at a red light when a car filled with white boys pulls up beside me. The white boy in the front passenger seat leans out his window.

"I hate you Indian motherfuckers," he screams.

I quietly wait for the green light.

1978: David, Randy, Steve, and I decide to form a reservation doo-wop group, like the Platters. During recess, we practice behind the old tribal school. Steve, a falsetto, is the best singer. I am the worst singer, but have the deepest voice, and am therefore an asset.

"What songs do you want to sing?" asks David.

"Tracks of My Tears," says Steve, who always decides these kinds of things.

We sing, desperately trying to remember the lyrics to that song. We try to remember other songs. We remember the chorus to most, the first verse to a few, and only one in its entirety. For some reason, we all know the lyrics of "Monster Mash." However, I'm the only one who can manage to sing with the pseudo-Transylvanian accent that the song requires. This dubious skill makes me the lead singer, despite Steve's protests.

"We need a name for our group," says Randy.

"How about The Warriors?" I ask.

Everybody agrees. We've watched a lot of Westerns.

We sing "Monster Mash" over and over. We want to be famous. We want all the little Indian girls to shout our names. Finally, after days of practice, we are ready for our debut. Walking in line like soldiers, the four of us parade around the playground. We sing "Monster Mash." I am in front, followed by Steve, David, then Randy, who is the shortest, but the toughest fighter our reservation has ever known. We sing. We are The Warriors. All the other Indian boys and girls line up behind us as we march. We are heroes. We are loved. I sing with everything I have inside of me: pain, happiness, anger, depression, heart, soul, small intestine. I sing and am rewarded with people who listen.

That is why I am a poet.

———

I remember watching Richard Nixon, during the Watergate affair, as he held a press conference and told the entire world that he was not a crook.

For the first time, I understood that storytellers could be bad people.

———

Poetry = Anger x Imagination

————

Every time I venture into a bookstore, I find another book about Indians. There are hundreds of books about Indians published every year, yet so few are written by Indians. I gather all the books written about Indians. I discover:

A book written by a person who identifies as mixed-blood will sell more copies than a book written by a person who identifies as strictly Indian.

A book written by a non-Indian will sell more copies than a book written by either a mixed-blood or an Indian writer.

Reservation Indian writers are rarely published in any form.

A book about Indian life in the past, whether written by a non-Indian, mixed-blood, or Indian, will sell more copies than a book about Indian life in the twentieth century.

If you are a non-Indian writing about Indians, it is almost guaranteed that something positive will be written about you by Tony Hillerman.

Indian writers who are women will be compared with Louise Erdrich. Indian writers who are men will be compared with Michael Dorris.

A very small percentage of the readers of Indian literature have heard of Simon J. Ortiz. This is a crime.

Books about the Sioux sell more copies than all of the books written about other tribes combined.

Mixed-blood writers often write about any tribe which interests them, whether or not they are related to that tribe.

Writers who use obvious Indian names, such as Eagle Woman and Pretty Shield, are usually non-Indian.

Non-Indian writers usually say "Great Spirit," "Mother Earth," "Two-Legged, Four-Legged, and Winged." Mixed-blood writers usually say "Creator," "Mother Earth," "Two-Legged, Four-Legged, and Winged." Indian writers usually say "God," "Mother Earth," "Human Being, Dog, and Bird."

If a book about Indians contains no dogs, then it was written by a non-Indian or mixed-blood writer.

If on the cover of a book there are winged animals who aren't supposed to have wings, then it was written by a non-Indian.

Successful non-Indian writers are viewed as well-informed about Indian life. Successful mixed-blood writers are viewed as wonderful translators of Indian life. Successful Indian writers are viewed as traditional storytellers of Indian life.

Very few Indian and mixed-blood writers speak their tribal languages. Even fewer non-Indian writers speak their tribal languages.

Indians often write exclusively about reservation life, even if they never lived on a reservation.

Mixed-bloods often write exclusively about Indians, even if they grew up in non-Indian communities.

Non-Indian writers always write about reservation life.

Nobody has written the great urban Indian novel yet.

Most non-Indians who write about Indians are fiction writers. Fiction about Indians sells.

———————

Have you stood in a crowded room where nobody looks like you? If you are white, have you stood in a room full of black people? Are you an Irish man who has strolled through the streets of Compton? If you are black, have you stood in a room full of white people? Are you an African-American man who has played the back nine at the local country club? If you are a woman, have you stood in a room full of men? Are you Sandra Day O'Connor or Ruth Ginsburg?

Since I left the reservation, almost every room I enter is filled with people who do not look like me. There are only two million Indians in this country. We could all fit into one medium-sized city. Someone should look into it.

Often, I am most alone in bookstores where I am reading from my work. I look up from the page at white faces. This is frightening.

———

There is an apple tree outside my grandmother's house on the reservation. The apples are green; my grandmother's house is green. This is the game: My siblings and I try to sneak apples from the tree. Sometimes, our friends will join our raiding expeditions. My grandmother believes green apples are poison and is simply trying to protect us from sickness. There is nothing biblical about this story.

The game has rules. We always have to raid the tree during daylight. My grandmother has bad eyes, and it would be unfair to challenge her in the dark. We all have to approach the tree at the same time. Arnold, my older brother. Kim and Arlene, my younger twin sisters. We have to climb the tree to steal apples, ignoring the fruit which hangs low to the ground.

Arnold is the best apple thief on the reservation. He is chubby, but quick. He is fearless in the tree, climbing to the top for the plumpest apples. He hangs from a branch with one arm, reaches for apples with the other, and fills his pockets with his booty. I love him like crazy. My sisters are more conservative. Often they grab one apple and eat it quickly, sitting on a sturdy branch. I always like the green apples with a hint of red. While we are busy raiding the tree, we also keep an eye on our grandmother's house. She is a big woman, nearly six feet tall. At the age of seventy, she can still outrun any ten-year-old.

Arnold, of course, is always the first kid out of the tree. He hangs from a branch, drops to the ground, and screams loudly, announcing our presence to our grandmother. He runs away, leaving my sisters and me stuck in the tree. We scramble to the ground and try to escape.

"Junior," she shouts, and I freeze. That's the rule. Sometimes a dozen Indian kids have been in that tree, scattering in random directions when our grandmother bursts out of the house. If she remembers your name, you are a prisoner of war. And, believe me, no matter how many kids are running away, my grandmother always remembers my name.

My grandmother died when I was fourteen years old. I miss her. I miss everybody.

"Junior," she shouts, and I close my eyes in disgust. Captured again! I wait as she walks up to me. She holds out her hand and I give her the stolen apples. Then she smacks me gently on the top of my head. I am free to run then, pretending she never caught me in the first place. I try to catch up with the others. Running through the trees surrounding my grandmother's house, I shout out their names.

––––––––––

So many people claim to be Indian, speaking of an Indian grandmother, a warrior grandfather. Suppose the United States government announced that all Indians had to return to their reservation. How many of these people would not shove that Indian ancestor back into the closet?

———————

My mother still makes quilts. My wife and I sleep beneath one. My brother works for our tribal casino. One sister works for our bingo hall, while the other works in the tribal finance department. Our adopted little brother, James, who is actually our second cousin, is a freshman at Reardan High School. He can run the mile in five minutes.

My father is an alcoholic. He used to leave us for weeks at a time to drink with his friends and cousins. I missed him so much I'd cry myself sick.

I could always tell when he was going to leave. He would be tense, quiet, unable to concentrate. He'd flip through magazines and television channels. He'd open the refrigerator door, study its contents, shut the door, and walk away. Five minutes later, he'd be back at the fridge, rearranging items on the shelves. I would follow him from place to place, trying to prevent his escape.

Once, he went into the bathroom, which had no windows, while I sat outside the only door and waited for him. I could not hear him inside. I knocked on the thin wood. I was five years old.

"Are you there?" I asked. "Are you still there?"

Every time he left, I ended up in the emergency room. But I always got well and he always came back. He'd walk in the door without warning. We'd forgive him.

Years later, I am giving a reading at a bookstore in Spokane, Washington. There is a large crowd. I read a story about an Indian father who leaves his family for good. He moves to a city a thousand miles away. Then he dies. It is a sad story. When I finish, a woman in the front row breaks into tears.

"What's wrong?" I ask her.

"I'm so sorry about your father," she says.

"Thank you," I say, "But that's my father sitting right next to you."

Head Shots

Steve Elm

I arrived in New York City in the autumn of 1991, a hopeful ingenue, if one can be an ingenue at the age of thirty-one. There was no doubt in my mind that the previous years spent training and working as an actor in London would provide a leg up on the competition here. Not that I had worked all that much in London. A voice-over here and there, small parts in a few films (Google me), some industrials, some scenes in a few plays; I was always hired as an "American." This proved to be quite touchy for me. I was Native American, and it was all I could do to impress upon polite and not-so-polite English society that there was a keen difference twixt the two. I insisted my agent put **Native American** under my name on my head shot. With raised eyebrows he acquiesced, and with that, all of the business would know I was **Native American.** This bright idea gradually resulted in two interesting developments: one, if they were looking for an injun, they called me; two, if they were looking for an American, they didn't call me.

Of course the injun parts called for me to affix synthetic braids to my head and remove my shirt prior to entering the casting office. I did it once and once only. At an audition on Carnaby Street for some bran flakes commercial, I spied a man outside the office dressed in full Lakota regalia. Sensing subterfuge, I boldly challenged him to reveal his place of origin, only to have him brazenly reply, "Barcelona." A few months later he was lustily eating cereal whilst riding a horse across my telly, in the same getup, four to five times a day.

I spent hours whiting out the **Native** part on my remaining head-shots, leaving only **American.** Within a few weeks I was dressed as an American fighter pilot on a film set, wearing the jacket De Niro wore in *The Deer Hunter* and paying my rent, to boot.

And with this, I arrived in New York City, and shortly thereafter, I got my first job. The play, in a major off-Broadway house. My part: "the Indian."

Six nights a week and twice more on the weekends I swung a real tomahawk onstage. And six nights a week and twice more on the weekends a metaphorical tomahawk swung at me. It did not miss. Who, you ask, swung that metaphorical weapon? "The Indian"— me, I swung it. I knocked myself so hard and it hurt so much and worse, it made me hate going on the stage. By the end of the run, the stage had become a professionally lit reservation where paying customers critically viewed how good an Indian I was.

Understand, this wasn't an acting job per se. The conceit of the play lay in its middle portion, where I, "the Indian," engaged in an unscripted debate with a Christopher Columbus acolyte. As for this debate, it was basically the acolyte insisting I, "the Indian," accept and embrace the superiority of Western civilization. In turn, I insisted that the acolyte, or more transparently, "the White Man," accept the West's role in not only decimating our cultures physically, but in savagely imposing the dysfunctional Western world-view on us. This went on and on, night after bloody night, with the audience either hooting and heckling or snoring loudly. None of us emerged victorious—the performers or the audiences.

Yet, I did not lose. In the months and years that followed the show's closing, I began to fully comprehend the implications of the experience. There I was, a Native man defending my right to exist as I see fit and on my own terms, as we have been doing for the past five hundred years. Only in this instance, I was being paid for it, I was on a stage, a Western medium; and more poignantly, the audience was mainly white. With this in mind, I began to analyze and in some way understand the limitations placed upon Natives in theater (and perhaps most contemporary art forms), and the role we sometimes unwittingly, and wittingly, play in them.

I was drawn to theater because I wanted to tell stories. At the time, and sadly, even today, there were very few stories about us being told on stages. What was in film was from a pained white man's point of view, usually a thinly veiled metaphor for American guilt in Vietnam (*Soldier Blue*), or epic tales of our victimization (*Little Big Man*). In the late seventies, early eighties, I knew of no plays of Native themes (I have since discovered several, produced in New York and Canada—*The Ecstasy of Rita Jo* and *49*, to name two, both by Native writers). I did not go to acting school to learn to be an "Indian actor." I trained to become an actor who would someday be known as an actor who happened to be Indian. I wanted to play all kinds of roles. And, I wanted the power that position would provide so that I might one day tell Indian stories on the stage, as either an actor or a writer, or even better, both. In London, I would receive a classical training.

On my first day of acting school I was given a piece of text to read in my speech class. The other students got Shakespeare, Chekhov, Arthur Miller. I got Chief Joseph. I instinctively put on my best stoic, sad voice, the one I learned from television and film, with *d*'s instead of *th*'s. Feeling myself blush as I tried to force a subtle tear to gently spill from my right eye, I realized I was in trouble. First of all, I was not subtle; nor was I stoic. In fact, I was rather hysterical at that age. Secondly, I realized that if I were to continue this falseness I would never become an actor. I asked my instructor why she had given me this particular piece, and she answered that she thought it would make me comfortable. Instead, it made me embarrassed. I felt like a phony. What to do? After all, I was Native American.

Now, I wasn't raised on the rez. The rez was a place to hear stories about and a place to visit relatives. I was raised suburban. Explaining this inconsistency to the image my fellow students and teachers had of Indians was not joyous. Their collective disappointment swelled, then settled sadly, like the heart of a rejected lover. I had betrayed them. I was not Native American. To them, I was American. OK, then.

It was touch-and-go the first couple of years. I understood Brecht and was pretty good with the whole epic storytelling thing. As for naturalism, trying to use an English accent in a Russian play from 1890 was a concept I did not, and this I understate, quite master. Still, I soldiered on, taking aim, sometimes hitting, sometimes missing. It was after one particularly wide miss that I received an illuminating piece of advice from a faculty member. I had failed miserably in a play in which my role was that of an insane Industrial Revolution–era capitalist with a Yorkshire accent who commits gruesome suicide. My performance was not subtle. Asked for feedback, the faculty member, with all good intentions, told me this: "You are not like most Indians I have met. Most that I have met have a strength and a silence that is missing from your work. You need to look to the Indian inside you, and use him in your acting."

The Indian inside me said *fuck you all*, and in my final year I concentrated on telling the truth with my own voice, one that was developed and nurtured mainly by the speech teacher who once gave me Chief Joseph. I graduated with a fine training, despite the identity-induced psychosis I battled throughout. Now I was an actor in London, England, and now I was ready to look for work. What I found were roles that required an unmistakably, overtly, over-the-top American-ness, both in looks and voice. Sometimes I wasn't American enough. My agent said I needed to refine my identity for casting purposes. I should carry myself as if I were that good-looking, rugged Jewish guy in *Thirtysomething*. Thus began another bout of identity-induced psychosis. Yes, I knew it was a business, but I was young, I had something to say, I had more to offer than stereotype. I had . . . the Indian inside me. Hence the head shots episode. Hence the journey to New York City, where I could be just an actor, albeit with a classical English training, yet!

Wouldn't you know that my first stop in New York City was the American Indian Community House, where I found a whole community of Indian actors, almost all with stories similar to mine? It was nearly 1992, the quincentennial, Indians were hot, and *Dances with Wolves* was coming out. How could I not? At castings I was told to grow my hair long. I was asked to speak slower, more Indian sounding. At one audition I wasn't asked to read; instead I was questioned about my horse-riding abilities. I witnessed actors out-Indianing one another, "I prayed for you in Boston last night." "I smudged and thought of you this morning." Once, after a late night where I had one too many, I showed up hungover to meet with a possible agent. She took one look at me, so sick I could barely mumble, and said, "Ah, I can feel the aura of an Indian man." Then, I got the play. How could I not?

After the play, I took myself out. If this is what they were hiring for, then I was the wrong Indian in too many ways. I got together with a group of like-minded young Indian actors with the aim of making plays about Indians. We did one play, written by a white man. Yes, it's ironic, but still, it was about us. A well-known play-wright, after seeing us in a workshop of the piece, stated that we had to decide if we were political or not. I vehemently disagreed, stating that we were simply actors who were Indians who wanted to explore Indian themes. I still remember her kind smile, and I thank her for not slapping my arrogant face. Of course, we had to decide. We ended up falling apart, some of us off to L.A. for the movies, others on to other, less demanding things. And of course, had we decided, we would have been political.

Merely acting in a play, being in a film, singing a song, making a piece of art, writing a text, is a political act if you are an Indian. Like it or not, a statement is being made. The statement either con-forms to what the general public thinks of Indians or it challenges their perceptions. It either comforts them or it unnerves them. It either makes them think or it don't. By "the general public," I include us as well. We are more affected, and effected, than anyone else when it comes to our images seen as art. Do we have a respon-sibility in this visibility? If so, what is it?

Spiderwoman Theater has for decades taken on the responsi-bility of exploring the lives of Native women. Coatlicue Theatre gives voice to the Native experience south of the border (sic). There are Native playwrights, writers, filmmakers telling Indian stories, and though many are not overtly political, all have themes that are shaped by the role policy and politics have played in our histories. We have more Native actors than ever playing Indian roles, a testa-ment to the talent and insistence of these people. Soon, I hope, these players will be given opportunities to be cast in roles other than those that demand Indian features.

As for me, my features get more Indian as the Indian inside me gets older. As editor of *Talking Stick Native Arts Quarterly,* published by Amerinda, out of New York City, I have the responsibility of raising the kinds of questions I raise in this piece, along with giving voice to the Native diaspora of artists that come to this city. It is a hard job, a job that seeks to take the quotation marks and italics away from our statements and, thus, our existence. As an actor, I am a teaching artist with City University of New York's Creative Arts Team, the New York City Wolf Trap Early Learning through the Arts program. I act with Only Make Believe theater company. I do voice-overs, I give lectures, I educate, I tell stories.

I was recently in Greece, with CAT/Wolf Trap, where I told stories in the ruins of a Roman amphitheater in Sparta. I told the Oneida creation story. As I was storytelling, I was also sharing one ancient culture with another. The Greeks listened to the story, the children acting parts of it out, all of them with the understanding that my story was not in quotation marks, was not in italics, was not merely of history. They heard it as they hear their own stories. Afterward, a girl of about eight approached me with her English-speaking mother. She wanted to know if Sky Man and Sky Woman were like Zeus. Both of our stories had helped us in becoming who we are. And we *are*.

Thinking I may take this storytelling thing on the road, I recently sat for some new head shots. How could I not?

IT WON'T PLAY—THERE'S NOT ENOUGH INDIANS

Diane Fraher

can't remember exactly when I first started working on my film, *The Reawakening*. It was sometime in 1990. I had just completed a successful public service announcement campaign, for print and broadcast, revealing the Iroquois Confederacy's influence on the formation of the United States Constitution. The project was the only officially recognized Native American project of the Bicentennial Celebration. American Indian Artists Inc. had worked closely with the traditional leadership on Onondaga Nation and the Ta-do-da-ho, the official head of the Confederacy, to develop and produce the idea. To our pleasant surprise, the mainstream media had finally embraced our idea and run a half-page ad in *People* magazine, and the major networks were cycling it in for broadcast. It was also being cablecast on two networks. MTV had even decided to run it.

The project had been my first foray into the mainstream commercial media world. The place where the Golden Rule—"Them that gots the gold makes the rules"—is the law. Heretofore I had worked in the New York City nonprofit arts world. The concept that there were perspectives other than European American was still relatively new at that time, and people in nonprofit arts organizations and institutions were at least open to the idea. Naively, I assumed that the mainstream media would be interested in hearing our perspective as well. I soon learned my expectations were indeed just that, only an assumption. The reality was much more brutal and unwelcoming.

When we approached with the idea of Native people's ideas influencing something as sacred as the United States Constitution, we were immediately categorized as suspect; the fact that it was a documented idea only increased our problems. A non-Native scholar wrote us blistering letters asking us who we thought we were, daring to share this information with the public. After all, he was the authority on the subject, who incidentally earned a lot of money publishing books and giving lectures about the subject, so we had better stop what we were doing. Wait a minute, was I missing something? We were a community-based Native arts organization, working with the Native Nations whose history and original construct had played this role in our collective history, and we were being told to cease and desist. The Great Law of peace and justice was meeting the Golden Rule.

Some publishers weren't much more enlightened. At one point we received a call from an editor at a major publisher with whom we'd had no previous contact, literally screaming at us to drop our silly project and find something better to do than dream up stupid ideas. It turned out he was the editor of a very silly series of books on the United States Constitution, who had stupidly not included any mention of the Iroquois Confederacy's influence on the forma-tion of the Constitution, even though it had been researched and documented by non-Native scholars who were the self-appointed guardians of these facts. The networks, when approached directly, weren't as angry at us. They just thought we were hallucinating and came up with a list of reasons why we couldn't place an ad on donated airtime. The first one being that we didn't have an annual budget over $100,000. The Golden Rule was being enforced again. We told them not to worry, we could go under the umbrella of the American Indian Institute, which had a large enough budget. When they saw we knew how to think, they went into high gear and sent us to a vice president for public relations whose job it was to humor folks like us until we saw the folly of our actions and repented by giving up.

Somehow, the way it always is with our work, we finally met some people at an ad agency who said they believed in the project and wanted to work with us. This relationship proved to be very productive, and things started moving. We produced the project, and a media buyer got the announcements placed. We later found out that the primary motivation of the agency owners had been to attract more business, and they were disappointed that our project had not produced enough of that for them. Fair enough, people go into business to make money, but since public service announcements don't generate direct income, the only possible gain is through industry-recognized awards, which they got. We never figured out how they thought the poorest folks in town were going to bring them in huge amounts of money. It must have been that "spiritual" power to make people rich that we were holding out on them with.

It seems to be human nature for the pain and struggle of something to fade in order to let the joy of long-held achievement into one's awareness. Whatever was driving my emotions, I was feeling really happy that it was finished, for one, and that we had succeeded against all the odds, for another. The joy that filled my heart gave me the courage to finally do what I had always wanted to do—make Indian feature films—genuine Native American cinema instead of genuine non–Native American cinema about Native Americans.

I had learned enough about how things work by now to know that a screenplay written by a Native American with a Native American storyline would never be taken seriously by the non-Native filmmaking industry. I got to work writing the script, and I wrote and I wrote and I wrote some more.

I was educated and had humbly accepted that I was blessed with a modest bit of talent that I was willing to work very hard on to keep improving, so on the journey of crafting the script I worked with more than one consultant. With one notable exception at the end, something kept happening over and over almost like clockwork during the consultative process. I wasn't getting hard-boiled critiques of what the script really needed. Instead, people kept wanting to rewrite the story into something that fit their preconceived image of what we ought to be: with characters that were children in search of a parent, a great white father perhaps, and a story that was more apologetic, where we needed non-Native approval for everything. The illusionary image of Native American people has been so firmly embedded in people's consciousness that the truth provoked a compulsive desire on the part of even well-meaning non-Native professionals to rewrite us into a cartoon in order to be validated.

During the entire process, I fell back on a more traditional Indian way of doing things and kept my elders close for advice and support. They must have thought I was a real daredevil trying to make a film. Hadn't I gotten enough abuse when we'd made the public service announcement? People gently prodded me to consider that if folks wouldn't give up their crazy ideas about us, getting them up off their money would be next to impossible. Remember, the Golden Rule is still operable here. What the elders were doing was helping me realize that if Indian people were going to make a film about ourselves, we were going to have to raise money in an unconventional way or else it wasn't going to happen. Our unconventional way was through philanthropic giving.

I applied for grant awards to individual artists and slowly began to receive them. How slowly? It took fifteen years to raise enough money to produce a film under a Screen Actors Guild "experimental letter of agreement," which has a maximum $75,000 production budget and which includes reapplying to some of the funders more than once to get support. The process was so long that I remember receiving a letter from a foundation and putting it in the drawer without opening it for four days because I just assumed that it was another rejection letter so there was no need to rush. I realized cynicism was creeping in when I finally opened the letter and found I had received an award. Elders did tell me to remember that if it was an Indian project it would be modestly funded because we are always last on the totem pole. I thought totem poles were an "ndn thang."

When I knew we had exhausted all the cash funding sources, I started reaching out to people for in-kind support so we could finally go into production. Eventually, events took their usual turn, but this time it was different: there were no hidden agendas. People read the script and they got it! They genuinely wanted us to make the film as much as we did. Kodak donated all the film stock, Le Moyne College agreed to house the cast and crew in the dormitory as guests, and the Onondaga County Sheriff's Department really stepped up with location, wardrobe, and prop support. There were many other individuals, businesses, and organizations, such as Syracuse Stage Company, who made in-kind donations as well.

The Council and the people of the Onondaga Nation were our partners in every way. We met with the leadership of the Nation and then left the script in the Longhouse for the people to look over. After reading the script and meeting with us, they opened their hearts and their homes to us and completely embraced the film. All of this felt wonderful and very scary at the same time. I had lived with rejection and alienation for so long that I had become comfortable with it. People's generosity challenged me to accept that I was on the threshold of a truly rare and extraordinary experience, an opportunity for Native people to produce a feature film about themselves.

When it was time to hire the cast and crew, it was like we had put up a sign saying we were giving away free drinks or, better yet, easy money. There were, of course, active alcoholics, hard-nosed bargain hunters, people catching a ride on their way to glory, born-again Indians who were professional actors, self-professed chiefs without a tribe, producers who were missing in action more than the alcoholics were, closet misogynists of the female director species, and de rigueur wannabes and people who were nuts beyond redemption that are part and parcel of every American Indian event or production. For some reason people who can't handle reality really feel at home with Indians. Maybe it's because Indian people take people as they are, and maybe it's because Native people have been politically exiled in America so the social outcasts feel they belong with us. Whatever it is, they always show up and they always make problems.

If all the others weren't enough to contend with, there were also plenty of people who knew what was best simply because I was a first-time director, a a title they used more than my given name during the shoot. I was used to non-Natives being nervous about Indians' competence, but these folks were worse than the ones we had encountered in the ad campaign. A very prominent Hollywood casting director offered me a few suggestions on a pro bono basis. It was very revealing to hear her suggestions. They were the polar opposite of what I knew the characters needed. The illusion of how non-Natives saw us was intruding once again. The expert syndrome was trying to creep in as well. It was obvious to me that she had become an expert on casting Natives by watching so many phony Indians in Hollywood films. I thanked her and reached out on the moccasin telegraph to Native actors and discussed the project with them directly. I also listened to elder Native actors who had read the script and knew who would be right to cast for the story. The result was an ensemble cast of actors who could work together without any time for rehearsal and precious little time for multiple takes on set to deliver performances that were always professional and at times individually wonderful and compelling.

Whatever the obstacles, whether real or manufactured, I had the unswerving support of my elders, the people of the Onondaga Nation, a fantastic cast, and a core group of Native and non-Native professionals on set. Together we prevailed, and the film was shot in only twenty-one days. The following year we completed post-production. My long-held dream had come true. Once again the joy of finally finishing and the hope of finding an audience over-came any bitterness and residual bad feelings.

For a film to be complete, it must be seen by an audience. So we set out to get our film seen by an audience. What we were told by theater owners—besides lies about the box office receipts and bills for nonexistent ads, was: "It won't play—there's not enough Indians." By that logic, non-Natives go to see films about Indians that are dead (historical period dramas), and since the Indians in this film were alive, well, they wouldn't go to see the film. Only Indians would go to see a film about Indians who are alive and, since there's not enough of us, it won't play. I had accepted that Native feature films, made by Natives, are by themselves edgy and confrontational to non-Natives, but I never expected to scare them all out of the theater. We protested that they were perpetuating a very insidious form of racism, that is, after we finally got their attention while they were continually congratulating themselves on being lifelong liberals. Some of them just came right out with statements like: "Oh no! A film about American Indians, not in my theater." Overseas distributors liked us even less. They assured our booking agent that "no one cares about those people." And all of these folks made these decisions without ever seeing the film. Europeans are reputed to deeply admire Native American culture, too. How come people only like Indians when they are dead or nowhere around?

Instead of an audience, we found an entrenched hegemony that dismissed anything that wasn't their idea. Hollywood had already made us into who they wanted us to be and it made them plenty of money and made us lots of heartache. Since an audience delivers box office receipts, the Golden Rule must be enforced when you try to distribute a film.

In spite of everything, I would do it all over again, not because I am stubborn, which I am. Because I'm an artist, and because the overwhelming resistance has shown me how important it is to tell stories that are about who we really are. I am rich beyond measure for having known and worked with many wonderful Native and non-Native people on the film, and I'm going to spend that capital by getting to work on another film. Someday there will be lots of people going to see films by Native filmmakers, and maybe some of the filmmakers will look back on *The Reawakening* as one of the independent films that helped start it all. The booking agent called today to say there are three theaters that have agreed to run the film.

Transitions in Haudenosaunee Realities: The Changing World of the Haudenosaunee as Seen in Historic Photographs

Richard W. Hill Sr.

My Own Family Album

My father is from a family of farmers on the Six Nations Reserve in Ontario. We can trace our paternal family ancestors back to the original tribal enrollment that was made in 1784 when those Haudenosaunee relocated to Ontario after siding with England during the Revolutionary War. It was then that most of our people received their English surnames—Smith, Johnson, Williams, and Hill, which speaks more of the old alliance with the English than it does with the imposition of a foreign culture. After nearly two hundred years of contact, my ancestors were hardly strangers to the Europeans. I am enrolled in that community as a Tuscarora, because in Canada, the government enrolls you under your father. My father is culturally a Mohawk, but is enrolled under his father, who was a Tuscarora. However, the Haudenosaunee trace their ancestry through the female bloodlines, so I am a Tuscarora because my mother is a Tuscarora. It is confusing at times, and it is these kinds of things that point out the mixed cultural identity that we are raised within.

After some of the Haudenosaunee who remained loyal to their English allies were relocated to Canada, each nation reestablished its own settlements. Each had its own Longhouse and community on that reserve. Until 1924, the reserve was governed by traditional Chiefs and Clan Mothers. My great-grandfather, Josiah Hill, and his brother, Richard Hill (the one that I am named after) were traditional Chiefs in that council. I came across a 1910 photograph of them sitting in a little council house. I had never been in that council house so I was amazed to realize that my relatives were there all of the time, working at maintaining the integrity of the nation. The photograph shows that the council house looks more like a courthouse, in the parliamentary style of the English. In the center is an Onondaga seated on a platform, holding the long strings of white wampum that represent the authority of the council. The other Chiefs are seated, wearing suit coats, looking directly into the camera. They appear to have wanted the photograph to be taken, as if it would legitimize their position. Across the back wall a huge Union Jack is hung, showing the ongoing loyalty to England shared by my father's relatives.

Lining the wall over the heads of the Chiefs are painted portraits of the two "royal" families. One was the queen of England and her relatives. The other was Joseph Brant, the notorious Mohawk warrior who had sided with the English during the Revolutionary War and led his followers across the Niagara River to settle in Canada. Like the treaty agreements of the past, two nations merged in that small council house. Josiah Hill sits with his hand on his notebook, for he was the secretary of that council and recorded the minutes of the council meetings for many years.

The photo connected me to my own legacy. Since then I have seen about a dozen photos of Josiah, but that first one sticks in my mind. It was an emotional moment to see that my father's male relatives were chiefs, active in maintaining the traditions of our people. It created a real connection to the past, to the Longhouse and the Haudenosaunee Confederacy. It also created a sense of loyalty within me to those very same things. As I looked at that old photo, another circle seemed to be completed. I was given a job to pick up where they left off. Whenever I come across a document Josiah recorded, I cannot help but think about his work and my own museum work, and how we both have worked for our own people in our own ways, but how we are also reacting to the work of the outside world to dismantle what we have as the Haudenosaunee.

Last year, to my surprise, as I surveyed the list of sacred wampum that the Haudenosaunee had requested be returned from the National Museum of the American Indian, one entry jumped out at me. One of the wampum strings was used to commemorate the death of Josiah Hill. Rarely was any one wampum string identified with one particular person. I couldn't help but wish I could obtain that wampum, as it is my real connection to the past. This wampum was not included in the first group to be returned, but it was eventually repatriated to the Haudenosaunee, and when I finally saw that wampum for the first time, it seemed ever so precious to me, thinking that it was used to condole the community at the loss of my relative. It seemed to make another circle complete in my own life, as it made those men in the old photos very real to me, even though I never met them.

One day, I was digging into a pile of photos that my mother had. She is from a family of farmers at the Tuscarora Reservation near Niagara Falls, New York. This is where I live today, on my mother's old family homestead. She had an old photo of her grandfather, Silas Hewitt, and great-grandfather, a Civil War veteran named Alvis Hewitt. They were photographed at the annual Border Crossing Celebration to honor the unique status of the Haudenosaunee in living on both sides of the border, but with special rights to cross that white man's border unmolested. They wore their Native

American clothes from that era, which included the unusual upright feathered headdresses. At first I thought they had adopted the Plains Native American war bonnet. It was not until I found more and more photos of the old-time Haudenosaunee that I realized that the headdress with the stand-up feathers was a Haudenosaunee tradition as well. The 1888 photo of the Onondaga man and two girls (NMAI #22318) shows a headdress that was the forerunner for what my mother's relatives wore. A beaded brow band with feathers attached to stand straight up is an old headdress of the Haudenosaunee. NMAI has a very old Great Lakes headdress of this type that is on view at the Customs House in New York. Considering the old paintings of the Haudenosaunee, that style has been in use since the eighteenth century.

There is an 1890 photo of a Mohawk dance troupe from Kahnawake, Quebec, that shows the clothing style of the times. These dancers are dressed in their fanciest clothes with elaborately beaded dresses and sashes, and beaded headbands with huge peacock feathers like that of Joseph Brant 150 years earlier. Another photo of a Mohawk man (NAA: 57245) shows the same kind of headdress. I am sure that this style was influenced by the headgear seen in the paintings of Joseph Brant, who was given peacock feathers while visiting King George. Brant wore those feathers with great pride, as did his descendants. We might laugh if we saw someone wearing such feathers today, thinking that it is not "traditional," but the photos show us that our ancestors were more liberal in how they interpreted tradition. If the feather fit, they wore it, anthropological authenticity be damned!

A Mohawk Chief Loft was photographed in the 1930s holding a copy of the treaty that gave my father's ancestors their reserve lands in Canada in 1784. His headdress shows a further modification of that style of headpiece. This all helps to explain the photograph of the leaders of the Indian Defense League (IDL) in a NMAI photo. Here we see all styles of headdresses in use. By this time, however, the Plains Native American headdress was chosen on purpose. Clinton Rickard, a Tuscarora principal in the IDL, chose to wear the war bonnet because it attracted attention. People assumed he was a chief, and he capitalized on that image. By wearing that kind of headdress, people knew that he was unmistakably a Native American. It also made a good image in the press, and more Haudenosaunee men began to wear such headgear in the 1940s.

The Iroquois Beverage Corporation of Buffalo, New York, founded in 1842, had adopted a logo for their beer that was a pro- file of a Native American in the western headdress. Their trademark became widely known across the territory of the Haudenosaunee. In the 1950s they used a painted portrait of a Native American wrapped in a colorful blanket, crested with a full war bonnet. Aloof and proud, this stoic image was seen in bars, magazines, and bill- boards for an entire generation. Hollywood kept that image alive, so that it is natural that Native Americans adopted that same image for themselves, at least in the political arena. It was effective for selling both beer and Native American rights.

Also in my mother's box of photos, I came across one of her mother in her Native American dress. She wears a headband with an eagle feather standing upright in the back. In one sense it also represents the stereotype reborn, as this was the image projected by Hollywood. Native American women were always seen as having headbands such as this. The story goes that headbands became predominant in Hollywood because the actors had to have some way to hold their long-haired wigs in place. For nearly a century, Haudenosaunee women wore feathers, recalling the Hollywood image, but usually the older style was a decorated headband with small feathers standing upright, similar to the male headdress. I found an old photo in the Canadian Archives (NAC #22168) of two little girls wearing the stand-up feather headdress. Are they wearing their own headpieces, or did the photographer ask them to put them on for the sake of the photo? You can find photos of different people wearing the same pieces. On some occasions the commercial photographers would have such cultural "props."

I found another photo of the Cayuga Chief Red Cloud, most likely from the 1901 Pan-American Exposition in Buffalo. Here, he sits tall and proud in front of a painted background of a Victorian parlor. This is the strangest mixture of images. He appears somewhat dignified, yet he has a ring in his nose. I had seen an earlier photo of a Seneca man wearing a silver pendant from his nose, but this ring was added for savage effect. But by whom? The photographer or the Native American? Red Cloud also has one hand on his tomahawk, recalling the older images we have already seen. I have seen other photos of Red Cloud that suggest that he traveled with a dance troupe. His outfit was assembled to cater to these public performances. In one photo, Red Cloud is seen swinging a tomahawk upon a white man, who in turn points a pistol at Red Cloud's head. It was captioned "A disposition to hark back," as if this was the relationship that would exist forever.

He wears beaded cuffs that reappear on a photo of a Haudenosaunee woman who was most likely photographed in the same studio, if not on the same occasion. Such beaded cuffs were popular on Haudenosaunee men's clothing starting from the 1840s. The beadwork does not match that on this woman's dress, suggesting that they were added to enhance the photograph. She also wears a man's beaded sash, draped around her shoulders for the same reasons. Imagine what cultural havoc would be wreaked if contemporary beadworkers used this photo for inspiration in making a "traditional" outfit, where men's and women's accessories are mixed. At the same time, her beaded dress is truly beautiful, and such elegance is seldom seen in today's clothing. Her dress was already influenced by the Victorian styles of a previous generation, so we have to be careful what we read into these photos. It can be extremely difficult to separate the Iroquoian reality from the photographic reality. More than likely, however, these old-time Native Americans would overdress for the photo, and might borrow other items that they would not regularly wear. They knew the difference. We might not.

My mother was quite a busy photographer herself, and her photo box had tons of little photos of her, my aunts and uncles, cousins, and, of course, her own very beautiful children. Every now and then we would pull out this box of memories and my mother would tell us stories about life at Tuscarora when she was our age. Some of the old houses were still there then. The old cars were gone. The farms were not as predominant. The boys had slicked-back hair. The girls had short, curled hairdos. Kids played with broken toys, worked the fields, dressed to go to town, puffed on cigarettes, joked it up, and appeared to be always having fun.

By my mother's time, the camera had become socialized among the Native Americans. The Brownie camera allowed Native Americans to photograph themselves. Among my favorites were the photos taken during the Second World War. My father had been drafted into the American Navy, and my mother, as a new mother, moved back to the reservation. There is one of my mother in her wedding dress that I couldn't help but compare to that of my grandmother in her Native American dress. Different tastes for each generation produce changes. When I got married in the Longhouse, my wife and I would be the first in our generation to have a traditional marriage, with my wife in her Native American dress, me in my Native American clothes. Yet, our Tuscarora clothing was very different from that of my grandparents. Not better, not worse, just different versions of the same idea.

Then there were the pictures of life with my dad's family in Canada. There, life was more rural, more isolated, and more focused on farming, hunting, and feasting. My father had become an ironworker and would take the camera to work. He had pictures of himself at work or of the other buddies that he worked with. Even ironwork had changed from those days to when I took my camera to work as a young apprentice ironworker. Being an ironworker, my dad took special pictures of the nature of the job, the things that it took to build the bridges and skyscrapers. He offered an insider's view of life as an ironworker. He seemed to enjoy telling us boys of the dangerous times he experienced, the complicated jobs he faced, and the craziness of his fellow workers. Those little photos brought that way of life to us young boys. Those ironworkers became our Native American heroes. We felt destined to follow in our father's footsteps.

The Tuscarora Anthropologist

In my travels as a curator, I came across the work of J. N. B. Hewitt and was pleasantly surprised by what I found. He was a Tuscarora and, as it turns out, a distant relative on my mother's side. He worked for the Bureau of American Ethnology at the turn of the century, documenting Iroquoian traditions and languages. He took hundreds of photos that are now part of the National Anthropological Archives. These are valuable sources of information about the period of change that produced the kind of lifestyle that I grew up with. Recently, while doing research on another exhibition, I came across some photos taken by Hewitt that were of my father's relatives in Canada. There was a portrait of Richard Hill (NAA-II-68), and it was an image that clearly showed the resemblance of this man to my grandfather and my father. While this photo would never be used in an exhibition on the Haudenosaunee—because he is not wearing "Native American" clothes, he is not dancing, nor is he doing anything "Native American"—this simple portrait is important to me. It allows me to connect to a relative I never met. What is strange is that the Tuscarora anthropologist is my mother's relative, photographing the Tuscarora chief who is my dad's relative. I get to know a bit of each of them through the photograph.

Hewitt also photographed hundreds of Haudenosaunee farmers, chiefs, clan mothers, and craftspeople during his tenure. His camera captured a people in transition, and he deserves more recognition as a photographer. He took a series of portraits of people from Tuscarora. Especially noteworthy are his images of the Tuscarora women selling their distinctive beadwork by Niagara Falls. His portraits are more relaxed, perhaps because he was himself Tuscarora and knew most of the people he photographed. I also think that he had a cultural mission in mind. He respected his own people on many levels. He found pride in beadworkers, nobility in farmers, and strength in ritualists. His own view of the world may have been too influenced by the Victorian thinking about culture, but the value of his research, his publication, and his photographs will be increasingly important as the Haudenosaunee become more distant from the farming and trading lifestyle that Hewitt witnessed and documented.

The Reason I Photograph

It was at art school in Chicago in 1968 that I was encouraged to use my camera to tell the story of my own people. I met Robert Frank, a photographer from Germany who had produced a series called "The Americans." He was interested in me because he wanted to know why Native Americans were the most difficult people for him to photograph. The Germans have their own stereotypes about Native Americans, and he was a bit disappointed in not seeing those noble Plains Native American warriors when he traveled across the country for his photo series. He was disappointed that the Native Americans did not welcome him and show him all of the colorful ways. We discussed the ethics of documenting people from other cultures. I realized that photographing Native Americans would also be the most difficult thing that I could do, if I was to retain a sense of dignity about myself and the people I photographed. I went to my first powwow at the Chicago Native American Center and took some photos. But I was not really connected to those Native Americans. They were doing things that I was unfamiliar with. I finally realized that to make the best use of my art, I had to take my camera home.

The Ironworker as Native American

The Native Americans that I knew were not like the Native Americans I saw in Hollywood movies, nor those I studied in school. I was born into a family of ironworkers in Buffalo, New York, in 1950. Since there were no steel buildings being erected on the reservations, my father had to go where the action was. He started ironwork at sixteen years old, with his brother-in-law, and he had some tiny, yellowing photos from his early days as an ironworker. Many Haudenosaunee men became ironworkers. In Buffalo, as well as New York City, Chicago, Cleveland, Detroit, Philadelphia, and Boston, there were small enclaves of Native American ironworkers. We lived on the west side of Buffalo in an Italian neighborhood. But my father's two sisters also lived in Buffalo, married to my mother's two brothers. In fact, one family of cousins lived right across the street from us in the city. We had our own little urban Native American community.

My father worked on many building and bridges. He was my first cultural hero. Those old photos were my avenue to daydream about myself as an adventurous ironworker. I would look at the photos and imagine myself as an ironworker. To my young mind, Native American men proved themselves through ironwork. It became our rite of passage. My dad attributes the birth of the urban Native American to ironworking, as several generations of ironworkers had to relocate to the city to follow the work. We were evidence of that process. He also believes that the Second World War changed the Iroquoian lifestyle forever. The young Native American men, sent off to war, saw a whole other world and gained skills, and after the war they wanted a piece of the action. There was a big migration into the cities after the war as the economic boom led to new jobs. The reservations were ignored in the postwar expansion. Additionally, many of the Native American women had worked off the reservation during the war. My mother, along with many of the other young wives at Tuscarora, worked in a factory while the men were off to war. They also developed a taste for the urban lifestyle.

The impact of ironworking on the Haudenosaunee family cannot be underestimated. For a variety of reasons, Haudenosaunee men made good ironworkers and gained a solid reputation as good workers. This led to a certain prestige and respect that was not experienced by other Native Americans during the 1940s and 1950s. It was good for the self-image. Additionally, it was very lucrative to be an ironworker. They were the highest-paid Native Americans among our people, drove the biggest cars, had adventurous lives, and became the male role models for several generations. I, like all other Native American boys of my generation, assumed that I would one day become an ironworker. And I did, starting at the age of sixteen, along with my two brothers. By then, my father owned his own company. His philosophy about work is ingrained in my own thinking: if you don't make a living for yourself, someone else has to make it for you; if you want the respect of the white man, you have to be better at your job than he is; you either work at the whim of someone else, or they work for you. Our family work ethic comes from my grandfathers, through my father and mother, to me. That work ethic has become a Native American tradition as well.

With camera in hand, I turned to the only Native Americans I knew, the Haudenosaunee ironworkers, and photographed the men at work around Buffalo. This included my own family. This series of works seems timeless for me because it recalls the stories I heard growing up about ironworkers, the times we spent on the job as kids and apprentices, the dreams and nightmares of my father and a way of life that continues for many Haudenosaunee families to this very day. We have been ironworkers for nearly one hundred years, yet few museums have any photos of the Haudenosaunee as ironworkers, as it is not perceived as a "traditional" pursuit.

The Longhouse People

To reconcile the accidental death of my brother Jim, I sought spiritual meaning to life and found connection to my ancestors on a spiritual level. It was only there that I found a way to cope with my grief. It was in the ancient condolence ceremony, recorded by J. N. B. Hewitt, that I would find hope for the future. That ceremony is a ritualized cleansing of the spirit. I studied it. Museums had photos of the old chiefs holding wampum strings from that ceremony. I saw the actual wampum strings at the Smithsonian and photographed them myself. I finally witnessed a Condolence Ceremony at Onondaga for a deceased chief and the installation of new chiefs. The ceremony said that the people knew the kind of pain that I was going through and that they would step forward and help console me. My own circle was complete.

This led me to want to learn more of the traditional ways of my own people. I received an artist's grant to interview Longhouse people and create a series of paintings of the stories they told me. It was as if I had personal cultural tutors. I still listen to those tapes now and then. I received another grant to photograph Haudenosaunee artists and craftspeople. This allowed me to visit nearly every reservation, and I benefited from meeting about fifty artists from whom I learned a lot about the arts, the stories behind the artists, and why I should work to keep it all going. I began to work in a historical museum in 1973 in Buffalo, New York. For the first time my work as a photo artist found a direct link with museum work on traditional culture.

I then met Jake Thomas, a Cayuga subchief of the Snipe Clan, also a noted singer, dancer, and ritual leader. He was the kind of person I wanted to be. He understood the things that I needed to know. I spent several occasions photographing his carvings and getting to know him. While he has come under some heat for carving and selling medicine masks, I still feel that I owe Jake a lot of respect for all that he has taught me of the Longhouse. I don't know where I would be without his knowledge and willingness to share it with me.

However, the most important lesson he taught me was patience. I was eager to learn and had a thousand questions for him. He would hear my concerns, translate into one of the five Haudenosaunee languages he knew, come up with an answer, then translate it back into English, then offer it to me. Sometimes I would ask him something and he would not answer for about ten minutes. I thought he was trying to ignore me at first. Or he would answer very carefully, measuring the meaning of each word he spoke. Other times, he would be deep in thought, trying to come up with an answer for me, and then say, "I can't explain that to you at this time. There is much you have to learn about first. The answer will come in time." So the photos I have of him have always reminded me of the need to take the time to learn, and not rush in seeking the answers. Ironically, I found a photo in the NMAI collection of another Longhouse elder from a century earlier. That man sits in the same position that Jake was in when I photographed him. It is not pure coincidence. I realized that I had seen many men sitting like that in the Longhouse. It is the way in which the men hear the sacred words, speeches, and messages from the past, take in their meaning, and reflect on them at the same time. They enveloped themselves in deep thought. They are hearing, thinking, and feeling at the same time. It goes back to the ancient notion of using the power of reason, what the traditionalists call the "good mind," to face the issues of the day. During the recitations of the Great Law of Peace, the Code of Handsome Lake, or any council meeting, you will see men sitting deep in thought just like these men in the photos.

Photos of the Artist as Native American

I want to end by sharing thoughts on some of the photographs I have taken of my own family that extend all of these ideas to today's generation of Haudenosaunee. I have learned not to try to make art out of our people's lives, or other people's visions about us. My photographs are merely momentary pauses when my family and friends and I share a common experience. Those experiences may be the artistic process, hunting, lacrosse, racing motorcycles, vacationing, or walking in the snow. These are simple moments out of the activity of our lives. They do not represent all of the Haudenosaunee, or all ways in which we express ourselves. They are singular instances when I felt that the camera would not intrude. People accepted me as a photographer, but knew me as a relative.

I tell you all of this to give you a more realistic picture of Haudenosaunee life since 1950. Too many people that I have met hold romanticized stereotypes of reservation life or of Native American life in general. In their view, Native Americans exist in a constant state of religious harmony, communing with nature, and dancing their hearts out at the drop of a hat. Such views are so deeply held that people are actually disappointed when they visit the reservation and find that Native Americans live pretty much like everyone else, in house trailers, not longhouses. We drive cars, not horses. We wear Carhartts, not buckskins. In reality, life on the reservation is as complex as life anywhere. We are faced with political, social, educational, economic, and ethical dilemmas all the time. We are not a unified people, we do not all believe the same things. We now fight over religion. But, we are the Haudenosaunee, the Haudenosaunee—the People of the Longhouse—and that common identity is enough to keep us going.

OLD STORIES FROM THE NEW WORLD

Susan Power

1 Do you know what it's like to be a sliver of the census pie in your own land, the numbers at the bottom of every statistical list, if you're listed at all? This is what it's like to be Native when you're born in Chicago in 1961: you exist in the mirror, in your mother's face, you exist in the angry poems that drizzle from the clutch of your pen, all your words upon words upon words, your exhibit, your proof of life, shouting with ink—we are here! Rose Maney who dances with cloud feet, Lizzie Wells, half blind with poverty, Big Tom who is only pretend-fierce and loves Albert, who wears his hair in a pompadour like Elvis. You scour the *TV Guide* for *Little House on the Prairie* mention of an Indian episode. You see *Little Big Man*, *Billy Jack*, on the big screen, even cheer Anthony Quinn playing Flap in a show called *Nobody Loves a Drunken Indian* because it's slim pickins to find some small shade of who you think you are. God help you if you read books! They haven't published Vine Deloria yet, or Louise Erdrich, or Sherman Alexie, so you're stuck with Peter Pan's girlfriend, Tiger Lily, who may be courageous but can say little more than "ugh," or James Fenimore Cooper's savages, lethal Magua, if they'd been *that* vengeful we wouldn't all be sitting here now.

Teachers applaud my promise, my chick of talent, but not my subject matter: the Indian ghetto in Uptown, the Indian bars on Clark Street, how we have our own Columbus Day Parade—the roaches march amid Relocation debris, a swirl of broken promises and day labor. Why can't I write about pretty things, they ask, don't my people like the natural world? And I don't know where to begin the biology-history-theology lesson of how far apart our idea of "natural" is. So I memorize Shakespeare from old recordings I discover at the public library, this mesmerizing snake charmer so Indian in his careful turns of phrase, his golden eagle tongue of grace. I chart my own backward-forward progression of resistance, write my own little-girl syllabus of everything I think I should know. Fill notebooks I will never bring to school with a voice persistent and wild as weeds, which I think is mine and mine alone until I learn better, wear glasses, and can finally see behind my shoulder all the ancestral ghosts who keep slipping me stories, tucking them into my hands and my pockets in that humble, unobtrusive way that makes you feel you're not their charity case.

In school I am shy, bookish, polite. I sit on my hands until the Indian in me erupts from her wooden post in the back of the room. Sometimes it's just too much, and I wave my hand in the air and hear myself speak with a vigor so unexpected it turns every head. They're praising Custer again, and his Shirley Temple–like curls of gold; it's the gold we should talk about now, his metal fever. They say we crossed the Bering Strait in a chilly migration from Russian lands when all of us know we grew from this ground like corn or fell from the sky like ripe seeds in the pockets of our mothers' dresses. They tell me our women were oppressed, worked like mules by lazy men, and they don't want to hear my grandma's name, or write it down: Josephine Gates Kelly, born 1888, tribal chairperson, head of the Standing Rock Sioux in the 1950s when other American women are trapped in the kitchen baking pies, martini-perfumed, with those red red mouths and cone-sharp breasts, chewing tranquilizers like mints to keep them still, help them like Ike, they fall into the laudanum bed of their day. It's Hopi, not Hoppy, I gently say, but I do not mention that as far as I know there is no tribe of giant rabbits in this land. And every November the gobbler art, turkeys and pilgrims and pumpkins, and Indians too, naked beneath their one stiff feather, cut from construction paper, unzipping the Thanksgiving myth that we ever broke even bread. My religion teacher, Mrs. Burns, says Puritans suffered the grim voyage from England to the black scars of Plymouth Rock because of persecution. And I know the intolerable weight of condemnation, where a ruling order declares that your God is not God, and your prayers are worse than futile, they are the sweet stink of burnt flowers—a devil's foolishness. Yet she will not acknowledge my hand, Mrs. Burns, when it peeps in the air, wilting, ignored. She already knows the questions I'll raise, why the sins of the fatherland are played out in the new world by folks who should have known better.

————

Thank God for my mother's Sacagawea-like sense of direction, she points north, this Gathering-of-Stormclouds Woman, her needle forever set magnetically on activism, trouble, people rise up and chase the moneychangers from the temple, dash their scales upon the stone floors! She helps me carve a space for myself and my voice in every white world I encounter from year to year, and grade to grade. This is how my head is patted, my face held in a brief gesture of hopefulness by Martin Luther King when I am three. This is how I find myself reading my middle school poems at age eleven and twelve with a lineup of literary angels like Tumbleweed, our Black-Creek friend with her pompom braids, and Dennis Brutus, just released from prison in South Africa, bearing his colored card, his BIA-like determination of how much blood makes you more than white in Johannesburg.

2.

For the past twelve years or so I've had a recurring dream about my country. I see our great cities underwater, the Statue of Liberty tipped from her pedestal, not *Planet of the Apes*–like buried in sand, but swallowed by the great ocean that washes her face with salt. Life is spent on long boats shaped like canoes, longer even than the imagination, and Natives man the oars, not rowing slavelike to a beaten drum, but purpose-driven all the same, bent by compassion. We travel this world of water to save our drowning relatives, black, white, we pluck them from the waves and sit them in the center of our boats where they huddle, stunned and chastened, ultimately grateful. I used to think this was a fiction of the mind, allegory, metaphor, or the less elegant labors of a brain churning the day's thoughts into a dull, confusing mush. But as the glaciers melt and superstorms, monstrous as Grendel, smash our houses and our lives, I see us rushing toward the future of these boats.

Listen to what Joy Harjo said in a book of poems: "Oh sun, moon, stars, our other relatives peering at us from the inside of God's house—walk with us as we climb into the next century naked but for the stories we have of each other. Keep us from giving up in this land of nightmares which is also the land of miracles."

———————

We were saved by stories—our crop that never dies, through every drought and dust bowl, every Himmler-like policy of death, every cultural root canal suffered in a boarding school. Don't you know we are the people of tinnitus? We cannot sleep for all the ringing in our ears: the ghosts of our ancestors sing us songs to keep us awake, awake, awake. Noisier than television, sirens, their voices gather in a crescendo of wisdom that bursts through time—a sonic boom to spill you on your ass. We have no choice but to listen eventually, remember who we were before the pain and the painkiller, the firewater and the diabetes, the bingo palaces and welfare programs, the Ivy League schools and powwow circuits, the American Dream. The strongest stories are homegrown. They didn't travel from another world. They weren't filtered through a test tube, microscope, Bible injection, calculus equation symphony of black quarter notes trapped on the page. Our stories surround us, whether we're rez or urban, whether our tribe was forcibly removed or stubbornly hid in the hills, in the woods, in the swamps. They twist inside us, remarkable as DNA, insistent, generous, a lifeline thrown to each generation. What's more, they are *true*, no matter how inventive or preposterous, no matter how much so-called magic is involved. How do I know? Because they peeled me down to the core, sloughed off stories I'd learned in school, crim law with Dershowitz, con law with Larry Tribe,

Stendhal, and even Walker Percy, a kind of exfoliation of the intellect and spirit where I find myself saying what I mean and meaning
what I say. Where I forget how to double-talk, bullshit, logic my
way into a righteous corner justified by footnotes citing evidence.

————

Our sovereign stories lead us to freedom. We make it through the
looking-glass world of all the upside-down, half-assed Indian policies that trot through history like a roll call of childhood diseases:
the Allotment Act, the Indian Reorganization Act, Termination, the
Indian Wars that never really ended but just changed venue. We
emerge from madness and arrogance, prejudice and ignorance, our
stories intact, stronger for the test of fire, the forge. We share them
in cars, at kitchen tables, poetry slams, and art exhibitions, in our
novels and chapbooks, in cheap motels and classrooms, in shake
tents and medicine lodges, funeral parlors and bars. Soon you will
hear us, too, buzzing hotly like bees. We will haunt you with our
tales though we are not ghosts, we are not finished, exterminated,
we are not conquered, we are not lost, we are not at the end of the
trail or the end of our rope, we are not a problem, a fad, a guru, a
channeling queen, a pet or a mascot, a jumble of bones in a
drawer. We are old stories groping forward into every new world.
We made it here by the skin of our teeth. No one can stop us now
from telling and telling and telling. It is our turn to run the schools
and teach you the anthem, the pledge of allegiance to every other
being on the planet, pull down the pyramid with a human face on
top (no, that's already happening without our intervention). Don't
you see we are already building the longboats with these words?

MARRY A DECENT GIRL

Gary Farmer

As an Indian kid growing up in Buffalo with Irish, Italian, and Polish kids, surviving meant being swept innocently into gang life as a means of creative survival; you had to unify with the locals to defend yourself, your neighborhood, your friends and family. Perimeters defined by city blocks, adapting Greek letters as shields of glory, just to define our existence. Tradition in the streets was wearing your "Magnificent Bastards" sweatshirt proudly down Grant Street. It's like we were bred to have an enemy. Not realizing at the time, it paralleled the foreign policy of the very country we were all pledging allegiance to every morning. The USA in combat, what appeared for time immemorial always engaged in war, Japan, Korea, Vietnam, Nicaragua, El Salvador, always against any enemy of the United States. And as you grew up, you realized what you learned was false and you struck out with violence illogically. Pulling people out of cars for driving badly. Attacking innocent victims of warmongering. Being a gang member was legitimized when you finally became an official officer of the law. The Buffalo police was the ultimate gang; countless ex–gang members moved seamlessly into carrying a badge and legalized guns. O'Malley, Lorenzo, LoTempio. It seemed to escalate in the street until finally automatic weapons entered the scene and death became a deterrent. After working for a living and being smart or lazy enough to carry on with your education, later realizing the gang life led to official duty. Legitimized by the badge of false honor. Corruption breeding corruption so naturally. But people pale when asked to justify acts of violence—that's when it seemed mediocrity led the bouncing ball. Sing along, marry a decent girl, and conform to societal pressures. It is so easy to play along, it became tradition, carrying forward the sickness to the next generation so willing to follow in your footsteps, not realizing or thinking about decisions made, fearful of being different, when your distinctness becomes a burden. Always striving for normalcy. Striving for prosperity. Luckily, I had a culture to fall back on . . .

———

When you live out in Indian Country, you live on the outskirts of town. You tend not to mind being different. Those of us not able to live without what society has to offer race out to drink, smoke, get crack, gamble, shop, and indulge in all the addictions of modern life. Some of those modern conveniences are readily available right on the rez, drive-thru booze and pot shopping. It's not until your water pipes freeze in winter you feel like an Indian. Living without is a way of life. No big deal, but always time for bingo. Always time to visit, less so these days. People on-rez are definitely more independent than ever, well, most people. I s'pose the traditionals are more traditional. One can only imagine. Everybody is not always friendly. Depends if they've heard anything about you or not. Sometimes it's good. Sometimes you're in favor, could be the time of year. Could be a movie they saw you in and liked. Could be a movie they saw and did not like. Especially when it's an Indian story. They easily could have been on the other side of the fence. We have differences on the rez, sometimes for years. Even if it was just a small thing to start, we could easily turn that into a larger issue, no problem. We are expert at feeling bad. It's like we all have chips on our shoulders. Treat yourself and try 'n knock it off, big shot! One could say I have a bad attitude about things. One could say I enjoy the animosity of living on the rez from time to time. Never a dull moment or could be a lifetime of dull moments. In a critically Christian church. Like a scary Christian church. Like a cult Christian church. Could be. We have sixty churches on the rez and I am sure there is some diversity among them. But I could not tell you what. I don't get out much.

———

I wonder about Indian casinos. Must be 160 of them across the USA. Some of them give money to the people. The people, never having had much money in their lives, find the most obvious places to spend it: limos, Hummers, Escalades, Mercedes Benzes, with Rolex watches to watch time pass. Some communities give money to the tribe and do good tribal things. Like build a health center or renovate the community hall or build a new arena. But most give away the money to development and the business of making more money. None of it gets into arts. Maybe Art Montour, Art Martin, Art Smith. But not the arts. The odd powwow prize monies. Cultural monies escape from time to time. But no organized arts activities. Like furthering education. Like a National Endowment of the Arts for the Indians. That is not the norm. In the communities that get direct monies, it's apparent the children seem less motivated to prosper in the arts. Why? The arts seem like hardship to most Indians. Like what for? Suffer for what? What the arts are about. Training in acting? Directing or producing seems not to matter. No access anyway. Well, in Canada, they have every reason to get in the arts with their own TV network. But stateside, we have no reason. Well, if you paint, you can go to the IAIA in Santa Fe, New Mexico. The place all artist types seem to go. The young ones who want to make films seem to find their way to the Sundance Film Festival, a select few. Many are not encouraged to pursue an arts career. Seems ludicrous. To be an artist, not real. Fake or sold out. Gotta leave the rez and go to college or university or do things the white people want you to do. You'll lose your identity and never be able to come home. Like nobody. You'll disappear out there. Better stay home or go into the Army or something. Go fight the Indians over there. All-new Indian war, you know?

THE STORY OF A CULTURAL ARTS WORKER ARTIST

Jaune Quick-to-See Smith

From very early in my life, I have memories of making things with my hands, mainly with mud, leaves, sticks, and rocks. In the beginning, I didn't have language to describe that process, nor what the future could hold, I simply knew that I entered another world, one that took me out of the violence and fear that dominated my life.

When I entered first grade, another world opened up to me that included paper, tempera paint, crayons, and library paste. As Indian children usually do with foreign substances, I smelled everything, tasted it, and proceeded to eat what seemed edible. Let me say this: crayons smell like a cross between Kiwi boot polish and grapes; however, once chewed they disintegrate into waxy crumbles and become most unpleasant. Library paste, though it wouldn't make the *New York Times* "Dining Out" section, had not only an enticing aroma but was quite palatable.

Serendipitously, I learned about the life of an artist when I turned thirteen. The Nisei family, the Yamadas, whom I had worked for since I was eight years old, took me and some other farmworkers to town in the back of a pickup to see a Saturday matinee. The movie was about the artist Henri Toulouse-Lautrec.

Shortly after that, I took axle grease from my dad's truck, placed it on a palette-shaped piece of cardboard, and smeared a goatee on my chin, flattened a hat into a tam, and asked the retired man down the road to take my picture. At that point in time, since I had not yet had an opportunity to see a woman in this role, I had to work with what knowledge I had. This was my way of entering the skin of an artist, of transforming myself, of attaining that personhood I so desperately wanted. Toulouse was recognized as a dwarf in those days; today he would be called a little person, so I knelt on my knees for the picture, thinking that would make me an authentic artist.

Totally on my own when I turned eighteen, I was able to manage my expenses by going to a community college in Bremerton, Washington, plus working in the school library and part-time at a veterinary hospital assisting in surgery. Luckily, I also received a Native American scholarship for tuition. There were no women in my art classes, only men students who received money from the GI Bill after the Korean War. At the end of the first year, the professor called me into his office and bluntly notified me that even though I was able to draw better than the men students, a woman could not be an artist, only men were allowed to do that.

For the next twenty years, I struggled to get a degree in art education, having resigned myself to the idea that if I couldn't be an artist, I could do the next best thing and teach art. While raising my two sons on my own, I attended school part-time in Seattle, Houston, Worcester, and Framingham, Massachusetts, and finally completed a master's degree in Albuquerque, New Mexico. My sons and I lived life on the "other side of the tracks" given our tough financial constraints.

My story is not so different from those of other Indian women my age. I often wonder how we developed our stamina to continue school under these circumstances. Most of us did not have parents who supported us in any way or even offered us any encouragement.

It is quite possible that I might be the first Indian to graduate with a master's degree from the Fine Arts Department at the University of New Mexico. They kept insisting that Indians did not get a degree from the Fine Arts but only from the Art Ed Department. Even though they turned me down three times, I kept going to school and accruing the credits needed for my degree. I also steadily worked at my art and was invited to join a gallery in Santa Fe, the Clarke-Benton, that exhibited works on paper by artists such as Susan Rothenberg, Pat Steir, Joe Brainard, and Roy DeForest. Also, my painter friend Susan Crile introduced me to Jill Kornblee in New York, who scheduled an exhibit of my drawings.

After all this took place and a review of my work appeared in *Art in America*, finally the art department acquiesced and allowed me to enroll. Now, of course, there are always Indian students in the Fine Arts Department.

As a mother of three children and now a grandmother of five, I believe that my activism and organizing people around common interests is because of the training I received with this job description. I began organizing as a political venture in 1976 with the Grey Canyon (a metaphor for the city) Artists, a group of contemporary Native artists who experimented with materials with no intent to appeal to the tightly controlled Indian Market. We would simply gather at my house for a bowl of stew and an evening of discussion about our work. We were controversial and visible for a period of four or five years.

In the mid-1970s in Santa Fe, I found that men, described as warriors, were the only Indians who were allowed to show in the galleries. Indian women were showing their work in trading posts, gift shops, and at Indian Market. I also found that if a woman were allowed to exhibit with the men, she was often isolated at the opposite end of the room where no one spoke to her.

So I had multiple reasons for organizing the Grey Canyon Artists. Certainly to bring more women onto the scene, but also to support experimental work that used new media. I made sure we had both men and women exhibiting in Grey Canyon, which featured contemporary art by Larry Emerson, Felice Lucero Giaccardo, Lois Sonkist, Emmi Whitehorse, Conrad House, Paul Willeto, and me. Often, we invited other guest artists, such as Harry Fonseca, Karita Coffey, Ed Singer, Linda Lomahaftewa, George Longfish, and others to exhibit with us in venues that I located around the United States.

Many people would ask what contemporary Indian art was or how it was different from traditional art and ask how you could tell that it was made by Indians if it didn't feature an Indian warrior or show traditional design.

I would patiently explain that education has a lot to do with the differences in Native art. Traditional art is similar to folk art, that which is taught at home and within the tribe. Institutionalized Indian art was and is a stylized form taught at the boarding schools such as at the Institute of American Indian Art or Haskell or Bacone, although in recent times they are breaking away from their stylized formats. Contemporary Indian art is usually made by a college-educated Native artist who may include imagery or design elements from art anywhere in the world in any media but may also reflect their own tribal arts. The important thing is for them to be true to themselves and their life experience rather than copy or mimic art for the sake of marketing.

The Grey Canyon Artists worked as teachers or at other jobs and were not dependent on the income from our art. We were free to write poetry, make our art, travel, and meet at conferences or collective places where young Indian scholars and artists would gather. We became a support system for each other in addition to mentoring younger Indians who wanted the same freedoms from the tightly controlled grasp of the museums, galleries, and white collectors of Indian Market.

While working with Grey Canyon, I also was traveling a lot to conferences or exhibitions or to lecture, and in the mid-'70s I began to network with other Indian artists and their communities. At various times through the 1970s and into the 1980s, I began meeting with Peter Jemison and Jolene Rickard in New York at the American Indian Community House; Janeen Antoine, Ken Banks, and Mario Martinez in San Francisco at the American Indian Community House; Joe Feddersen, Jim Shoppert, Larry Beck, and Gail Tremblay in Seattle; George Longfish at the C. N. Gorman Museum at UC Davis; Alyce Sadongei and Erin Younger in Phoenix.

I founded another co-op on my reservation in order to tour work to exhibits outside Montana. This network across the United States, though informal, is still active today, and of course, younger artists have joined in as well.

Just to give an accounting of how powerful a small group can be: I was at a conference in North Dakota when a Menominee man asked me if I knew the Grey Canyon Artists. When I said yes, I founded them, he was obviously very pleased. He asked how many artists there were in this famous group, fifty, maybe more? I responded with a smile, "On good days there are ten members and on bad days there might be four."

I've served on many boards over thirty years; they include the College Art Association, Salish Kootenai College (the tribal college on my reservation), and the Institute of American Indian Arts in Santa Fe, as well as many Native arts organizations such as American

Indian Contemporary Arts in San Francisco, ATLATL in Phoenix, and MICA, Montana Indian Contemporary Arts.

Consistently, for thirty years, I have organized and curated exhibitions for Native artists or consulted on exhibitions for museums, galleries, and arts agencies. Some of the notable exhibits have been "Women of Sweetgrass, Cedar, and Sage" the first touring exhibit of Native women's art and the first touring exhibit of Native American photography, both of these in the early 1980s. The average exhibit has twenty-four to sixty artists. Most of these exhibits were and are done on a shoestring budget; all I need is an invitation from a willing director of an exhibit space, and often by cajoling them I can get the exhibit to tour to at least two other venues.

My most recent exhibit, "Offerings from the Heart," was picked up by the North Dakota Arts Council from Peg Furshong's gallery at the North Dakota State University and traveled for nearly four years through North Dakota, South Dakota, Minnesota, Iowa, and Montana. There were twenty-four younger Indian artists who live in isolated locations and who rarely have the opportunity to exhibit their work. I always hope that some work will sell or perhaps some of the artists will be invited to show again. I do know the shows are well attended, and often visitors return again to view work that is filled with soul, meaning, and personal stories.

I always request that the museums invite some local Indian artists to join our exhibit so that they have an opportunity to see their work on a museum wall, too. Often this is the only time they have had such an experience, and they attend the opening with parents, siblings, aunties, and cousins to admire their artwork.

Rarely do I have money for a catalog or even a brochure, but on rare occasions, such as the "Women of Sweetgrass" exhibit, I have. After sending the catalogs out to the women artists who lived in large urban areas and remote reservations, I received a letter from one of the artists. It was short but very touching. She said that she had not met many Native women who exhibited their work and when she received the catalog, she leafed through the pages touching the faces of the women, and finally she laid the catalog against her cheek and cried, because she had no idea there were so many Native women out there and she no longer felt so alone.

This is another reason I encouraged the Heard Museum in Phoenix to create a contemporary arts biennial. There needs to be a space in every Indian museum for the contemporary arts. With the advent of the tribal colleges, there are more young Indians who attend college now. In the early 1980s the Heard Museum curators hired me for a daylong consultation with them because they were considering a "ten best Indian painters" exhibit. My point was that they could educate their community, boards, and collectors in an ongoing process by hosting a contemporary arts biennial. I suggested the framework for jurors, a catalog, and how to locate contemporary artists across the United States. My hope was they would collect from each exhibit and thus create a collection of contemporary art over time.

In the eighties, I looked at and read about earthworks or site artworks and kept thinking that for thousands of years we Native peoples have been involved with spiritual earthworks that delineated the seasons, such as the medicine wheels, or that made a demarcation of something that Coyote did. Finally in the nineties, MICA found a coal tax grant and I suggested we use that money for food and gas money to travel to Flathead for a weekend encampment to make art. We slept on my cousin's floor, Jerry and Lois Slater's, ate our meals together at Salish Kootenai College, while Vic Charlo, our famed Flathead poet, read to us through meals.

Jaune Quick-to-See Smith: *Celebrate 40,000 Years of American Art*

There were incredible in situ pieces, such as Ernie Pepion's medicine wheel of red tempera atop blocks of ice, which melted in the sun and replicated the fragility of life. Dwight Billideaux created a large picto image of a horse on a hillside with dried knapweed and set it on fire after sunset so we could witness the slow crawling line of the fire as it drew the image for us and left us with a smoking trail. There were other meaningful pieces, too many to recount here, but perhaps over and above the art was the social aspect of the gathering. It brought contemporary artists and traditional artists together, families, relations, neighbors, and tribal people, too. Rocks, sticks, poetry, mud, food, humor, water, and emotion were all mixed together. For Indian people, in art making the process is always more important than the product.

Some of the changes in the contemporary Native art community that I've personally witnessed include seeing more Indian women involved, and young university-trained Indian artists and scholars appearing everywhere across the United States. A disappointment is the lack of major (over one hundred pieces) collections of contemporary American Indian art, either by private collectors or public and private museums. Further, there are no scholarly books on contemporary Native art; the few that mention contemporary work at all are 90 percent artifacts and traditional art from history. There has been no major touring exhibit with a significant catalog of both men and women's contemporary art like the multiple exhibits of African American or Latino art.

We live under a colonial system that is still controlled by white anthropologists who continue to use hegemonic language like "pre-history"—which means there was no history happening in the Americas for thousands of years, until whites got here. The colonial phrase that we "came across the Bering Strait" was a total fabrication made up by Samuel Haven, a lawyer in Massachusetts and a weekend pot hunter. Yet every anthro continues to tout this myth in every book they write. Under a colonial system, bad scholarship is never questioned.

Our way out of this colonial dilemma will be when we have our own Native anthropologists and art historians writing interpretations about our art, our history, and our culture. African American and Latino artists are in that place now; they have credibility with the major museums, which collect both folk art, that of the *mestizaje,* as well as the contemporary art. Their anthros and art historians have coined themselves a new title, which is cultural critic. This allows them to write about art and culture as well as politics and sociology. They have the freedom to name themselves, describe themselves, and interpret themselves. That's where we're headed, too; it's just taking us longer to shake off the doldrums of the colonial myths. We are the only original land-based people in the Americas, and thus our relationship with the U.S. government is way more complicated than that of any other immigrant group, and it is taking us longer to achieve the same acceptance.

Working as a cultural arts worker artist for nearly forty years, I can look back at how far we've traveled, and it is truly phenomenal. No matter what art styles have come and gone in New York or around the country, contemporary American Indian art still delights me, touches my heart, speaks to me, and enriches my life. I believe that it will be discovered someday soon and that museums and collectors will find a treasure trove of unexplored art that will dazzle them in the most unexpected way.

THE BONES OF THE SKY

Diane Glancy

B y reason of the multitude of oppressions,
they make the oppressed to cry;
they cry out by reason of the arm of the mighty.

—Job 35:9

What is it I do, speaking from the margins? More than anyone, I
have been influenced by Gerald Vizenor. The trapezoids of space
he builds in his words. Who pursues the invented Indian in his
writing. Who disrobes the inventions of disguise. Who uninvents
the invented. The rest of the world invented Indians. Well, in name
it's true. Also in the earlier stereotype that all Indians were Plains
Indians with buffalo, tepees, and feather bonnets. In the civilized
tribes, it was corn and robes and turbans. The Cherokee had an
early written language and an ability to assimilate. To shape language to shape.

I am an invention of my invention.

One of the early ways of making a signature in the ledger-book
drawings was a head at the bottom of the page with a bubble going
from it in which was drawn the symbol of his name. My writing is
a bubble going from my mouth.

What do I do from the outskirts?

I am no immediate presence in the tribe. I am not in immediate possession of tribal ways.

For *Pushing the Bear*, a novel of the 1838–39 Cherokee Trail of Tears, I have received commendations. I also still have people say, the removal trail wasn't that way, and to them it wasn't, but it was to me after research, after traveling the nine hundred miles of the removal trail, after hearing the voices in my imagination. There are multiple stories, as many as those who walked the trail.

I work with this inventive history.

I do nothing directly for the tribe in this new stance of tribalism in which one identifies with an individual tribe and not with the overall Indianness, which was Plains Indian, the migratory buffalo hunter, the tepee dweller, and not the corn-farming Cherokee.

I do not know the Cherokee language. I do not take part in the ceremonies of the Keetowah fire. I do not live on Cherokee land of northeastern Oklahoma.

Yet the stories of the Cherokee fill my pages.

Other tribes also infiltrate the marginality of my appropriations. I wrote about the Shoshoni in *Stone Heart*, a novel about Sacajawea, who accompanied Lewis and Clark on their 1804–06 expedition. I wrote about the late-nineteenth-century Ghost Dance in *The Dance Partner*. I wrote about Kateri Tekakwitha, a seventeenth-century Mohawk/Algonquin girl who was converted to Christianity in *The Reason for Crows*. The crows, of course, are the Jesuits who came from France. I even have a chapter on the rough crossing where one priest suffered a terrible seasickness. Is there nowhere I will not overstep?

The past is given in a knot of unknowns.

Of its own, but still—

This wagon I am hitched to—this baggage of Indian history I pull. Not directly connected with, but tongue and wheel. Giving voice to those who did not have a chance to speak their side of the story gives me a chance to speak also—to know, to restore through the art of language.

———

Woods Lewis, my full-blood Cherokee great-grandfather, was born in 1843 near Sallisaw, Oklahoma. The courthouse later burned, and records are gone. I know he was in trouble and fled Indian Territory just before the Civil War. In Tennessee, he joined the Fourth Cavalry. His Union records are in the National Archives in Washington, D.C. After the war, he tried to return to Indian Territory, but could not because of his crime. He settled in Viola, Arkansas, had nine children, and is buried in the Hand Cove Cemetery above Norfork Lake. One of his children, Orvezene Lewis, was my grandmother, who later married Dr. William Jasper Hall.

That is what I know. That is what I am. A great-granddaughter of a renegade. Still fleeing the laws of the English language.

———

What I know is_____. What I am is this airway. This air.

All my life has been an erasure of who I was—am. A part-native heritage surrounded by Europeans, and most of them European several generations back. They too were erased from what they had been. Nonetheless, they had the dominant fork. They knifed and spooned their way through family dinners and their side of history. My native heritage was amputated. Yet the ghost ache of it was there. Withering, dying on the vine. My writing would reinstate the limb—would re-grape the vine.

———

Much of my writing, up to now, has been about restoration. In a collection of my stories, *The Voice That Was in Travel*, the last story in the book is called "America's First Parade," with overtones back to the Trail of Tears. The setting of the story is Tahlequah, Oklahoma, the new Cherokee capital. I had to go back and look at the story to find the main character's name and realized that she is left unnamed. She owns Redlands Café with her former husband. Her son is getting married to Janet Gillette. The traditional Christian ceremony is shaped with Cherokee customs. "Why hadn't she seen the renewal in the Cherokee? She had that restlessness she'd seen in her father, but she couldn't blame it on him. The only thing she didn't want was to stand still. The anger at herself. The guilt. She belonged to the generations between her grandma and her children, who were finding their way back to what she and her parents had thrown away. Now it was facing her in its loveliness."

It is in their finding that I also find. The past still inhabits the land.

"Sometimes the spirits were so thick, she couldn't walk from her house of an evening."

In the story, I also include a passage in Cherokee from an early translation of the New Testament book of John. It shows the direct translation of the word order. "John first written by him that from the beginning one that lives we have heard our eyes we used what we saw and our hands what we touched word life it happened and we saw we are speaking of that which ends not . . ." I have used passages of the old Cherokee and its direct word-for-word translation in several of my books. It restores my soul.

Many of the Cherokee were converted by early Baptist and Moravian missionaries.

As Maureen Konkle asks in her book, *Writing Indian Nations*, how can an Indian who is a Christian and writes in English still be an Indian?

I hope that is one of the contributions to my tribe and the over-stepping of my tribe to other tribes—an explanation ceremony of faith. That—and an intertribal, innovative Native American writing in which oral tradition is re-created in written form—or a facsimile or something that would bring to mind what oral tradition could have been.

Next week, by the way, I return to Native Voices at the Autry in Los Angeles to continue work on a new play, *Salvage*, about a Blackfeet family in Montana. The man has an accident, and events keep happening after that to unravel their lives. It is about the sudden and irrevocable change in a way of life that encapsulates the history of native life.

I have the thought sometimes, why am I crossing these borders? But these border crossings are what my writing is about.

———

I recently opened the *Writer's Chronicle,* October/November 2006, to an article by Elizabeth Oness, "Poets as Independent Pub-lishers," where she quotes her husband, I assume, C. Mikal Oness.

"In an oral traditional setting, oral formula and type-scene trigger different resonant meanings only because there's a physical and psychological locus that contextualizes the 'text'—the verbal production requires a 'performance arena.'"

What is he talking about?—was my first question. But I kept reading.

"My aim, as a printer, is to recall that notion of performance arena by concertizing the images, binding, and verbal text to allow for a similar dynamic of meaning making as would occur in pre-literate, traditional setting."

There is something in that I like—and that I get on some level. Native oral tradition now dances also in the arena of the book, and in outward readings wherein an image or tone or sense-of-what-was lives again—or it ghosts the audience as state parks use the ghosting technique to rebuild fort sites, reestablish a sense of what was from whatever evidence is left.

I like to work in the vast space between signifier and signified. I like to work with a transposition. An illiteracy. A shifting meaning, a tilting of words, a transformage, a slippage, dippage (of one into another). A scrambled past retrieved in scrambled form.

———————

I have a novel, *Designs of the Night Sky*, which is an explanation tale for written language. The spoken word is more important, of course, but we live in a printed world.

The book is written in broken texts as if the scattered sections were stars in the night sky—or patterns of stars in the night sky. The idea for written language came from the stars—the constellations are seen as paragraphs in a story.

In the book, I combine a contemporary story of the Ronner family with old excerpts from "Emigrating to the West by Boat" (original in the National Archives, Office of Indian Affairs, Washington, D.C., "Cherokee Emigration" C-553 "Special File 249") and "Poor Sarah, or Religion Exemplified in the Life and Death of an Indian Woman," by Elias Boudinot, a Cherokee leader born in 1802.

The dialogue in the book is in the form of drama—

ROBERT (*at first, he can't speak*). She died in her sleep.

WAYNE (*he is broken up also*). Somehow she let go.

RAYMOND. She kept the peace in the family.

ADA. She came to the last page and her book closed.

The indirectness or rerouting of the novelistic expectations is a technique of poetry, the renegade genre. There is subversion of text. In the novel, all genres work together. It is a light working, but the novel echoes drama and poetry. I am interested in one form becoming another, or how in one form there are echoes of others. I like the subjectification of text. Historical writing become *hystorical.* An illogic outside logic. All the missing emotion.

Shape changing is common in native thought. *Designs of the Night Sky* is a shape-changed novel. There are exact places and exact situations in the book. The Iguana Café, the setting I walked in Tahlequah, Oklahoma taking notes, taking names. The Manuscript and Rare Book section of the Northeastern State University library where Ada Ronner works is there. The old texts are kept in a small cage in a corner of the library behind something that looks like chicken wire. Indian country also has dysfunctional families.

I also iron out a lot of wrinkles in *Primer of the Obsolete,* a poetry collection. It is a way my grandmother thought—she could not even write her name, but she was the bridge between the old Cherokee and the coming English. In the poetry book, the new world is painted over the old world, the new paint is not quite dry.

Surely native history is a book of Job.

———

In my travels, which is my main form of research, I rake over the land which is a repository of voices that lived upon it and are buried in it. It is where I find these voices—these bones of writing. It is where I transform the thought of language into bones of the sky. Story is something solid in the unsubstantiation of this airway where I find myself.

The message is there. The connection to the past. Job lost all he had, but his possessions were restored, even his eight children, though they were different children.

Acculturation is rough. The generations still cry out from the oppression of poverty, alcohol, substance abuse, neglect. The loss of what was floats through the airways into my dreams from time to time with an overwhelming sense of grief. And yet the skeleton—the furniture of restoration is present also. Through education, mainly. "Get over it" is a line used several times in *Salvage*. In the overall plan of the universe, and it seems to me there is a plan, a battle plan, maybe, I make new ledger drawings, which writing is.

I am an outsider of the outsiders, though I see Indian tribes as integral to the space of this country. Kernels of the past on the new cob of the Cherokee staple—corn. It is what is growing in the field I have planted. A field that is fragmentary. Abrupt.

four

ROLLING THOSE SOVEREIGN BONES

Zero
      to One
             White
      to Purple
Bead
      to String
             Bead
      to Pull
Breathe in
      to Out
             Beat
      (to pause)
Beat again

There are no guarantees that you
have any more than the last breath
you exhaled, the last blip
running the river of your wrist

      so roll those bones across the dirt
      take a chance on every dust particle, every
      star alignment and face of grandmother moon

you can find, put on a little English
spin them from your digits
release them out into the world

gamble on these stories of ours arranged
like vertebrae each one building
on those that have come before
reaching ever higher toward the sun.

Accept the odds work against
us, and take their charms we chance
along the way, electronic pulse,
magnetic tape, movable type
like Bead
    to string
        then Bead
    to breathe in
to breathe out
    to Beat
        then pause
    to Beat
to purple
    to white
        then pull
    to One
to Zero

Ernie Paniccioli: *Ancient and Modern*

A New Enemy

Ernie Paniccioli

ndigenous people are now faced with a new and perhaps cul-ture-destroying enemy. A disease that is so technologically advanced and insidious as to be virtually undetectable. The virus of which I speak is altering how we see ourselves and even how we relate to ourselves, as well as how we view our ancient cultures.

Before you dismiss this as fear-mongering or paranoia, read on. For the first time in our history, we are ingesting images of our-selves created for us by people other than us. We have always cre-ated our own images, our own music, our own methods of speech and dress and submitted only to our own rhythms, memories, and inherited traditions. Now we follow ugly caricatures and stereo-types of how we should walk, talk, look, dress, and even dance. These blueprints are made for us by those who understand the least about us and who have the lowest image of us.

What has always sustained Native culture has been our deep-rooted love of family, respect for elders and our parents, and close ties to our unique identity. Travel around this land now and you'll see our children mimicking African Americans, Whites, or even Chicanos. It is clearly evident in their musical choices, dance, walk, and slang. As a Native man who has documented hip-hop culture for over three decades, I am in a unique position to give this warning. Young people from rezes around the country send me their music CDs to listen to. Almost all sound like straight copies of Black music.

For any rap (rap is one of the four elements of hip-hop culture, the other three are DJs/graffiti/dance) music to have authenticity it must reflect the life, lifestyle, and experience of the person rapping the story it is trying to tell. We come from a totally misunderstood people who have endured and survived so much for so long. Our backgrounds can provide us with a wealth of rare and powerful poetic imagery, so much so that we need never copy anything from anybody. Losing that identity by copying corporate cartoon images spoon-fed us by the mass media, TV, and youth-driven, clueless outlets like VH1 and MTV, will be the final nail in the coffin of assimilation and destruction against which we have fought so hard, long, and bravely.

COMINGS AND GOINGS IN INDIAN COUNTRY:
SPIRALING FROM A BLOG*

Joy Harjo

I needed to be out in the ocean, in the canoe. Thought off-season practice was at 5:30. It was at 5:15 and when we drove up the canoes were filled and pushing off. So headed to the gym to work off grief by pushing weights.

Why grief? It's there and palpable and I don't know who, how, and why, though mentally I can find many sources. Early this morning I got up with an apocalyptic dream. It was the kind of dream that is a possible future. These kinds of dreams embody a certain kind of tone of dream reality. The earth was shaking. Seconds blossomed to minutes. I watched across a bay and thought San Francisco; it wasn't. The shape of the city was different. I watched a phallic black glass-and-steel building of offices, apartments, and people plummet. Everything was crashing around all of us. And then the ocean heaved back, then forward. It was sick with pollution. A tsunami consumed the disaster.

That's one source of the grief.

We all know there's a shift. We know what's called civilization has gone too far without proper gratitude and care. We're all a part of it. We were put here specifically to take care of this place. We turned from the responsibility. It's difficult when prevailing rulers believe the earth and all nonhuman inhabitants are dead, when they pretend we no longer exist. We are invisible as we follow the masses into slavery to this system. It's difficult not to be swallowed by the tsunami of false culture bearing down on us.

I know, brother. I know, sister, I think when passing those who have given it up for drink, drugs, food, sex, or television. I understand the weight of grief, of shame.

I scan the internal horizon for other sources: childhood, my brother who is on disability and can't get on Medicaid, or the words of a paddling coach who said she and her girls have recently paddled past human excrement dumped from cruise ships into the ocean.

Even grief gets hungry and demands more grief.

I turn the other direction as the sun heads into the sea. I acknowledge grief. And we both keep moving.

———

Yesterday I talked to my sister early in the evening. She's in Oklahoma taking care of our mother, who had a successful knee replacement. Our mother is doing relatively well; however, she believes, like so many in this country, that a pill will cure everything, so she goes to two or three doctors and gets various prescriptions because she believes more medicine will make her even more well. We think that's the cause of her slurring yesterday morning, and her comment that took her back in time to forty years ago: "Is Joy still ironing?"

The behavior is frightening, but we had to laugh. I told my sister Margaret that it's terrifying to consider that somewhere in memory I am still ironing and will always be ironing. My mother showed me how to iron when I was tall enough to reach the ironing board, and from then on I ironed everyone's clothes, including my mother's restaurant uniforms, my stepfather's heavy khakis, and my school clothes. I even took in ironing to make money when I got older. Ironing was stacked in piles, or should I say mountains, in my sister's and my room. No matter how much I ironed, the stack never seemed to diminish. I won't go near an ironing board now.

———

Thursday night of the Creek Nation Festival, after we filled ourselves up with plates from Charlie's Chicken, my sister and I dragged our chairs up to the stomp dance circle to enjoy the music and the company. Usually I'm right in there with my shells. That night I just took the spirit of it all in as the music carried us: the ongoing stories of friends, and the prodigious growth in the nation. I was in mourning for a beloved friend, a Mvskoke citizen who was buried just hours before, far away from the nation. He had left Wagoner with his family when he was eleven. Later he joined the military, married a Hawaiian woman, and stayed in Honolulu. Bill Tiger made a community in the islands for many of us. He embodied the spirit of *vnoketckv*. And because of him when people far from Oklahoma think of the Mvskoke they'll think of Tiger: tall, outgoing, and generous.

When we leave the tight circle of the nation in Oklahoma we become emissaries of a sort, whether we are officially appointed as such or not. Anywhere we Mvskokes go, we're often the only Mvskoke anyone ever meets, or even the only Indian. And you can be sure that wherever you are, at the grounds, in church, or on a street halfway across the world from Oklahoma, someone is always watching to see how you act.

I left Oklahoma late summer of 1967 for high school at the

Institute of American Indian Arts, a BIA Indian school in Santa Fe, New Mexico. Everything I owned was packed into my brand-new army green footlocker. Richard Ray Whitman, Euchee Creek, was a student there, as were the Fife sisters: Phyllis and Sandy. I left again with a Cherokee husband, son, and stepdaughter in 1970 in a car whose trunk slid off every few miles. We frequently ran out into the road and retrieved it. Since then I've lived mostly in New Mexico and Hawaii. I've gotten to do a bit of traveling to perform, from Argentina to a music festival north of the Arctic Circle in Sami country in Norway. What always strikes me is that no matter where or how far away from Oklahoma I travel, though we may be few and far between out there, I always meet up with Creeks.

I'll never forget Alex Posey's granddaughter being wheeled up to meet me at the Heard Museum in Phoenix. And some years back, when I was feeling a little bewildered in the middle of Pennsylvania, Rosemary McCombs Maxey came up and introduced herself and made me feel at home. I was in New York City a few years ago and was proud to catch Tim Sampson appearing in his father, Sonny Sampson's, classic role in the Broadway show *One Flew over the Cuckoo's Nest*.

Breakdown

I resolve not to post any more poem drafts. They reveal the raw and chaotic inside of the creative process. It isn't pretty, though the inspiration is able to keep me moving through the muck and flaws of physicality, of humanness, of flaccid, first attempts at language. This is why I haven't posted, though I write every day. I'd rather work something through until it shines. So I suppose I could loop back and post the cleanest rewrites. Mostly I haven't been very sat-isfied with the poetry or much of my writing. I am in that state between states in the creative imagination. How do I get from stomp dance to this island, through strands of jazz, blues, and heartbreak ballad? How do I negotiate sacred thinking with the rhetoric and guns of a president who has announced he's going to build a fence along the border? How do I find "the" story from all of those who are vying for attention?

I'm in the middle of a breakdown that carries similar elements as the first, when I was a painting student at the University of New Mexico in my early twenties. It was dusk at the height of going-home-from-work traffic and I was crossing the street as I had crossed the street for thousands of times with no worries. It was an ordinary task. I couldn't. I hung onto the narrow island of dirt, weeds, and a little grass as I knew I would die if I crossed. I couldn't go backwards or forwards. Eventually I had to think myself across the street. And had to will each step the nearly-mile home. I couldn't swallow as those muscles wired to panic.

I did not have the luxury of a breakdown. I had small children, a job, and classes. So I thought myself through each small incre-ment of movement. I knew that if I didn't, it would all blow apart. When I took the wheel of my car I had to fight for control so I would not drive off the road.

This time was marked by a ban enforced from my mother's house because I called my stepfather a terrorist. I wrote it in a letter to my mother. He opened up all of her mail before she did. This was one of the many ways he kept her hostage. During this time my daughter's father was alternately binge drinking, writing beau-tiful and necessary poetry and political treatises, and collecting hippie-girl lovers. It was also marked by extreme creativity. I began the path of poetry. I put down my painting brushes.

Chaos. This is a different layer of the spiral. The elements are here. Some aspects have diminished, like the panic.

Each morning I ask for a blessing by the sun. I keep my eyes and heart open. I see the journey for what it is—the complicated layers of time and memory pulse. I go out and ask the workers next door to turn the radio down to a notch below "blasting." They're local guys. They do.

––––––––

We've finally landed in winter after a long summer and fall. Here on the Rio Grande flyway, geese and cranes have been passing over. Only thing is, they aren't always headed in the right direction. I've watched several layered vees of birds head south, then turn back north. Others fly east or west in a confused manner. Strange. I never saw this growing up in Oklahoma. In the fall, birds flew south. In the spring, they returned. Since the hard freeze of the last few weeks they are definitely and quickly flying south. No question. At least the sun still comes up from the east and sees us through until nightfall, and returns again. A *mvto*, or thank you, for the sun.

We just survived Thanksgiving. Most people don't know that it's a holiday based on a fabricated story of a sit-down dinner with Pilgrims (a mispronunciation of the word *pillager*) and Indians. The Pilgrims weren't too friendly, were rather grim, not the sort to hang out and eat with Indians. The holiday was an invention fostered by the writer of the poem "Mary Had a Little Lamb," Sarah Josepha Hale. Maybe the poem should have been, "Mary Had a Little Turkey." Did her family own a turkey farm? Of course, most of us enjoy any kind of excuse for a day off, for eating lots of good food with family and friends, and for some (not me) an afternoon of football games. And it's always good to take time to express gratitude, and even better to make it a habit every morning before getting up, or before sleep. I take issue with the compromised premise, and with all of those people dressing up as fake Indians. For most of the world, turkey feathers in the hair and buckskin equals Indian.

Once, years back, in a class, we studied images of Indians. One of the students took sheets of paper and markers to a preschool class in Boulder. She asked the children to draw an Indian. They all drew one of two images: a warrior on horseback brandishing bloody tomahawks, or delicate princesses, most of them on horseback. They weren't human beings, rather symbols, and the children had already internalized them.

When my daughter was three, just before she went into Head Start, we went to sign her up at a preschool in Iowa City (where I was attending graduate school). The children surrounded us and danced around doing that Hollywood war whoop, you know the one. Their teacher was embarrassed. I was amazed that children that young had already taken in that false image that had nothing to do with being Indian, or Mvskoke, or Acoma, my daughter's other tribal affiliation.

We're still mostly portrayed in those flat images in art, literature, movies, and not just by non-Indians or three-year-olds. The worst culprits are often our own people. Of course, we do have warriors on horseback, and I saw a little tomahawk-brandishing in my early days, and most of our princesses aren't so delicate. They like to eat.

A few years ago I carried a fussy grandson, accompanied by his older sister, for a stroll around the Santa Fe plaza, while their parents (and the rest of the diners) finished dinner in peace. Desiray, who is Mvskoke, Acoma, Navajo, and most decidedly "Indian looking," paused in front of a Plains headdress displayed in an Indian jewelry shop for tourists. "Look Nana," she said. "Indians."

Identity is a complex question. How do we see and define ourselves, and how do others define us? What do governments have to say about it, and what does the wisdom beyond the foolishness of small-mindedness have to say about it? I understand there are many in the tribe who believe tribal membership should be made up only of full-bloods. Yet many of these same people sing hymns and espouse a religion that isn't Mvskoke in origin. There's a contradiction here. I have no issue with people talking with or worshipping God in whatever manner or form. Diversity in form describes the natural world. And I'm convinced we all carry a part of the vision. No one person or culture carries the whole story.

What I take issue with is the rigidity and hurtfulness of an exclusionary vision. Such a plan to limit tribal membership is not only racist, it's genocidal. It's what the makers of the Dawes Act had in mind in the first place, like a sustained-release genocide pill. And many have bought into it. Self-righteousness stinks, no matter how it's dressed. Behind this are some real issues and concerns about what it means to be a real Mvskoke person, about our responsibilities, and about having some say in the shape of the future of our nation. Who is taking care of the spiritual, mythical, and familial center? Who is carrying forth the stories, the songs, and making new ones to fit the needs of the time? Many of those who know are dying off.

Our experiences have been different, and race figures greatly into how one moves about the present world. Consider that we didn't define ourselves by race before the coming of the Europeans. We must remember where we came from as a nation, and have a shining idea of our direction. A fearful approach doesn't work, in governments, societies, or our individual lives. We bring about what we fear as surely as we bring about what we love. Both carry the same charge. Let's try some common sense and compassion. We need to be open to hearing each other.

I've talked to many of our tribal members in Oklahoma and elsewhere in the country who have expressed concern that their children and grandchildren are being denied a place in the family, our Mvskoke Nation. Is this who we want to be, a people who throw their children away? If we look with the mind of the vastness and complexity of the viewpoint of the stars, then we will see and know wisely.

As I write this I am on a late flight to Albuquerque. We were delayed from Tulsa, missed the connecting plane in Dallas–Fort Worth. Alfred Berryhill, our second chief, was also on the same delayed flights, so we had plenty of opportunity to visit. I was impressed by his cultural knowledge and his love of our Mvskoke language. Ask him sometime about how to get from "aerodynamics" to "arrow dynamics." Mostly we talked of the need for a refreshing vision for the people. We agreed we need to see ourselves as who we are, not in that false mirror of misrepresentation that has been forced on us. When the Europeans first arrived they were amazed by the way we lived, by our democracy, our lack of a need for prisons, for our social systems, our finely crafted homes. In a relatively short time we have forgotten our true legacy as Mvskoke people. It's still here, within us.

———

Friday night in Albuquerque. Jammed on saxophone. I am listening beyond sound to understand sound.

More rains. Thunder and lightning. Cornfields ruined at Laguna and Acoma. Floods. I watched the clouds gather all afternoon. Tall thunderheads in the blue. They don't usually hang around here like this. Never did in all the years I lived here since Indian school in the late sixties.

A few hours ago I sat at my favorite kitchen table, in Isleta Pueblo. We shared green chili stew, chocolate cupcakes, and stories about all these changes, from strange weather to this terrible legacy of war brought to us by a particular reigning family. This country will never be the same. (There is a connection between all of the above.)

I remember, years ago, walking straight into an airport and getting on a plane with no "security." Then security machines were installed. Then, after 9/11, we were searched and screened though we had not committed crimes. The worst were the smaller airports. I was picked "randomly" (the only Indian) in Bellingham, Washington, and was forced to stand in line with huge orange tags clipped on my bags and me. Everything was taken out and unwrapped, in front of everyone. I tried to have a sense of humor about it, and told myself that people were "just doing their job." So was the U.S. Cavalry, so were the guards at the concentration camps. Then, a man had the makings of a bomb in his shoe, and we were then forced to remove our shoes as we moved through "security." I've even had my bare feet wanded, for security. Now, it's lipstick, deodorants, shampoos, and perfume. Now there's a machine that is going to be installed in Phoenix that will reveal the completely nude body. If word gets out, there'll be a rush of men signing up for airport security jobs.

Watch out. Be careful. This is how it happens. We will forget to even question why.

Now I should be like my favorite comic and friend Charlie Hill. He makes people laugh about all this. The poet attempts a resonating chord between the soul in here and the soul out there. So does the comedian, or, some of them (and some poets). I told Charlie he and I were standing at the back of the line when careers were given out: he took comedy, I took poetry (and a strange jazz-like native root music).

Suspended

Once I was so small that I could barely see over the top of the back-seat of the black Cadillac my father bought with his Indian oil roy-alty money. He polished and tuned his car daily. I wanted to see everything. This was around the time I acquired language, or even before that time when something happened that changed my rela-tionship to the spin of the world. My concept of language, of what was possible with language, was changed by this revelatory moment. It changed even the way I looked at the sun. This sus-pended integer of time probably escaped ordinary notice in my parents' universe, which informed most of my vision in the ordi-nary world. They were still omnipresent gods. We were driving somewhere in Tulsa, the northern border of the Creek Nation. I don't know where we were going or where we had been, but I know the sun was boiling the asphalt, the car windows open for any breeze as I stood on tiptoes on the floorboard behind my father, a handsome god who smelled of Old Spice, whose slick black hair was always impeccably groomed, his clothes perfectly creased and ironed. The radio was on. I loved the radio, jukeboxes, or any magic thing containing music even then.

I wonder what signaled this moment, a loop of time that on first glance could be any place in time. I became acutely aware of the line the jazz trumpeter was playing (a sound I later associated with Miles Davis). I didn't know the words *jazz* or *trumpet*, or the concepts. I don't know how to say it, with what sounds or words, but in that confluence of hot southern afternoon, in the breeze of aftershave and humidity, I followed that sound to the beginning, to the place of the birth of sound. I was suspended in whirling stars, a moon to which I'd traveled often by then. I grieved my parents' failings, my own life which I saw stretched the length of that rhapsody.

My rite of passage into the world of humanity occurred then, via jazz. The music made a startling bridge between familiar and strange lands, an appropriate vehicle, for though the music is predominately west African in concept, with European associations, jazz was influenced by the Creek (or Mvskoke) people, for we were there when jazz was born. I recognized it, that humid afternoon in my formative years, as a way to speak beyond the confines of ordinary language. I still hear it.

* These pieces were culled from Joy Harjo's blog at www.joy-harjo.com and from Joy Harjo's "Coming and Going in Indian Country" column for the *Muscogee Nation News*, the newspaper of the Muscogee Creek Nation of Oklahoma.

THE NATIVE AMERICAN MOVES INTO CONTEMPORARY LITERATURE: DISCOVERING A VOICE WHICH MAY NOT BE NEW BUT IS AUTHENTIC

Maurice Kenny

Remembering back to traditional, tribal literature which is composed of song, poetry, story, and oration, the fact appears that these genres were oral in presentation; I rediscovered this truth. Not just the creative voice of the writer, but a particular voice, the persona, was known and used on a regular basis. Often the singer is not the creator of the song or poem. The song, or perhaps story, is ancient and handed down over centuries. Consequently, the speaker is oftentimes simply a "chosen" voice to sing or tell the story or recite the poem. The song, or poem itself, and certainly the narrative and dramatic monologue, are usually of the persona genre. It can be assumed that on occasion even the lyric poem could be recited in the voice of another. Perhaps this persona has less to do with the creation, and the song or poem is more often than not changed by a shaman, a holy person, and not he or she who might be the subject or the author in question.

It must always be remembered that the community is at the forefront of traditional, tribal concern and purpose in all events and experiences of any nature. The people were always protected and honored but expendable without the community or tribe, sometimes known as a band; individuals might die through war or disease or by adoption into another band or Nation at the conclusion of some feudal war. The community is of utter importance, not necessarily the individual person nor group of peoples. Without the Nation, there is no reason; there is nothing. It can survive without the single person, yes even an important chief, but it cannot survive without its center, the community that contains a complete culture through its language rather than its genes.

Hence, the singer or poet created beautiful songs and poems, told stories, or chanted a sacred moment for the entire community, though the prayer may have been designated for healing an individual suffering from an illness or possibly dying, with hope the sick might survive the illness, combat wound, or witchery of black magic. The composer will sing celebration, an honor song or poem, to celebrate success in war, the hunt, a vision quest, exactly in the manner Virgil wrote *The Aeneid*. Persona was, and is, not far off from genres of Native American literature. An example of a collection of song and poetry is *Singing for Power: The Song Magic of the Papago Indians*, by Ruth Underhill; other collections that may also be cited are: *The Winged Serpent*, edited by Margot Astrov; the classic *The Sky Clears: The Poetry of the American Indian*, edited by A. Grove Day; and a more contemporary approach to Native American literature, *Iroquois Voices, Iroquois Visions*, edited by Bertha Rogers.

Many years past, in the early 1970s, I discovered, as a poet, a new voice of my own. Like all English literature majors, I, too, studied Victorians and particularly poets such as Matthew Arnold, Tennyson, and Elizabeth Barrett Browning and, of course, Robert Browning. As a young reader, Arnold and Tennyson had little appeal for me. I avidly read Elizabeth Barrett Browning and Robert Browning. In that Victorian class, I quickly began to discard the sentimentality of Elizabeth to discover the great beauty and joy of Tennyson and especially Matthew Arnold, and not merely his magnificent "Dover Beach," which I continue reading to this moment. Then Alfred Tennyson took my poetic eye, and at night in my rooms I would read his poems aloud to my roommate who, in turn, read passages from the Bible over my head. I lay prone on the pillow, eyes shut tight, hoping dreams would carry me away from Bill's droning voice and his biblical, fundamentalist posture. Bill was a fine young man, but his penchant was to believe we were all sinners, particularly our landlords, a Mr. and Mrs. Davidson (he an attorney, and she manager of a lady's dress boutique). I was, without a doubt, a sinner, for I read not only poetry but poets who wrote about, or while on, drugs: Tennyson's "The Lotos-Eaters" and Coleridge, who puffed opium and composed numerous poems under its influence, among many others. There was one other poet who influenced my thought and my poetic form far more than I ever suspected he would, certainly at the time. I was quietly enamored of Robert Browning. He hid under the guise of the dramatic monologue, or what we currently speak of as a "persona." I enjoyed these brief dramatic exercises immensely. They were a joy to read. I thoroughly enjoyed his love poems and swooned while reading them. Remember, I was not only gullible, but young and most impressionable.

I have always held a flair for the dramatic, the ham in me persists, and I took easily to Browning's personae—what I call his quick, blackout plays such as "My Last Duchess." In the 1970s, I wrote a poem entitled "Sacajawea" and considered it fairly successful when my good friend and fellow poet, Rochelle Ratner, exclaimed in a somewhat excited manner, "You have created your first persona poem." Rochelle, at the time, was deeply interested in the persona form, and was actually writing an in-depth study on the use of form. It seems to me now that she wrote something about my collection *Blackrobe: Isaac Jogues,* which was mostly composed in persona. I had totally forgotten Browning; she brought him back to my attention. Also, at about the same time, I was introduced to Robert Peters through Kirby Congdon, both immensely fine poets, and Peters was certainly experimenting with that form himself. Here, I thought I was the only poet in the world doing such work. What a shock! Apparently, my good buddy Rochelle discovered many modern, contemporary poets working in persona. I was excited being in such good company.

This new form led to my new voice, though it remained lyrical and slightly narrative. I, however, refused to admit that I was a storyteller; I believed I should leave that up to my betters, such as Peter Blue Cloud, Simon J. Ortiz, and the masterful Leslie Marmon Silko, all friends. Surely I must have realized (I did hide behind the mask) that in order to write *Blackrobe* it was necessary to tell his life story, however brief, or rather, allow it to be told by means of the voice, persona, of the other players circling him. I spent several years researching the book and was extremely pleased to almost instantly find a press eager to publish it, though the book was not yet completed at the time. The problem with the book could be found in the characters and particularly in Isaac Jogues himself. I thought him fraudulent from the start. He was an ordained Jesuit who came to the Americas to save souls, those of "pagan" Indians of North America, especially those in what became New York State along the Mohawk River and in southern Ontario, Canada. He was put to the club, killed because of his interference with the minds of the women and the children of various tribes on October 18, 1646. It was sheer joy to create these persona poems. I was able to rid myself of a major nightmare that the Catholic nuns and teachers had forced into my sleep—for instance, placing the guilt of his assassination on my quarter-blood Mohawk head. I was also able to put away my apprehensions of the church's tenets. When I was a very tiny lad, my awfully Catholic aunt had insisted to my parents, and particularly my father, that I become a Catholic priest—horror upon horror. My sinfulness saved me from that fate. Basically, I was in the position to right wrongs. To this moment I believe with all my poetic heart and soul that poetry deals with truth and beauty, but first truth and only then beauty, the beauty of chosen and charged language. Unlike T. S. Eliot, I was angry with traditional Christian belief, as it had put so many wonderful and spiritual rites and celebrations of the true energy of life—for lack of more appropriate terms, the Supreme Being—to death. Traditional Christian belief had killed the idea that all creatures were equal and that, if I had a brain, the tree and the wolf and the bear had brains as well—a solid Native idea, belief.

In *Blackrobe*, not only was I dealing with religion, the Catholic faith, my own lack of Christian belief, and newly rediscovered foundations in a strong, traditional faith or spiritual belief—many years later a Catholic nun accused me of having no religion, to which I responded, "You mean your religion"—I was also working with as factual a history as I could possibly conceive, even though I considered the lives of people in a very fuzzy reality of American history, characters only *thought* to have lived, such as my character "Wolf Aunt," an alleged Mohawk woman who, at least temporarily, helped slow Jogues's penalty of death. She had been thought lost to historians because her act was not appreciated by other Mohawks in her village, who forgot her. The book, to my delight and surprise, was comparatively successful, critically and financially speaking. Within the thought process of the composition, I allowed myself the pleasure of writing with reference to the abysmal practice in America's history of genocide of its original people, the Native American, through whatever means, especially religion, war, smallpox blankets, rum, European disease, etc., to again tear the dishonesty from our eyes, a function I have attempted to continue in my writings, where the polemic might quietly slip between lines or words.

I did not realize at the time that *Blackrobe* was a departure, and that departure is necessary in writing: a change of form, perhaps, say, from sonnets to free verse, or from the personal to persona, for example; it is what James Joyce suggests we do as we grow in age and accomplishment and, as we develop, it becomes part of that development. Consequently, I continued writing my poems, my stories, or what is designated as fiction, some book reviews, a tad of literary criticism in the form of essay, and surely, deep and abiding interest in American history, which, I hope I do not need to explain, cannot be separated from Native American Indian history, as it is exactly the same to this moment and depends upon the other for its support and continuum.

In 1985, I found myself on the Akwesasne Mohawk Reservation working on the newspaper *Akwesasne Notes* with such poets as Peter Blue Cloud, Rokwaho, Alex Jacobs, and also Doug George who, at the time, was more interested in "law" than in poetry. It was Doug who suggested that I write something, in some form or other, on the life of the great Mohawk woman warrior Tekonwa-tonti (She-Who-Is-Outnumbered). She came into history as the wife of Sir William Johnson, Molly Brant, older sister of the famed Joseph Brant. Doug thought a study of this woman was overdue. He was correct; I began the study of her life and place in American history. I also began writing poems dealing with that life and that history. Twelve years later, White Pine Press published the collection of persona poems, *Tekonwatonti: Molly Brant: Poems of War.* What a tremendous job, an eighth of a lifetime's work, an all-consuming labor of love. I thought, believed implicitly, that I did not write personally and only persona-ed. Indeed, in this new venture, bright experience, and living through a perhaps surrealist experiment, I would surely hide, escape within her life and times. I did exactly that, or so I thought, until a young Native Creek PhD candidate acquired a copy of the book, read it, and decided that the epic story of Molly Brant was not as critically impersonal as I had planned. Craig Womack, the young Creek, in researching my own biography and looking into the activities of both Molly Brant and her Irish husband, Sir William Johnson, the machinations, and the tenure of the times, found that the book was actually far more personal than I had ever suspected. His belief was that Sir William was a near cutout of my father, who was of both Mohawk and Irish descent, and that if Molly was not actually based on my birth mother, then she was surely the mother I had always "desired." My mother has Seneca, not Mohawk, blood, but she held no understanding of her Seneca lines, with the possible exception that her father, my grandfather, collected Native American (then Indian) artifacts and donated the collection to a North Country museum near where he lived and died.

He collected arrowheads from the back lots of his dairy farm in the Cape Vincent area of northern New York State. My mother was a direct descendant of the Seneca Parkers. Now, reconsidering Craig Womack's study, I agree that, certainly to a point, my father shared certain characteristics with Sir William besides blood. They were both philanderers, industrious and poor upon arriving in the States—my father was born on the Canadian side of the political border—both amassed a small fortune, commanded others, and saw that less fortunate peoples were helped in whatever way they needed.

My mother was certainly a different kettle of fish. She shared fewer characteristics with Molly Brant than my father did with Sir William. Molly was somewhat well-read. Her life was lived in the thick of survival, not only for herself and her children and household, but for her Nation, the Iroquois/Mohawk; she eventually believed that this survival was more attainable via the royalists and the crown of England than through the revolution and the soon-to-become Americans, though she actually trusted no one. Molly never even trusted her stepson, John, who eventually evicted her from his father's mansion at William's death in 1774. Molly was dominant, forthright, strong-willed, passionate, knew anger fervently, and reveled in it with sweet savor. She knew the scene and could track as well as any man. She knew the wiles of the European, Brit, and rebel. She was a Mohawk of rich blood and tradition and became a protective panther-mother of eight children.

My biological mother held some of Molly's traits, but only a few. She showed certain weaknesses, specifically in her relationship with my father, whom, I believe, she adored as strongly as Molly adored Sir William. Unlike Molly, my mother had no leverage to keep him in her bed, as Molly did Sir William, being not only a Mohawk woman, but important in and to the Nation, if only at the tribal council, where her opinions carried weight. My mother had no such power; she could merely drop her tears onto the shoulders of a friend. My mother was an industrious and hardworking woman; she possessed the wonderful talent of baking, made very pretty doilies for the bedside stand, the cocktail table, the chair arm; she was a whiz picker in the berry field. As political consultant or lobbyist she was a total failure. My sisters and I often considered her a weak mother, good woman that she was.

I suppose there is some truth in Womack's deductions, that there is much of the personal in *Tekonwatonti: Molly Brant* that, if one looks deeply enough, a line of blood to both Molly and Sir William might be discovered, if only in the wish that my mother could have shared more of the strengths that Molly possessed . . .

A new discovery, a new voice, a new way of viewing things and life, the past and future, history and art, literature and recollection, love and lust, war and politics, peace and death, revolutions and bondage, heaven and hell, religion and spirituality. Traveling into the unknown, a trail blazed by many but influenced by Ambrose Bierce of *Devil's Dictionary* fame. A journey, or sojourn, into magic and poetry.

In August 1999, I traveled to Mexico and then returned to my home in Saranac Lake in the Adirondacks to finish my book, *Collage of Recollection: Conversations with Frida Kahlo*. I had my vision focused upon the past, my college years, and the influence of Whitman. I could write the way I needed, thirty-three books of poems, fictions, and essays, later.

A new, and once old, voice. I rediscovered the past; could write of dreams and magic, visions and fantasy; could interlope prose and verse, talk to the dead and hear answers, could be dead or unborn. I could at last sing in my true voice. I could ride the old mares of my youth and ride them as deep as I wished into the imagination, the richness with which the Supreme Being had enhanced my life—I was free. Did I not need to write my life in this new work? Life itself holds restrictions and is anything but formless, even when you only consider conception, or birth, and death. But within those parameters, oh my, what hell you might create, what glory you might sing, what words of vocables you might hurl upon the world, what joy you might come to know, suck into your spirit, your being.

Consequently, two hundred pages later, I have a new and old voice, hopefully perfected over the juvenile product, and still maintain my intended approach to art, to poetry, to truth, and to beauty. I have managed to maintain my sights and visions on Native culture, the continuum, and have also paid homage to the great Keats and to the all-important influence of not only Walt Whitman but also of William Carlos Williams, who in his own fashion lifted from Native American culture: song, story, and form.

This creativity: adventure, discovery, celebration—whether it is Emily Dickinson finding flies or Simon J. Ortiz telling his young son to protect the newborn mice of the southwest desert. This is my return to Native culture, the visions of the past looking into the future by way of poetry, song, and recollection for the good of the community and the spirit of mankind—yes, even the individual— obligation, imagination, industry, exhaustion . . . success.

E-Socials: Cultural Collaboration in the Age of the Electronic Inter-Tribal

James Thomas Stevens

The Iroquois social (read: powwow), a mainstay of Haudenosaunee tradition, allows for tribes and peoples to come
together and share dance, food, and song. Ironically, today
the Internet is allowing for this same kind of interaction on a
global scale, aiding in recording cultural traditions, sharing ideas,
and even preserving languages.

I recently embarked on a poetic collaboration with Samoan
poet Caroline Sinavaiana. This electronic call and response took
place between the years 2002 and 2005. Our goal was to play a part
in preserving our respective languages, and to share and enjoy
elements of our cultures. The collaboration resulted in the publication of the book *Mohawk/Samoa: Transmigrations,* published by
Subpress in 2006.

I first met Sinavaiana while attending a humanities conference
in Honolulu. A poet friend of mine had invited me to teach a
class at the University of Hawaii at Manoa, and later I attended a
dinner with Sinavaiana. I was immediately struck by a familiar
Nativeness—her calm manner, easy smile, and thoughtfulness.
Upon my return to the mainland and upon reading her book
Alchemies of Distance, I knew I had found a kindred soul. I wrote
to her via e-mail, and proposed a poetic collaboration involving

something I had been working on in my own work. I had deemed it "sui-translation," translations for the self. They were not meant to be literal translations—though I do offer these to the reader in a parallel format—but translations to create personal relevancy.

I had been working with traditional Mohawk songs and chants, not religious in nature, but more along the lines of work songs or traveling songs, a canoe song for instance. Part of what has always interested me about the oral tradition is the element of change—change that is necessary to create relevancy. I had been questioning the relevancy of the canoe song in particular: of what use is a canoe song to a Mohawk professor living in the twenty-first century? It occurred to me that while I can't say I often find myself in a canoe, I do find myself trying to navigate a steady stream of people and personalities that are sometimes smooth and at other times full of dangerous eddies and snags. Using the original song, I created a rewrite or translation that was relevant to my life.

I proposed to Sinavaiana that I would send the original poems in Mohawk and their literal translations, but not my sui-translation. I asked her to consider the originals and make her own connections, responding with a poem. She, in turn, would send me Samoan songs or chants in translation, and I would respond to these. The "call and response," as she would come to call it, appealed to both of us. Sinavaiana, being from an oceanic culture, a seafaring people, is a traveler by nature. I had just come into overseas travel in the last five years, but in that time had traveled to China, Scotland, England, France, Jordan, Sweden, Denmark, Iceland, and, most recently, Turkey. Sinavaiana, a devout Tibetan Buddhist, was often traveling to ashrams in India and Tibet during these years of collaboration. The timing from call to response was often sporadic due to distances and constraints from personal obligations, but it was always with great expectation and joy that we viewed each other's responses.

I came to see the interaction/collaboration/correspondence as a kind of dance—a social dance, where hands unlinked as the line of dancers (ancestors) split off, shuffled off on their circular pathways until hands were relinked, and a circle was completed. As I received Sina's (as she is known by her friends) responses from India in an Internet cafe in Grenoble, France, I would wonder at the technology that allowed this cultural exchange—both hating the computer and admiring it—as some new kind of time/space travel. Sometimes, sitting by my window, looking out over gray train tracks along a frozen Lake Erie shoreline, I pondered how two cultures so vastly different in environment, a northeastern Native from a land of six-month winters and a Samoan Native living in the warm blue Pacific, where the Manoa Valley poured forth its flowery scent, could meet in the fertile field of poetics.

Then it happened quite naturally. The poems began to flow, though sometimes they caught on the ice floes of the lake, while at other times they moved swiftly on warm Pacific currents:

> *Ice crystals*
> *slice a fingertip*
> *trying to clear the way.*

> *Pulse—like the watery*
> *stir of stars*
> *slouching across this lake.*
> *And*

> *Fly canoe to blue reefs.*
> *Sing to bonito*
> *swimming in green shadow.*

Let your chant angle
through deep water.

Obviously, we were working from different climates, both geographically and in genetic memory. Where my "wampum bird ascended in / purple / and white clatter," Sina's "chant angled / through deep water. / A hook for the ear / of fish, a line . . ."

I know that personally, it was a challenge at times while traveling to ignore the scenery surrounding me while writing and to remain intent on only the songs. How does one put the color of sandstone and the sound of horse carts racing through Al Siq to the ancient city of Petra out of mind? I had to focus on the eastern woodlands. In all likelihood, there are emotions and images that slip into the poems from many places, but this, in part, is what makes them sui-translations.

Recently, I had the opportunity to do a reading at Bogazici University in Istanbul, and I was impressed with the number of people there interested in Native American studies. I had heard before that Turks hold the belief that genetically and culturally, we are one people.

This was made evident to me as, over and over, I met people who stated, "We are the same, you know?" Many Turks believe themselves to be the people who crossed over the land bridge of the oft-disputed Bering Strait theory. One thing that was made clear to me is that they are serious about Native American studies there. The Turkish professors I met who teach Native studies have lived and spent time on reservations in North America. They are also very serious about language preservation and its importance to cultural preservation.

When I read in foreign places, I always begin by reading the Mohawk song poems from *Transmigrations*. There is a certain obsession I have with reading these poems in spaces that I know have never contained the sounds of our language. It feels like I am leaving them there to reverberate for all time. This was true of my reading at Bogazici, and the response was overwhelming. A Turkish professor immediately approached me about the import of language, telling me how he had lived on the San Carlos Apache Reservation for two years and had seen firsthand how instrumental language is to culture. He asked if I had recorded myself reading the poems so they could be taught elsewhere with the benefit of hearing the pronunciation and intonation. This is something I will be proposing to Sina in the near future. The beginnings of a translation project are now in the making, as once again, these words will be electronically shuffle-dancing their way to Turkey in order to be translated into Turkish.

The circle widens. The round-dance opens—more tribes, more peoples, and more collaboration.

THROWING MOCCASINS

Kristi Gansworth

The first time I sat down and made a pair of moccasins with my grandmother, I was a neurotic mess. I had watched her for weeks preparing the deerskin—scraping the fur and flesh off it, soaking and draining it, rubbing it down with bacon grease to get the soft texture she pursued relentlessly. She'd explain with every motion that if you didn't partake in this step or that, then the hide would come out a disaster, and all the time invested would be wasted and the skin would have to be trashed. Left out for the dogs to gnaw at as a chew toy, or else frozen for further work at a later date, if it came down to that and you just couldn't invest the time to do it properly. She believes in doing things right the first time, and making sure that there is nothing half-assed about any given project, whether it is tanning the hide of a three-hundred-pound deer, cleaning the kitchen floor, preparing a tray of deviled eggs, accepting the world and yourself as they are.

I couldn't have been older than ten or eleven years old, and I had always wanted to be a part of her work, to learn how she made the fancy footwear, churning out pair upon pair with little effort, her house a factory of sorts, stopping only for meals, as she and my aunt would sit for hours on end sewing and designing with new and old patterns based on what people are doing these days, what colors are popular, what finishing touch would complement the final look. I wanted to make a pair of baby white deerskin moccasins with rabbit-fur lining, and she complied right away, excited that finally, someone would be adhering to the specificity of her intricate instruction.

She laid out the pattern for me and explained how to do it, and just as I was finishing the rabbit fur, I pricked myself with the needle and blood seeped into the gleaming white border and down onto the side of the moccasin. I, of course, was enraged, lost all patience, and swore off the idea of ever attaining the skill and wisdom she emanated with seemingly no forethought. Rather than focusing on my infantile temper tantrum, my aunt walked to the other side of the room and picked up the moccasin, suggesting that I remove the fur and instead bead small red flowers on the side of the flap; that way the stain would be covered and "no one would even know that you put your blood into it!" So I took her advice, and, with her help, made a nice pair of moccasins, for a beginner, and ended up giving them to my first niece when I met her.

Lingering irritations remained, because all of the moccasins I had ever seen for babies were lined with the fur, and in the row of completed pairs mine looked slightly off—though there were different shades and variations of animal skin, mine was the only pair with beads. However, my mentors both encouraged me to think of that as a good thing: uniqueness. How significant that every time I pick up a needle or see anyone else doing the same thing, I remember throwing that moccasin clear across the living room and renouncing the idea of ever picking one up again.

But I have, and have learned how to make them, and many other things, even recently trying my hand at the meticulously rewarding craft of quillwork, remembering always that mistakes will be made, and there are ways to repair them back into something presentable. I've learned from these women, and from my family as a whole, that particularizing a craft and making it your own is something that will build strength and power in you, and will give you the ability to focus on creating rather than on stewing and being blindly angry or upset, tarnishing your destiny and your work in one fell swoop.

It wasn't until recently that I had a chance to apply those principles outside the admittedly rare instances where I accomplish bead or leather work, but transfiguring the concepts has been key to understanding my role as a human, and the path my life will take as I grow with the years. I've spent a dizzying amount of time being unproductive, incensed by the way that life can often daunt a person into believing that something as crucial as hope is off the menu, unavailable, out of stock. That, frankly, is a lame way to live, think, and execute a life's work, and I say this as a person who has been just that for many years. I blamed white people, my parents, family, the education system, the DMV, whoever I could for the multitude of confusions that I've faced through the years in not being able to make a purposeful, thoughtful determination of what it is I want, how I'm going to get it, where my beliefs lie, and where I ultimately belong.

The political and social realities of my people, vast and diverse and multiplying ad infinitum, are not going to bog me down, I've decided. The fact that many Americans who surround me, Caucasian and otherwise, are ignorant of the suffering and devastation that have been inflicted on my people is not going to stop me from respecting them on an idiosyncratic basis and allowing myself to be open to connections outside my own culture, where I've personally endured persecution and nonacceptance, from reasons as various as tribal lineage to my choices in friends to my taste in music and clothing. None of that criticism and negativity matters to me anymore, because I've studied many of the ancient teachings of the Ojibwe, the Onondaga, and the Lakota, all tribes from which I derive in one way or another, and I have found that when those cultures were thriving, and even they experienced demolition, the principles I believe in are there—and that's what is important to me in keeping the concept of tradition alive. I feel that I am able to relate purely and timelessly to my ancestors, however gradually and awkwardly that relationship grows.

The most devastating things inflicted upon human life and the power lying within it are loss, death, annihilation, and the inability to grow; misfortunes like this are commonplace in the histories of myself personally and all those that preceded me, yet we still live, and thrive, and find that among all of the bureaucracy and absurdity of indigenous politics and spite and failure, there is much to be gained. For me, this has been an intellectual journey that starts with introspection and ends there as well. It takes a long time, I think, to find the peace within oneself to be absolutely honest enough to admit that as a Native, it really isn't the fault of [insert racial group here] that we have met with such suffering. Some are lucky and have it right away, but starting there, as an artist, has been paramount to my crossing into the ability to be honest with myself about other, equally important facets of life.

It's funny, actually, that when I was younger, high school age and even well before, social acceptance from other Natives was not something that I had at all, and yet I would still rage against white people and popular culture as if I were standing right alongside those who despised me, arms crossed, defiant in my refusal to grow past such a simplistic preconception. However, as a whole, I've learned that this society and culture that was forced upon me, upon my ancestors, and upon whatever comes after me, is rife with possibility, in rare delicacies of beauty, truth, and creativity. There is so much awesome postmodern stuff to revel in, even if it is derivative of the need for social change—punk rock for instance (I mean the real stuff—late '70s, not this Green Day, MTV-ed, homogenized assembly-line three-chord crap) creative nonfiction, independent filmmaking, fashion design, body modification, photography, the subtle evolution of poetry which for me is a necessity not unlike air, culinary artistry—these are all fabulous ways of people expressing their most basic desires, hopes, and fears, and though they technically are, in essence, products of so-called white culture, as some people in my community (to include me at one time) would see it, I have a relationship to those things and many others, such ideas and inspirations, that is strong, healthy, and significant.

I don't believe that, creatively, there is anything more dangerous than anger; the seething, insensate wrath that strips a person, this one anyway, of the freedom to expand past that numbing nothingness to a place where the opportunity for growth presents itself, as it invariably does, inviting choice: to become a useless, wasted, blood-encrusted replica of things already done, or to become something similar but different, original, and capable of standing on its own among such a plethora of variations. It was OK to bleed all over that moccasin and then cover it up, to create a new style from the remains of a previous attempt that had ended in failure.

FROM BETTY CREEK:
WRITING THE INDIGENOUS DEEP SOUTH

Janet McAdams

I t rains today. The first of a week of rough mountain storms, a rage of water and wind, distant thunder and lightning. Pine trees crash in the forest around me, trees already half dead from an infestation of pine beetle that began a few years ago. It is too wet to walk today, but I walk anyway, push away the rhododendron, wish that waterproofing my boots wasn't one of those tasks I continually put off. I am in a rare place: a six-hundred-acre artists' retreat in Rabun County, Georgia. Rabun County is mostly National Forest land. I am surrounded by a green world largely uninhabited by human beings. As I walk, I am aware of the road to the north, the main house up the road, but I see no one, though I walk for several hours. If I were willing to do a little bushwhacking on this wet day, I could escape every trace of humanity. This is the fifth week of my seven-week retreat in these north Georgia mountains, Cherokee land—this *used to be* Cherokee land, people tell me—where I try to sort out the life story of Anna Packard, the Creek mixed-blood heroine of the novel I'm writing.

Like mine, Anna's roots are in Alabama, not Georgia. Disenfranchised from her own tribalism by the same historical forces that nearly obliterated indigenous America, Anna's Creek mother leads the life of many urban Indians, a nuclear family, a city

(Atlanta), a life of not quite passing. The South was hit hard by the genocidal practices of European invaders and settlers. When I teach about the indigenous South, I point out on the map of present-day Native America the large white space in the heart of what is now Alabama, Georgia, the Florida panhandle, noting how the nations were pushed not only west, but north and south, in the Removals of the 1830s. There are a handful of reservations in the Deep South, as well as state-recognized tribes and bands. Anna's family, though, represents the other faction of the indigenous Southeast, those families and individuals acutely aware of their Native ancestry but disconnected from a tribal community.

This disconnection is one of the many things Anna and I share, along with Alabama, Georgia, and Central America, but Anna is not me. Although the novel was originally sparked by my experiences living for a year in El Salvador during its civil war, Anna went her own way months ago, pages and pages ago. Whatever path I might plot for her forks or twists, leading sometimes into a thicket so dense I'm not sure how to find my way out, and sometimes into a clearing, ringed by brush but open to the sky. Other characters in the novel are equally resistant to being told what to do. Someone in a writing group once suggested I make Anna "more Indian." "Have her eat some *sofke* or something," he said. But Anna resisted, and her grandmother went on packing her the same lunch to take to school: bologna on white bread, an apple cut into four quarters (probably a golden delicious), a Moon Pie or Little Debbie.

The retreat's resident artists—we are writers, painters, sculptors, composers—gather for dinner at the main house, and someone asks if it's true that I'm "part Indian." "How much?" she wants to know, assuring me that the more Indian I am the better. Other residents nod, watching as she scrutinizes my face, ignoring my white skin, assessing my cheekbones, my dark hair and eyes as definitely

Indian. The group talks about bear hunting. Georgia is one of the few states with an open season on bears. A short season, thankfully, and the bears, knowing the acreage of the retreat is protected land, huddle down in these woods during the two weeks hunters and their radio-collared hounds try to tree them and shoot them down. A young bear runs across the drive just before dinner. We are reminded to wear our orange safety vests, to report any signs of hunting we see on retreat land. Someone mentions a Cherokee guy down the road who takes white guys on bear hunts. The carcasses hang, skinned and bloody, like lumpy human bodies, from the porch of the Cherokee hunter. *Guide,* the white customers likely call him, when they return home with their prizes, their authentic Indian experience.

My studio sits just off Betty Creek Road and not too far from Betty's Creek, named after Little Betty, a Cherokee woman who evaded the Removal by moving deeper into the mountains. There is some talk of Betty Whitecloud one night. Many of the residents are from other parts of the country; while they've heard of the Trail of Tears, they don't really understand that a Cherokee woman could not have simply stayed in north Georgia after the 1830s, not without difficulty, or concessions, or both. What happened to her? I wonder aloud. Did she stay? Was she taken to Oklahoma? Or did she die along the way? No one seems to know.

Later, I Google Betty Whitecloud, only to find some confusion between "Betty Whitecloud," who lived along the creek in the 1920s, and "Little Betty," a Cherokee widow, who petitioned for the 640 acres she was entitled to under the 1817 treaty, a treaty that guaranteed the Cherokees the right to stay on their land in Georgia. A treaty even more short-lived than the many, many abrogated treaties between the Indian Nations and the United States. According to the Dillard Family Association, Little Betty was the widowed matriarch of a large family. When white settlers encroached, she moved farther up the creek that bears her name. Did she stay? Are her descendants living on in the Southeast? I can't help but hope so.

An Alabama Cherokee friend tells me she is "Cherokee, Creek, German, and English" but that "Southern is a layer over all of that." She's not suggesting a hierarchy here, but pointing to something I, too, know well. That Southern mixed-bloods don't exist at intersections of identity categories; "Southern" isn't something that taints an otherwise authentic Creek—or Cherokeeness. One is indigenous *through* one's Southern-ness. This construct, though, can't necessarily be inverted. Because in the Deep South so much Indian land remains occupied by settler descendants, indigenous-ness is marked by a peculiarly simultaneous disenfranchisement and acceptance. Among many Southeastern mixed-bloods, an Indian grandparent or great-grandparent is worth noting, but it is a marker of specialness, not otherness, an ornament, not a different body.

My own parents affirm their Indian blood but think of themselves as white people with Creek and Cherokee ancestors. An aunt responds with horror when the topic comes up, having been taught by some past minister that miscegenation is strictly forbidden in the Bible. My mother considers me her "Indian daughter" and has identified me that way to others. In this, they are not unusual. Mixed-blood families in the South approach their Indian ancestry in all kinds of ways. My Alabama Cherokee friend, whose life work as a psychologist has focused on the experiences of Native children, comes from such a family. Her brother has served as chief of a state-recognized band in Alabama, but several of her siblings could sit next to my aunt. No, they say, we are not Indian. We are white.

And the indigenous Deep South shares with the non-Native South its peculiarities, the tragic, comic world of the grotesque depicted by Faulkner and O'Connor. Once, while I lived in Atlanta, I talked two friends into accompanying me to a "reenactment of a Creek village"—perhaps I hoped that I would meet some long-lost cousins. I found a village of the small square houses Creek people lived in before the Removal. Interesting to stand inside one, thinking about sleeping there, dreaming over the ancestors who would've been buried beneath the floor. Yet outside one of the houses was a half-excavated grave, a skeleton topped with long, fuzzy black hair lying in it. Horrified, I complained to a staff member, who reassured us that it wasn't a real skeleton. It and its accompanying long black Halloween wig were from Toys "R" Us.

"I'm part Creek and it doesn't bother me," the staff member told us. "In fact," she added, in a baffling non sequitur, "we're all a little bit Indian." To be fair, one of my friends has a distant Powhatan ancestor, but the other can only be descended from that secret Indian tribe living in the Czech Republic these last hundred years or so. I am wary of the word *authentic* and the way notions of authenticity drive imperialist nostalgia, how they divide the dis-empowered from each other, yet there are moments when the weight of the *in*authentic pulls down the very air around you, thick, tangible, undeniable. Moments when you could just as easily weep or laugh or turn away.

Like the rest of Native America, the Deep South contends with Disneyfication, the foam rubber tomahawks and face paint of Atlanta Braves games, the simultaneous erasure of living Indian people and the celebration of comic-book versions of them. While the emphasis among academics and activists in Indian country these days tends toward the recognition and rearticulation of Indians as sovereign citizens and not hyphenated Americans, this

Disneyfication, particularly in its internalized form, is still troublingly powerful in the Deep South. Powerful for many reasons, among them the post-Removal habit of hiding, since, until the passage of the 1924 Indian Citizenship Act, it was illegal to be Indian in most of the Deep South. In addition, the South's shameful and highly documented anti-Black racism obscures the presence and history of other cultures, Native American and, more recently, immigrant cultures. The South's historic racial white/red/black hierarchy exacerbates the problem for Black Indians. For Deep South Native and mixed-blood people, hyphenation might be a step up. Hardly ideal, but it beats representation as a bewigged plastic skeleton in a fake grave.

In this soup of paradox and simulacra, how to discover and transmit the important stories? It isn't that I don't write about and from the South in every piece of writing I produce: poetry, fiction, class lectures, letters and e-mails, this essay. But the world that poetry makes is a slant one, where there is metaphor instead of map, image in place of sentence. The heart of a poem appears to me indirectly, the way some stars can best be seen by looking slightly away from them, stars that may have burned out years ago. Sometimes we understand our stories as they rush around and through us, but more often they unfold in the telling, or with distance, the way, in telling a dream at the breakfast table, a dream that had seemed merely an extravagant and fanciful story upon waking, its meanings reveal themselves with shocking clarity.

The indigenous South is not a subject I have taken on with much directness in my poems. In "A Map of the Twentieth Century," a sequential poem in my first collection, I consider the very southern phenomenon of my grandfather, who had one Creek grandfather and one who, according to family lore, kept his Klan robes hidden under the mattress. (Those who tell this story are adamant that the robe never left its hiding place, but whether this is factual or white Southern apologism, it's impossible to know.) "Three generations later we are pale as sand," I wrote. We and our pale history, for the poem is less about my grandfather than the failure of history to tell us who we are exactly, than the grief over the "past we own [existing only] on stone and white paper."

My second collection, *Feral*, is a book about wildness, about what gets tamed and what cannot be tamed, only destroyed. I first called the collection "The Children of Animals," believing that one key to our destruction is something crucial that white culture has forgotten, this simple fact: that we are animals, children to them, siblings, kin, and they to us. But a friend renamed the collection *Feral*. This book is wild and fierce, he told me. Now a wolf races across the cover. In "Earth, My Body Is Trying to Remember," the long anti-epic that concludes the book, a people undertake a long journey toward what they believe to be their homeland, toward land that remembers them, land they are trying to remember.

Our deepest metaphors are the furniture, language, oxygen of that other world, the "unacknowledged" world. It is a life's work to understand them. It is the lifework of a poet to write them down. If autobiography is that which seeks to transmit the facts of one's life story to others, then I have never written an autobiographical poem. I had to find a different form to write about these issues that bear so greatly on my life, yet continue to elude me as a poet. Fiction remains for me a more secular process. I write down Anna's story at least in part to try to understand the lives of Southeastern indigenes, and to try to make sense of the currents that run north and south in Native America. Anna is the locus of sorting out years, centuries even, of material history, of stories that can be mapped and remapped, followed and perhaps understood, if only a little.

Meanwhile, back at the retreat, yet another resident wants to know. How much? he asks, *How much?* the question that seems to obsess so much of non-Native America. I keep thinking about Little Betty and *her* retreat with her children, farther up the creek, deeper into the mountains, in the hope that Andrew Jackson's soldiers wouldn't find them. I hold up my smallest finger—about this much, I tell my fellow resident—or colonist—since places like this one are, after all, also known as artists' colonies. He nods, satisfied. Or maybe a little more, I continue, shaking my left leg in his direction, realizing too late it's the leg with the crisscross of scars across the skin over the patella and the hip that pops when I attempt something too fancy in yoga class. An interesting choice, to designate the land called "Indigenous" on the map of my body. If this were an after-school special, I suppose I could thump my chest just over the heart and say, "Here! This part." But this is real life, which is inexact and messy, and I am not sure how irony will play here, in this milieu where Indianness is simultaneously sentimentalized and ignored, in this place that *used to be* Cherokee land.

This place that is, that always will be, Indian land.

BEYOND REPATRIATION
Wiley S. Thornton

So you think you know all about Repatriation and what it means to Native Americans and the ramifications that come from it. But, not so fast, my friends and relatives. The general view of Repatriation is that museums and federal institutions have to return Native American human remains, funerary objects—which is another name for grave goods—and sacred objects or objects of cultural patrimony such as false face masks and medicine bundles to lineal descendants, culturally affiliated Indian tribes, and Native Hawaiian organizations. It all sounds good. Some of our sacred objects and human remains have been returned, and it has been good for our people to get them back from museums and universities.

Sadly enough, there are also people against Repatriation. A large percentage of archeologists, scientists, and museum curators oppose the return of human remains and our sacred objects. They want to keep the bones of our ancestors and our cultural patrimony for future generations to study until the end of time. Native American remains have already been studied, cataloged, and photographed to death. This group of experts doesn't want to give them up, so many of our sacred objects are still in museums and other cultural institutions. So, some have been returned, others are in the process of being returned, and many will never be returned to our people.

I worked for the National Museum of the American Indian in the 1990s when tribal delegations came to the museum to look at objects that came from their people. Many times these elders were saddened by the things that were in the storage vaults of the museum, and they hardly ever wanted to look at the human remains. A lot of these objects had been lost on the battlefield, stolen, or sold by our people for pennies to survive those years of our cultural genocide. The last time I was home, my cousin talked about those years. He said the Osages almost did not survive them.

Indian people couldn't practice their religion anymore, speak their language, or live as our ancestors had for generations. I was at a powwow in Tulsa one time when they asked an elder of the Iowa Nation to give the opening prayer. He said he was ninety years old and nobody could understand Iowa anymore. But, he said, God could still understand him, and he then proceeded to give the prayer. The missionaries told us about God, but we already knew about God. Like my mom told me, we had been worshipping the "Great Mystery" for thousands of years before the White Man landed on these shores. Our elders passed many things down to us, our ceremonies, our languages, how we pray, and how we see the world. The elders told us how the old people did things in the past. The knowledge that has been passed down to us always ends with, "That's what the old people said." The government wanted to kill the Indian in us and make us like them, or kill us off in the process, but it didn't happen.

We have survived like the coyote and the lively otter. The Native American population is one of the fastest-growing in the country. But, we can't go back into the past because those days are gone forever, and even if I could become in fluent in Osage and learned all the songs and dances and all the ceremonies, it still would not be the same. The world has changed, and we have to change with it. Change is part of life. I think we are too hard on ourselves when we compare our lives to those of our ancestors. The old people wanted us to survive and prosper. They prayed for the coming generations and, like my elders, told me prayer goes a long way. Our experiences and the things we do now are important to our generation and to the generations that will come after us. Native American people have to carry on. The Osages have a word for this: *Wa-shkan*, "try hard, do your best." Someday our descendants will look on us as the old people.

In my opinion, our new pride in ourselves started in the late '60s and early '70s after the occupation of Alcatraz, Wounded Knee, and the Trail of Broken Treaties. Across Indian Country, the people were standing up for our treaty rights and our grandmother, the earth, and it gave Native American people renewed pride in ourselves. We suffered too long from low self-esteem and lack of confidence in ourselves because we were a conquered people. American Indians had become a minority in our own country. Our homeland security back then, like today, was lacking.

These political events in the '70s made us realize that nobody of our generation had been conquered; none of us had been on a Trail of Tears or rounded up and put on a reservation of barren land. Native people today look on our reservations not as islands of poverty in a sea of plenty but as our homes, where our relatives live and everybody knows our name like on *Cheers*. It's where our parents and grandparents are buried and where we have our religious ceremonies and dances. I remember a poster from the '70s with the words "The People Are Standing Up," with pictures of Indians at Wounded Knee, Alcatraz, powwows, and pictures of smiling Indians graduating from college. It was a keen poster, and I miss the '70s today for the idealism of the time and my youth.

————

I attended college in 1970, but I did not have high hopes for my academic career because my draft lottery number was 33, which meant my days as a civilian were numbered. In 1972 while in Germany as a military policeman, the news that Wounded Knee was occupied by AIM made me happy, and my army buddies said that if they were in America they would join the Indians against the sheriffs and federal troops. Many good things have happened in Indian Country since those days. One very important thing is the number of Native American colleges that have been established across North America. There are now thirty-two Native American colleges in the United States that serve about thirty thousand students. Treaties were made between Native Nations and Congress that said that in exchange for our lands, the government would provide health care, education, and other services for our people. The funding for these colleges comes from Native American Nations, the federal government, and philanthropic giving. These colleges support the sovereignty of each Nation and help preserve the languages and culture. Many times Native American kids don't finish school—they drop out, party too much, or get homesick when they attend non-Native educational universities. Indian students do better in the Indian colleges; the classes are smaller and there is lot of peer support.

Haskell Indian Nations University, as it is now known, was founded in 1884 as the United States Indian Industrial Training School. At the time of its founding, it was a boarding school for children in grades one through five. There were many of these government boarding schools around the country to assimilate our people. My father went to Chilocco Indian School, located north of Ponca City, Oklahoma, and south of the Kansas state line. My dad said the first thing they did to the Indian students when they arrived was to cut their hair. The young Native students couldn't speak their language or practice their religion. They taught my dad and my uncle how to be stonemasons. The schools did give those students a trade, and many students ended up falling in love with their classmates and getting married. That's why you'll find people today with blood from northern and southern Nations.

Another good school is the Institute of American Indian Arts or, as we say, "IAIA" with an Indian accent. IAIA is located in Santa Fe, New Mexico, which I always like to visit because there are so many brown people living there and because of the mountains and the Mexican food. IAIA has been really good for our people, in my opinion. I know many artists here in New York City and back home who went to school there and got their degrees. Most Indians I know like to draw and paint and know how to make their traditional clothes. "Our best clothes" like they say back home. Their mothers and fathers and grandparents taught them how to make their mocs, leggings, and headdresses. So this school is like the next step in their journey to express themselves.

We are saving our languages, too. The Osages have a language program in place, and there are workshops all over the country where all the different Nations meet to talk about their programs and find out what's working and not working. Our parents' generation was the last generation that was still fluent. We almost lost our languages when we lost our parents. The same thing happened on many other reservations. Now, the languages are coming back all across the country. Universities in states with large Native American populations are also working together with the Nations to bring them back. The University of Oklahoma has classes in five languages: Cherokee, Cheyenne, Choctaw, Creek, and Kiowa.

At home we are building an immersion center where you can only speak Osage, and other Nations are doing the same thing. They use a tape of my grandfather talking at a dance back home in the language program. When he talks, there is no hesitation on his part. He doesn't have to think of a word or phrase. It's a very exciting time for our people all over the country, bringing back these languages. We are rediscovering a new world that we were a part of but we couldn't reach, and now we can.

The funding for these language programs and other programs on different reservations comes from casino revenue and government grants. Casinos have been popping up around Indian Country like mushrooms in the forest after a heavy rain. I look on casinos as good and bad. They can provide money for tribal government, housing for elders, jobs for tribal members, and income for tribal members. Many reservations are in rural areas, and some of them are small, especially in California. Native American people are sovereign, and whatever each individual Nation does to take care of its people in whatever way it deems right is all right with me. The bad things about casinos are prostitution, drug abuse, and making money off of people's weaknesses.

There are now large contest powwows all across the country. These powwows are good for Native people and give so much in return: good fellowship, a chance to make money while having fun, and going on Indian time for a weekend. I dance at them and know many Indians on the powwow trail. It would be fun to go on that powwow highway and be on one long road trip, going from reservation to reservation and city to city with your friends and making new ones along the way. The journey, not the destination, is what is important in life. Native People of all ages go from coast to coast to these powwows and they have fun whether they win or lose. It's always good to hear the drum, dance on the grass, and visit with my relatives from Oklahoma.

The drum has a spirit to it, and it picks people up. My grandma always said, "If you feel bad, dance around the drum three times and you'll feel better." It's true—it really does make you feel better. There are many drum groups, and their names reflect where they come from: Yellowhammer, Stony Park, and my all-time favorite, Rose Hill. Those young Native men sitting around those drums learn the old songs and compose new songs about the world Native Americans live in now. They compose songs about the Iraq War, snagging at the powwow, and everyday life on the reservation. Seeing the lady singers around the southern drums always reminds me of my favorite '49 song, "Indian Girls." I have seen up to fifty drum groups at some of the big powwows.

Native American people have come a long way. I have a secret to tell you, but shhhhhhhh, don't tell anybody. We are doing better than the general population of Americans. We have health care for our people, housing for our elders and families, and jobs with job security because you are always a member of the Nation. We now have language programs, Head Start for our kids, commodity programs, and our own court system when we get in trouble with the tribal police.

My dream is that Native Americans can buy land to expand our land base and build alternative energy resources and organic farms, and that all the Native American Nations bring back our brother, the buffalo, for food. Eventually Native people can buy back our own "country"—what a concept. Most importantly, we still have our traditional life. We all enjoy our dances and ceremonies, it's part of who we are as a people. I'm a member of the

Native American Church of Oklahoma, Osage chapter, and at midnight we make smoke in our meetings. One of the firemen takes the tobacco and rolls a cigarette for the Road Man and he takes it and smokes and prays for the people. He always says it's a new day. Whatever happened yesterday is passed. It's a new day and a new beginning for our people. We always remember the past, but we look forward to the future. I saw a movie about John Trudell earlier this year. The late Kiowa guitar player Jesse Ed Davis was in his band. Trudell's band is on stage performing in one scene and Jesse tells the audience, "It's good to be here and it's good to be an Indian." That's how I feel. It was good to write these words and it's good to be Osage and Cherokee.

Wah-ka-nah.

Studio Sweeps and Rendering the Fatback

Phil Young

I went into my studio tonight and mentally swept up memories in the finished works themselves as well as the in the brushes, paint, rocks, and written notes, artifacts of my creative life. I think I should go in with a video cam or at least a digital voice recorder and follow where it all leads me. I would have a series of small narratives that could both open up and ground the realities that I find hard to express in the fragility of words. Remnants of haircuts and red earth patina the floor of my studio, waiting to be swept up into pieces yet to be born.

It is hard to render the fatback without discarding the remembered taste. When the fat of that favorite family (bacon) hog meat is cooked away, I always wonder if I am losing something essential in the translation to leanness of the small crispy slivers. Morsels. It's like taking my stories, writings, and art and trying to cut them down into something essential and clear, a fear of losing the savor.

Sometimes my words are worn-out paint rags, feeble, full, incapable even of removal. They feel like polyester trying to be cotton or linen. They are flat, like an overstarched, over-ironed shirt, desperately seeking refinement and life, yet burnt in the refiner's fire till only ashes of pretense are left. Where is the Phoenix? I identify myself as a human being, an artist/teacher/mixed-blood and co-creator within this ongoing multiverse of the Creator. In breaking with earlier artistic training, I have come to a freeing and enabling conviction in my work, a "soft" dogma that affirms that "all art and teaching is collaborative." Though I take responsibility for the work I make, I am indebted to much larger circles of communities of ancestors known and unknown, family, teachers, artists, and the largest circles of the Land and the Creator, all of whom draw me in, sustain and gird me each day. For my paintings, for example, I do not make the brushes, nor did the brush-maker "harvest" the sables' hair, nor did the fur cutter make the sable, etc. I am clearly reliant upon those who first ground earthly dust with water, egg, and urine, and upon great paint makers today who creatively perform their alchemy from the organic and synthetic gifts of the Earth. I am also a papermaker, though I first pay homage to the very first papermaker, our wasp kin. I am also not the farmer or the ginner or baler or weaver, much less the creator of the cotton or flax; and am deeply indebted to a first century BCE Chinese mixed-media craftsman who formed the first paper out of macerated water and recycled fabric.

Deep within the memory of the earth a cacophony of marks competes for a sacred place of legibility and truth.

I grew up in love with the land and early on experienced it as a sacred place, to be revered and thanked, with whom I had an intimate relationship. The red clay that farmers grew to hate has been a magnet that has not let me go since early digging times and clod fights. My scrounging, pack-ratting and dragging home of a variety of discarded materials that now surround me have led me to a lifelong obsession that still leads to Dumpster jumping and other "fine art" activities. I was curious about the

original history and meaning of these materials, and in spite of periodic questions from some family and friends about the why and what of these actions, I was always supported and encouraged to experiment and play without fear of censorship.

Smoke houses were private museums of family histories, corrugated tin roofs held tight during the worst hailstorms and tornado sirens from the Wetumka fire station. Every frozen rainstone was a percussion maker, while swallow gourds, once used by Creeks to keep mosquitoes away from summer camps, swayed till the storms passed. Mason jar and Folgers can vitrines spilled over with dense collections of rusted nails, bolts, and nuts, and occasional paper-shell pecans were cracked open by rodent clans. There were no cloth sacks of flour or corn or millet to feed these kin who could squeeze through any space, only large rusted traps, which my grandparents never set. I used to climb upon the dusty saddle, worn smooth by my dungarees. It hung from a thick rope, like a hog waiting to slowly become a hot, sugar-cured ham. Grandpa Conner would pull it outside and mount it on a sawhorse so I could ride off into the sunset. According to my mom, he never owned a horse. Then who was Old Chubby? All this on a saddle for a horse they never owned, with traps he never set, in a smokehouse that never smoked meat. This small, dark, windowless, hotter-than-Hades-in-the-summer shed at the end of St. Francis Street generated more important light than all that seeping through its significant cracks. It became one of my earliest artist playgrounds, conjuring up fantasies for the next performance.

Grandpa stomp-danced a jig across the flowered vinyl floor
paths worn down nearly to tongue and groove,

while Grandma poured fatback gravy thick as wallpaper paste
over biscuits cut from tin cans and two eggs over easy landsliding
from cast-iron skillets onto pink depression plates collected from
oatmeal boxes.
"Coffee isn't strong enough unless you can cut it with a knife," she said
to me, a four-year-old with his first cup in hand.

MIXED BLOOD ~~DOUBLE VISION~~

or

<u>MIXED BLOOD DOUBLE VISION</u>

~~DOUBLE VISION~~

To desecrate the land is to vandalize culture. The strong, yet fragile Body
of the earth, from which emerges the mysterious and enigmatic, the
embodiment of the numinous, the Holy, continues to be ravaged by the
twin monsters of greed and "progress."

"Poodle Grooming and Indian Jewelry Just Ahead"

"See Genuine Indian Weavers and Dinosaur Tracks at Cherokee
Tepee Trading Post—2 Miles"

Strings of Closeout Sale banners break across the space on frayed
turquoise wires, insulation like my Dad and I used to repair, which are
now myelin sheaths broken by my internal, corrosive disease, Multiple
Sclerosis. Beneath the struggle between plastic and the living skin, the his-
tory of the sod is sanguine. Trading posts are desecration sites in the body
of the Land. Touting "Genuine Indian" items made in Hong Kong and
Taiwan, these are sanctuaries for the unholy marriage between greed and
stereotypes. The "Noble" and "Ignoble" Savages are sidekick Siamese
twins, replicating side by side, shelf after shelf . . . The search for the

"Genuine" is itself part of the distorted mirror image with a historical lineage arising from the time of Columbus.

Four golden eagles caught the updraft from the floor of Junction Overlook, rising out of the canyon to briefly form four points just above the ridgeline. I reached into my backpack to grab my camera, looked up and they were gone. It was more than good fortune that I took the time to sit and attend to their gift. These drawings and these words in my sketchbook indelibly found a memory place, which hasn't corroded. These winged relatives led me to embed my MS figures literally into the larger paper pieces impregnated with red ochre sandstone.

At times I sensed this wall with its history of holes and patches like trying to repair myelin, a palpable skin, already scarred, pockmarked and receptive of near undecipherable, inverted white writing in Cherokee and English and even small electronic resistor bristles. The life-size handicap icons on the floor have an ambivalence of materials and meanings. Shredded copper wire, hair, and feathers are mixed with crusted artifact syringes collected from over nine years of daily injections, leftovers of feeding the MS shark to try to keep it from progressing so quickly. "Palimpsest" red sandstone from Oklahoma and mica from New York are tentatively secured with Sprite and spittle—later to be blown and slowly and ceremonially washed away with cleansing water that has also been used as a weapon against indigenous people.

In the left side outback of the celebrated Meteor City Trading Post, remains of the first foundation are buried under prairie grass, cockleburs and twisted rebar. Septic tanks are leaking down into several pools, barricaded from public view by fragile deteriorating plywood fences. To the right, an entangled caricature of a hoop dancer loses his grip as he peels away from the silhouette of a sunset butte cliché. A hydrant hose coming out of the disinte-grating mural unravels on the ground like a coiled-up snake drooling out venom, "Unpotable, Do Not Drink." I used the Johnny (Wayne?) Port-a-Potty for customers that was right next to it. It was a relief to get out, and a shock to be confronted by a six-feet-high garrulously painted "Chief Generic Head" whose exag-gerated nose was smelling the stench leading all the way from the seeping septic to the newly painted entrance. The sign read "Beware of Dog!" My sketchbook cartoon said, "I'm Having a Bad Dream Catcher Day."

Phil Young: *Arizona Maps Spotted*

Within histories of removal and immigration to Indian Territory, Cherokee/Scotch sharecroppers on my dad's side (Sorry, No Princesses!) and Irish farmer immigrants on my mother's side, united in Wetumka, Creek Nation, Indian Territory. I was born into these vast extended families in 1947, at Henryetta, but raised for three years in Weleetka, Oklahoma. Jim Shoulders and Troy Aikman are famous since they're on the billboards into Henryetta. One of my kids asked me one time why my name wasn't on one of those big signs as we took the Beeline around town to I-40 toward the turnoff through Pharaoh. "Where you're born matters, but not as much as where and how you're raised," I said. I guess I was just passing through to back to where my folks first lived with me. Maybe that's what I'm doing right now. Having been blessed with knowing family on both sides, each with a tradition of great storytellers and makers, I have experienced the resistant and resilient power of re/membered family story/lineage/role models to reconnect, even disconnected by illegibilities and disabilities, and the enabling humor to usurp and reclaim integrity and healing.

Fragility and strength are mixed with vulnerability and resistant hope.

When my Grandma Conner was a little girl, she lost sight of one eye when a cow swished its tail while she was milking. She also had a bad case of rheumatic arthritis that left her back curved and her hands often swollen at the knuckles. This did not keep her from pressing butter in a patterned wooden mold, or placing it under a beautiful carved glass dish on a well-set table, or teaching me how to sew and how to weed the flower and vegetable gardens. Unbeknownst to her, she helped me find the seeds, alive in wrapped brown paper packages, after her death. It was her penciled handwriting that showed me what was inside them and in her good-natured dignity in spite of physical obstacles. Grandpa was born in Alabama, one of three sons of a young Irish immigrant who was conscripted during the potato famine to work on the southern railroad, landing off a cattle boat into a South not warm to those they derided as "Potatoheads." He was taken with one brother from Wetumpka, Alabama, to Wetumka in the Territory. His Cherokee uncle by marriage was contracted by the Creeks to survey their land before the federal government carved it up, because Creeks didn't trust them. He showed me how to knock down pecans from the large sprawling tree in the front yard, and to crawl under tight fences and onto a cot in the cool cellar on a blazing August day.

IT: IDENTITY THEFT IN INDIAN TERRITORY

The architecture of removal and allotment was laid out as a calculated genocidal map, from North Carolina to Indian Territory. Freshly ironed flags line the topography of this Trail Where We Cried. A continuous undulating contour of systemic violence is drawn open-eyed over the land/the People from Jefferson and Jackson and Dawes to the current day. The plans are drafted on one long infested paper as modular variations on the theme of superiority destined to be manifested, often disguised as "salvic," "protection," and "natural law."

As far as I know, neither my great-great-grandmother, Martha Mary Penesda Lane Thomasson, nor her children were on the Trail of Tears. My grandma and grandpa Young were born in White County, Arkansas, in the area between the Arkansas and White rivers, the land given to the first Cherokee "Old Settlers" and near one of the routes of the Trail. They were still in Arkansas during the U.S. government enrollment period led by the Dawes Gang. When they arrived there, "the Card" agency was closed by these "Friends of the Indian." They didn't qualify for the 0 percent APR loan, though they were allowed to get commodities. (Sure loved the cheese, but not the peanut butter with all the oil on top.) Our oral history confirms stories of allotment papers of Grandpa's grandmother, seen by relatives, only to be found again, shredded into tiny pieces by mice who got into a family trunk. One day Grandpa took off on the long trip to Muscogee to get the family enrolled, only to turn around in a little while, unhitch his team, hang his head, and silently retire to his bedroom, never to speak of it again.

Your mule is too damn slow and you're just living too damn far to ever get to Muscogee in time, and your family accounts can't be trusted, and you don't even have a bit of that birth certificate you claim was burnt up in the Searcy courthouse. You can't read or write and can't afford a lawyer. You don't have a chance. Besides you don't look like no Indian to us. You're already light enough to pass, and too mixed to seem legit. Don't matter some of your thirteen kids look like they have the signs of the "disability." Some may be Goldilocks' descent, but it don't matter. In this government life, you're allotted just one chance before the offer expires, gotta be in the right piece of government-approved land and enough measurable blood to get your landgrabstake. Just gotta be there at the ripening time, when the harvest comes in. Can't wait until cotton is hoed, much less till it is ginned. Can't stay round tilling and having one more kid, 'cause if you keep sharing, you're gonna lose out. Go back to your hoe and "Brown Mule." This BloodCard's not for you. Go straight back to

Cherokee Stripped QuantumNeverLand, no squares on the checkerboard for you and your kin.

Both grandpas spoke some Creek, Grandpa Conner bilingual enough to sell at the coin store in town. Grandpa Young, though, used to teach it to us, but when we asked him if we were Creek, he would say "No, we're Cherokee and don't tell anyone." With thirteen kids scraping a living "on the shares," denial became a means of survival. We were not taken to boarding schools where we were punished by lye in the mouth if we spoke our own tongue; but somewhere along the line, the Cherokee language of my ancestors was cut off from my family.

I've tried to learn to reclaim it through a tape. One day the voice repeated the phrase, "Do you speak Cherokee?" which I painted in the syllabary at the top of a collaged paper series. I yelled back in frustration, "No, I cannot speak. I cannot speak. I cannot speak, but I can write Jeep Cherokee" . . . in another, "I cannot speak Cherokee, but I can draw perspective."
"I didn't ask you if you could speak, but if you can understand," the tape said. "Clearly you have not," said the tape.
"Rewind and start all over again."

As of now, we are united with those deemed illegitimate.
Our Cherokeestrippedblood measured out,
Discarded without the Card.

In spite of the attempts to completely cut the cord, I've found the lineage of the *Ani yun wiya,* "the Real People," survived and was passed on through a fiery cord that did not burn up nor consume us when we grasped it.

Selu is reborn as hope in the scarified, sanctified mounds
burying historical amnesia, family confusion,
and the invasion of corrosive disease

If you haven't figured it out by now, my true identity, which I am fully revealing this day before you and the U.S. government is . . . that I am a

MIXEDMEDIABLOODDOUBLEVISIONSCAPEARTIST
member of the FACADEBUSTER clan.

The Card, well, I always leave home without it, but I can never leave *Ah-gway-nuh-suh* ("my home") behind.
For further information, visit my website at <u>desecration/</u> <u>sacrilege.com</u> or call toll free, <u>1-800-GENUINE.</u>

Through writing this essay, I have come to more clearly under-stand that the significant reasons that I identify myself as a mul-timedia artist are rooted in my mixed lineage and early childhood experiences. Whether the work is complex on-site installations or of two-media pencil and paper, it is all mixed to me. Consistent pursuit of series is part of many traditions, and is certainly not unique.

In spite of my Upstate New York residence, the land, the red clay of Oklahoma still runs in my veins.

I am truly blessed.

This is written in honor of the Creator, the Earth, our non-human neighbors, my family, and the communities from

which I come, some of whom are still disconnected. It is also meant as a recognition of years of grappling with cultural outrage and an affirmation of the powerful, loving beauty of this variegated world and my family story to reclaim history and identity with hope, humor, and health.

Wa do.

Sherman Alexie (Spokane/Coeur d'Alene) is the author of eighteen books; the most recent is the novel *Flight.* His poems, fiction, and essays have won him an international following since his first book, *The Business of Fancydancing,* was published to great acclaim in 1992. *Smoke Signals,* the film he adapted from one of his stories and coproduced, enlarged his audience still further. Alexie's honors include awards from the National Endowment for the Arts, the Lila Wallace–Reader's Digest Foundation, the Before Columbus Foundation's American Book Award, and the Washington State Arts Commission, as well as a citation as "One of the 20 Best American Novelists under the Age of 40" from *Granta* magazine. His work has also been included in *Best American Short Stories 2004, Pushcart Prize XXIX of the Small Presses,* and *O. Henry Prize Stories 2005.* He was also three-time winner of the World Poetry Bout in Taos, New Mexico. He lives with his family in Seattle.

Pena Bonita (Mescalero Apache) is a writer of short stories and poetry. She has been a regular contributor of both fiction and nonfiction to *Talking Stick Native Arts Quarterly* since 1999. A prolific writer, Pena has also written essays and a full-length screenplay. Born and raised in the Southwest, she now lives in New York City, where she is a founding member of the American Indian Writers' Workshop and is active in the national Native American arts community. Ms. Bonita began her artistic career as a visual artist and later photographer, and she has exhibited and lectured extensively in the United States and Canada. Her work is reflective of Native American values and experiences. In 2004 she was a recipient of the National Foundation Book Award.

Michele "Midge" Dean Stock (Seneca) passed into the spirit world at an early age in May 2006. She was a gifted beadworker, basket maker, and singer. Her recordings of traditional social dance songs are available on *Songs My Elders Taught Me* (Oyate Records, 1997). She was writer/actor/producer of the video series *Keeper of the Western Door*, and she appeared in *How the West Was Lost*. She served as education director for the Seneca Nation and director of the Seneca-Iroquois National Museum in her hometown of Salamanca. She was justly renowned for her educational presentations on Seneca and Iroquois culture and history, and for her beautiful voice.

Steve Elm is a member of the Oneida Nation of Indians in Wisconsin. He is editor of *Talking Stick Native Arts Quarterly*, published in New York by Amerinda. He has worked as an actor, writer, and director for such companies as Chuka Lokoli Native Theatre Ensemble, American Indian Youth Theatre Project, New York Theatre Workshop, and, in the UK, Common Body Theatre and Manchester University. Steve is a teaching artist with the Creative Arts Team at CUNY and is a master artist with the Wolf Trap Foundation for Early Learning in the Arts in Vienna, Virginia. Along with providing educational counseling at American Indian Community House in downtown New York City, he also lectures and gives talks on Native America to schools, community groups, local governments, and corporate concerns. His work was recently featured in *Genocide of the Mind*, an anthology of urban Native American writing published by Nation Books.

Heid E. Erdrich (Turtle Mountain Ojibwe) is the author of two collections of poetry: *The Mother's Tongue* from Salt Press and *Fishing for Myth* from New Rivers Press. She co-edited *Sister Nations:*

Native American Women Writers on Community. Her next book is *National Monuments,* forthcoming from Michigan State University Press. She cofounded Birchbark Books Press and the Turtle Mountain Writers Workshop. Heid is the curator of Ancient Traders Native Arts Gallery in Minneapolis. A wandering poet and teacher, her home is in Minnesota.

Louise Erdrich (Turtle Mountain Ojibwe) is the author of eleven novels as well as volumes of poetry, children's books, and a memoir of early motherhood. Her novel *Love Medicine* won the National Book Critics Circle Award. *The Last Report on the Miracles of Little No Horse* was a finalist for the National Book Award. She cofounded Birchbark Books Press and the Turtle Mountain Writers Workshop. She lives in Minnesota with her daughters and is the owner of Birchbark Books, a small independent bookstore.

Gary Farmer (Cayuga) was born in Ohsweken, Ontario, into the Cayuga Nation and Wolf Clan of the Haudenosaunee/Iroquois Confederacy. Farmer attended Syracuse University and Ryerson Polytechnic University, where he studied photography and film production. Farmer is known for his role as spiritual Native American guide Nobody in *Dead Man.* He reprised the role for a cameo in *Ghost Dog: The Way of the Samurai,* from the same director. He also was the publisher of *Aboriginal Voices* magazine and is an avid supporter of Native media projects in film, radio, television, and the Internet. He has won numerous awards and nominations from many Native film festivals, as well as Canadian film awards. Farmer has performed in both the film and television adaptations of Tony Hillerman's novels. He played Cowboy Dashee in the 1991 film *The Dark Wind* and Captain Largo in *Coyote Waits* (2003) and *A Thief of Time* (2004). He was nominated for Independent Spirit

Awards for his roles in the movies *Powwow Highway, Dead Man,* and *Smoke Signals.* He also has a band called Gary Farmer and the Troublemakers. The band consists of John Longbow on bass, Gary Farmer on harmonica and vocals, Denton McCabe on lead guitar, Nick Mendoza on rhythm guitar and vocals, Arne Bey on drums, and Neon Napalm on vocals.

Diane Fraher (Osage) is the writer and director of *The Reawakening,* a contemporary dramatic feature film about a Native man's struggle to identify with traditional values. She also wrote and directed *You're Looking at the First Draft of the Constitution,* the award-winning public service advertising campaign for print and broadcast on television. Ms. Fraher is a contributing author to *Genocide of the Mind: New Native American Writing,* published by Nation Books, and *Creation's Journey: Native American Identity and Belief,* published by Smithsonian's National Museum of the American Indian; and she wrote the afterward to *Mean Spirit,* Linda Hogan's novel of the Osage oil murders. In 1987, she founded American Indian Artists Inc. (Amerinda), a nonprofit organization governed by an all-Indian board of directors, dedicated to promoting the indigenous perspective in the arts to a wide audience, and is its director.

Eric Gansworth (Onondaga), professor of English and Lowery Writer-in-Residence at Canisius College in Buffalo, was born and raised at the Tuscarora Indian Nation in western New York. His books include the novels *Indian Summers, Smoke Dancing, Mending Skins* (PEN Oakland Award winner 2006); a book of poems and paintings, *Nickel Eclipse: Iroquois Moon;* and the cross-genre book *Breathing the Monster Alive.* His poetry, fiction, nonfiction, and visual art have been printed in numerous anthologies and in the journals *Kenyon Review, Boston Review, Cream City Review, Shenandoah, Cold Mountain Review,* and *American Indian Quarterly,* among others. Additionally, paintings and photographs of his have appeared in a number of exhibits in New York State, including the Herd About Buffalo public arts project. He has been an artist in residence at the Associated Colleges of the Twin Cities, the Seaside Institute, and the Just Buffalo Literary Center, and was a recipient of a Constance Saltonstall Foundation Individual Artist's Grant. He served eleven years on the board of directors for Hallwalls Contemporary Art Center, has served terms on the literature panel for the New York State Council on the Arts and the Artists' Advisory Committee of the New York Foundation for the Arts, and has been a peer panelist for the Administration for Native Americans. A second collection of poems and paintings, *A Half Life of Cardio-Pulmonary Function,* will be published in 2008. A fourth novel, *Extra Indians,* is also forthcoming.

Kristi Gansworth is an enrolled member of the Kitigan Zibi Anishnabeg reservation in Maniwaki, Quebec. She received her bachelor's degree in English from the State University of New York at Buffalo, and lives among the Haudenosaunee in western New York. She writes fiction, poetry, short stories, and creative nonfiction about contemporary indigenous culture, exploring the self and the process of growth within and outside of her own life.

Diane Glancy (Cherokee) has written poetry, scripts, essays, and fiction that have earned her numerous literary prizes, including an American Book Award, the Minnesota Book Award in Poetry, the Native American Prose Award, and a Sundance Screenwriting Fellowship. Glancy is a professor at Macalester College in Saint Paul, Minnesota, where she taught Native American literature and creative writing. She is now on a four-year sabbatical/early-retirement program. Glancy also taught in the Bread Loaf School of English MA program on the campus of the Native American Preparatory School in Rowe, New Mexico, in 1999. She was the 1998 Edelstein-Keller Minnesota Writer of Distinction, University of Minnesota, where she taught Topics in Advanced Poetry. Glancy also was the Native American Inroads Mentor at The Loft in Minneapolis, where she taught creative nonfiction in 1997. Her books include *Rooms, New and Selected Poems, In-Between Places, Designs of the Night Sky, Pushing the Bear, The West Pole, Claiming Breath,* and *The Dance Partner, Stories of the Ghost Dance.*

Joy Harjo, a member of the Mvskoke/Creek Nation in Oklahoma, is an internationally known poet, performer, writer, and musician. She has published seven books of acclaimed poetry, including such well-known titles as *She Had Some Horses, In Mad Love and War, The Woman Who Fell from the Sky,* and her most recent, *How We Became Human, New and Selected Poems,* from W. W. Norton. In Harjo's first music CD, *Letter from the End of the 20th Century,* she is featured as poet and saxophone player. Her second CD of original songs, *Native Joy for Real,* crosses over many genres and has been praised for its daring brilliance. Her third release is a spoken-word CD: *She Had Some Horses.* She has won numerous awards for her poetry and writing, including the Arrell Gibson Lifetime Achievement Award, Oklahoma Book Awards; the 2000 Western Literature Association Distinguished Achievement Award; the 1998 Lila Wallace–Reader's Digest Award; the 1997 New Mexico Governor's Award for Excellence in the Arts; the Lifetime Achievement Award from the Native Writers Circle of the Americas; the William Carlos Williams Award from the Poetry Society of America; and the Eagle Spirit Achievement Award for overall contributions in the arts, awarded by the American Indian Film Festival. Harjo has performed internationally, from the Riddu Riddu Festival held north of the Arctic Circle in Norway to *Def Poetry Jam* on HBO, from Madras, India, to the Ford Theater in Los Angeles. She is currently the Joseph M. Russo endowed professor in creative writing at the University of New Mexico, where she will be in residence every fall through 2007. When not teaching and performing, she lives in Honolulu, Hawaii, where she belongs to the Hui Nalu Canoe Club.

Allison Adelle Hedge Coke is of Cherokee, Huron, Creek, Metis, French Canadian, Lorraine, Portuguese, English, Scots, and Irish descent. She grew up in North Carolina, the Great Plains, and Canada, and worked horses, tobacco, in commercial fishing, construction, and factories. She is a MacDowell Colony and Black Earth Institute fellow, a professor of writing at the Institute of American Indian Arts, and a faculty member of the summer MFA intensive at Naropa University. Hedge Coke authored two volumes of poetry from Coffee House Press, *Dog Road Woman* (American Book Award) and *Off-Season City Pipe* (Wordcraft Writer-of-the-Year Award), and the memoir *Rock, Ghost, Willow, Deer* (University of Nebraska Press); and has a new poetry release, *Blood Run* (Salt, UK); she has edited five anthologies, and is a poetry contributor of *Political Affairs*. Hedge Coke recently performed in the XV International Poetry Festival of Medellín, Colombia, and the third World Poetry Festival of Venezuela. She mentors troubled and incarcerated youth; urban, rural, and reservation K–12 and elderly students; institutional and shelter clients; and laborers and working-class writers. She also works in negotiations, mediation, and peacemaking, and teaches transformation, dignity, and peace through poetry, philosophy, performance, and life.

Gerald L. (Jerry) Hill was born and raised on the Oneida Reservation in Wisconsin. He is a member of the Bear Clan. After six years in the United States Air Force he stayed in California, eventually becoming an activist in the '60s. In 1969 he went to Alcatraz for several months, after which he was recruited to higher ed at San Fernando Valley State College, which subsequently became Cal State Northridge. There he received a special BA in linguistics in 1973, and was then recruited by the American Indian Law Center at the University of New Mexico in Albuquerque and was admitted to the University of California, Davis, from which he earned a JD in 1976. He then returned home to Oneida, Wisconsin, passed the state bar exam, and became the first chief counsel of the Oneida Tribe, retiring in 2000. He considers himself an Oneida language activist and promotes the use of technology by Indian communities to produce their own language materials. He is the president of the Indigenous Language Institute, headquartered in Santa Fe, New Mexico, and has been a member of the board of directors for eight years. He is now a solo practitioner as well as a writer and yo-yo champion.

Richard W. Hill Sr. (Tuscarora), born in Buffalo, New York, in 1950, is a painter, photographer, carver, beadworker, and basket weaver. He attended the Art Institute of Chicago from 1968–70, and the State University of New York at Buffalo, where he obtained an MA in 1980. Through his work as a writer, curator, and advocate, Hill has contributed inestimably to the critical discourse and advancement of First Nations art and artists across North America. He has held numerous museum positions, including the directorship of the Institute of American Indian Arts Museum in Santa Fe, New Mexico, where he curated the notable 1992 exhibition "Creativity Is Our Tradition," and is a consultant for the National

Museum of the American Indian, Washington, D.C. Hill is also assistant professor of American Studies at State University of New York at Buffalo.

Alex Jacobs (Karoniaktahke) was born in 1953 on the Akwesasne Mohawk Nation (St. Regis Mohawk Indian Reservation). In 1975, he attended Manitou Community College in Quebec. In 1977 he received an AFA in creative writing and sculpture from the Institute of American Indian Arts, Santa Fe, and in 1979 received a BFA from Kansas City Art Institute in creative writing/sculpture. From 1980 to 1986 he worked as an ironworker across the country while raising a family: Cyndi, Duran, and Ciera. He was an editor for the Mohawk Nation international journal, *Akwesasne Notes*, 1972–75, 1983–86, and 1995–96. In 1986, he cofounded the community paper *Indian Time* and the Native Arts journal *Akwekon*. Jacobs was a DJ, talk show host, news director, program director, and assistant manager for CKON, Mohawk Nation Radio, from 1986 to 91. He has read poetry and done spoken word performances from New Mexico to New York. He has a twenty-year collection of poetry to be published and currently has a spoken word CD with the last ten years' of performance. In 1995, he won a New York Foundation of the Arts poetry fellowship. His Web site is: http://groups.msn.com/alexjacobs.

Maurice Kenny, born in Watertown, New York, in 1929, is one of the most celebrated Native American poets of all time. He has published over thirty books of poetry, fiction, and essays. His *The Mama Poems*, an extended elegy, won the American Book Award in 1984, and his books *Blackrobe: Isaac Jogues* and *Between Two Rivers* were nominated for the Pulitzer Prize. Kenny considers his most important work to be *Tekonwatonti, Molly Brant,*

1735–1795, a historical poetry journey in many voices that honors the Mohawk figure Molly Brant and explores an important time in American history when the British, French, Iroquois, and colonists were engaged in a monumental collision of cultures. For the past four years, between New York and Mexico, Kenny has extended his method of historical poetry in writing a new book, *Conversations with Frida Kahlo: Collage of Memory.*

Oren Lyons, a member of the Onondaga Nation, is a Faithkeeper, a guardian of traditional knowledge, and a professor of American studies at SUNY Buffalo, where he is the director of the Native American studies program. He holds a degree in fine arts from Syracuse University. He worked in New York City as a commercial artist, and served as planning director of Norcross Greeting Cards. Lyons has exhibited his works extensively. Since returning to Onondaga in 1970, he has been a leading advocate for Native American causes. On May 25, 2006, the trustees of the New York State Department of Education awarded him their highest honor, SUNY Distinguished Service Professor.

Scott Richard Lyons (Ojibwe/Mdewakanton Dakota) hails from Leech Lake Reservation in northern Minnesota. He teaches Native American literature at Syracuse University and is a columnist for *Indian Country Today.*

Janet McAdams grew up in Alabama. Her first book, *The Island of Lost Luggage,* won the Diane Decorah Award for Poetry from the Native Writers Circle of the Americas and was published by the University of Arizona Press in 2000. Praised by reviewers as "closely crafted" and "achingly beautiful," the collection received the American Book Award in 2001. Her second collection, *Feral,* was published in Salt's Modern Poets Series in 2007. She teaches at Kenyon College, where she is Robert P. Hubbard professor of poetry, and is completing a novel set in the indigenous Deep South.

John C. Mohawk was a member of the Seneca Nation from the Cattaraugus Territory. He was an associate professor of American studies at the University at Buffalo and director of its Indigenous Studies Program. He received his BA from Hartwick College and his MA and PhD from SUNY Buffalo. He served as representative member of the External Affairs Committee of the Haudenosaunee, Six Nations Iroquois Confederacy, in 1990 and 1991, and was responsible for representing the affairs of the Grand Council as requested. He was editor (with Oren Lyons) of the books *Exiled in the Land of the Free* (Clear Light Publishers); *A Basic Call to Consciousness* (Akwesasne Notes); and *The Red Buffalo* and was publication editor for *DayBreak* and *Akwesasne Notes*, official publication of the Mohawk Nation. His books include *Utopian Legacies: A History of Conquest and Oppression in the Western World* and *Iroquois Creation Story: John Arthur Gibson and J. N. B. Hewitt's Myth of the Earth Grasper*. John passed into the spirit world in December 2006.

MariJo Moore (Cherokee/Irish/Dutch) is an author/poet/essayist /editor/publisher/anthologist. Among her many published works are *Spirit Voices of Bones, The Diamond Doorknob,* and *Confessions of a Madwoman;* she is editor of *Genocide of the Mind: New Native American Writing,* and *Eating Fire, Tasting Blood: An Anthology of the American Indian Holocaust.* She resides in the mountains of western North Carolina. Her Web site is www.marijomoore.com.

Sara Marie Ortiz is a young Acoma Pueblo writer, poet, and scholar born and raised in Albuquerque, New Mexico, and currently residing in Santa Fe. She is a recent graduate of the Institute of American Indian Arts with a BFA in creative writing and is working toward her MFA in creative writing at the University of New Mexico. Ms. Ortiz is the recipient of several prestigious awards, among them the Truman Capote Literary Award and a first-place award in creative nonfiction, which she won at the age of fifteen, from the SouthWest Writers Workshop. Her latest publications include works of poetry and creative nonfiction in *Letters from Young Activists*, published by Nation Books, "A New Vision of Native Literature" published in *THE* magazine, and *Scrimshaw: Neo-Modern Literature* from the Institute of American Indian Arts, of which she is also co-editor.

Simon J. Ortiz, Indigenous poet and writer from Acoma Pueblo, currently Richard L. Thomas visiting professor of creative writing at Kenyon College, is a professor of American Indian Studies and the department of English at Arizona State University. As the author of *Woven Stone, After and Before the Lightning, From Sand Creek, Speaking for the Generations, Men on the Moon, The Good Rainbow Road,* and *Beyond the Reach of Time and Change* and a member of the 1960s generation of Indigenous poets and writers, he is a proponent of Indigenous literary nationalism.

Ernie Paniccioli (Cree) is the author of *Who Shot Ya?—Three Decades of HipHop Photography* (HarperCollins). Regarded by many to be the premier "hip-hop photographer in America," Paniccioli first made his foray into the culture in 1973, when he began capturing the ever-present graffiti art dominating New York City. Armed with a 35-millimeter camera, Paniccioli has recorded the entire evolution of hip-hop, much in the same way Gordon Parks recorded the civil rights movement, or akin to the manner in which James Van Der Zee, the documentary photographer of Harlem in the 1920s, met the energy and spirit of the times head-on with his picture-making. And like Edward S. Curtis's monumental prints of the Native peoples of North America, Paniccioli, himself a Native American, has found a beauty and resiliency in a community often ignored by mainstream society.

Susan Power is an enrolled member of the Standing Rock Sioux tribe and a native Chicagoan. She is a graduate of Harvard College, Harvard Law School, and the Iowa Writers' Workshop, and is a recipient of a James Michener Fellowship, Radcliffe Bunting Institute Fellowship, Princeton Hodder Fellowship, and United States Artists Fellowship. Her first novel, *The Grass Dancer,* was published in 1994 and awarded the PEN/Hemingway Prize. Her second book, *Roofwalker,* was published in 2001 and awarded the Milkweed National Fiction Prize. She currently lives in Saint Paul, Minnesota.

Melanie Printup Hope is of Tuscarora descent and was raised on the Tuscarora Indian Reservation in western New York State. She earned her BFA in graphic design at the Rochester Institute of Technology and her MFA in electronic arts at Rensselaer Polytechnic Institute. She is currently completing graduate studies at the Cooperstown Graduate Program in history museum studies. She lives in Schenectady, New York, where she owns her own graphic design business. She is currently associate professor of graphic design at The Sage Colleges (Albany, New York) and has also taught at the University of Minnesota, Banff Centre for the Arts, Rensselaer Polytechnic Institute, and Skidmore College. Her video, multimedia, and installation work has been shown throughout the United States, Canada, and Europe. She received a Rockefeller Foundation Intercultural Film/Video/Multimedia Fellowship in 1996 and has received additional awards and fellowships from the New York Foundation for the Arts, the National Endowment for the Arts, the Andy Warhol Foundation for the Visual Arts, the Jerome Foundation, the New York State Council on the Arts, and the Lyn Blumenthal Memorial Fund. Her biography has been included in *Who's Who among America's Teachers, Who's Who of American Women,* and *The World Who's Who of Women.*

Jaune Quick-to-See Smith (Enrolled Flathead Salish, member of the Confederated Salish and Kootenai Nation, Montana) uses humor and satire to examine myths, stereotypes, and the paradox of American Indian life in contrast to the consumerism of American society. Her work is philosophically centered on her strong traditional beliefs and political activism. Smith is nationally known as an artist, curator, lecturer, printmaker, and teacher. She was born at St. Ignatius Mission on the Flathead Reserve. She holds three honorary doctorates, from the Pennsylvania Academy of Fine Arts, the Minneapolis College of Art and Design, and Massachusetts College of Art. Her work is in collections at the Whitney Museum, the Metropolitan Museum, MOMA, the Brooklyn Museum, SAAM, and the Walker.

James Thomas Stevens is a member of the Akwesasne Mohawk Nation in upstate New York. He attended the Institute of American Indian Arts and the Jack Kerouac School of Disembodied Poetics at Naropa, and received his MFA from Brown University. He is the author of *Tokinish* (First Intensity Press, 1994), *Combing the Snakes from His Hair* (Michigan State University Press, 2002), *(dis)Orient* (Palm Press), *Mohawk/Samoa: Transmigrations,* a collaborative book of poems with Samoan poet Caroline Sinavaiana (Subpress 2006),

Bulle/Chimere (First Intensity Press, 2006) and *A Bridge Dead in the Water* (Salt, 2007). He is associate professor of English and director of the American Indian Studies minor at the SUNY Fredonia. Stevens is a 2000 Whiting Writers Award winner and a 2005 finalist for the National Poetry Series. He has done readings from Stirling, Scotland, to Grenoble, France, and from Amman, Jordan, to Istanbul, Turkey.

Wiley S. Thornton is Osage and Cherokee. He is from the Deer Clan, a Committee Man of the Hominy I'n-Lon-Schka, and a member of the Native American Church of Oklahoma, Osage chapter. A graduate of the University of Oklahoma, he works for the National Park Service. A contributing author to *Talking Stick Native Arts Quarterly* and *Genocide of the Mind: New Native American Writing,* he is currently working on several different writing projects. He resides in New York City.

Clifford E. Trafzer is professor of American Indian history and director of the California Center for Native Nations at the University of California, Riverside. He is of Wyandot and German descent and has worked with American Indian communities throughout his life. He has published several books, including *Earth Song, Sky Spirit, Blue Dawn, Red Earth,* and *Native Universe.* He is currently editing *American Indians and American Presidents* with the National Museum of the American Indian, and he is completing "Changing Medicine: Intersection American Indian and Western Medicine in Southern California, 1900–1950."

Jeanette Weaskus is an enrolled member of the Nez Perce Tribe of Idaho. She received a BA in English from Lewis-Clark State College and an MFA in creative writing from the University of Idaho.

Ms. Weaskus is currently working toward a doctoral degree in rhetoric and composition from Washington State University. She enjoys dancing in powwows as a traditional dancer and Rollerblading.

Ted C. Williams (Tuscarora) was born at the Tuscarora Indian Nation in western New York in 1930. After graduating from LaSalle High School in Niagara Falls, New York, Ted spent four years in the United States armed services as a paratrooper. Under the GI Bill he studied trumpet and modern jazz arranging at the Knapp School of Music. He later toured the country as a professional archer. Ted's hobbies included stone carving and ceramics. He was employed as a crane operator for the Eastman Kodak Company in Rochester, New York, later moving to North Carolina. He is the author of *The Reservation*, a modern classic of Iroquois literature. In September 2006, having just finished his follow-up volume, *Big Medicine from Six Nations*, he passed into the spirit world.

Annabel Wong (Salt River Pima) was born in Tucson, Arizona, and raised in San Francisco. In 1996, she received an AFA degree from the Institute of American Indian Arts in Santa Fe, New Mexico. In 1997, she moved to New York City and completed her BFA degree in photography at the School of Visual Arts. Annabel currently works in New York City with artists and art dealers producing fine art prints and assisting in digital and organizational solutions.

Phil Young is of Cherokee and Scotch-Irish descent, born in Henryetta, Oklahoma, in 1947. As a member of the "Façade Buster Clan" (sorry, no princesses!), his work affirms the necessity of "on/site for insight," geophysically/culturally/autobiographically. "Cultural raids" into Tourist Trading Posts of the Southwest have become sources for performances, paintings, drawings, and mixed-media "Genuine Indian Burial Sites." The latter parodies have been temporarily installed on canyon rims, in museums, and in galleries. Satirical text accompanies the collected and fabricated items that unmask, subvert, and celebrate the demise of the "inauthentic—GENUINE INDIAN," perpetuated in trading post breeding grounds. Additional recent sources from the disabling effects of multiple sclerosis have entered the mixed-blood bodyscape. He says, however, that "having been blessed with knowing family on both sides, each with a tradition of great storytellers and makers, I have experienced the resistant and resilient power of re/membering family stories, and the enabling humor to reclaim integrity and healing." He was awarded a Millay Colony residency, a Joan Mitchell Foundation Grant in Painting and Sculpture, and a New York Foundation for the Arts Fellowship in Sculpture. Currently he is professor of Art at Hartwick College in Oneonta, New York, where he has resided since 1978. In spite of his upstate New York residence, he states that "the red clay of Oklahoma still runs in my veins."